ENDORSEMENTS

"While moving money, choosing products to buy and strategies to use are all important, our mindset and approach to things can and does make all the difference. The authors provide us much context to handle all of the above in this well-done book."

—*Kim Butler, Author, Founder, ProsperityEconomics.org*

"*Financial Blindpot* gives nonfinancial managers the confidence to understand the nuance beyond the numbers. 10/10 would recommend if you want to know more about our current financial system."

—*Bruce Ellemo, Author, Speaker, Personal & Corporate Coach, bruceellemo.net*

"*Financial Blindpot* combines readability with well researched and understandable examples. I now feel much better equipped to speak with my own financial advisor and ready to ask him questions and encourage him to consult experts in the various 'products' which may be useful to better serve my family and make the most of the money I earn from my efforts."

—*Mike Lenz, CBI Author, Partner, Business Intermediary, Chinook Business Advisory Ltd., chinookmabb.com*

"Through stories, analogies and metaphors, the authors illustrate how financial blindspots contribute to poor financial decisions. *Financial Blindpot* is an easy read, full of proven strategies and tactics that lead to positive financial outcomes. Financial stability is an important contributor to overall happiness. *Financial Blindpot* will help you spend enjoy and share your money."

—*Norm Trainor, President & CEO, The Covenant Group,*
Strategic Consultant | Executive Coach | Speaker | Author,
Covenantrgroup.com

"*Financial Blindpot* take you on a journey to help you see what you don't naturally see – blind spots. You will likely be amazed to discover some beliefs you thought to be true are in fact not true. So, if this is the case, when would you want to know what your blind spots are?"

—*Dean Harder, Founder of H, Author, www.deanharder.com*

"The authors provide a valuable resource by enlightening the reader on aspects of their thoughts or behaviour - conscious or subconscious - surrounding money. Understanding the basics, not only what an RRSP or 401(k) actually is, but how money works and what it is to you, provides a foundation for any reader's career in wealth accumulation."

—*Robinson Smith, President of Smith Consulting*
Group Ltd and best-selling author of Master Your
Mortgage for Financial Freedom

FINANCIAL
BLINDPOT

FINANCIAL BLINDPOT

*Insider Secrets for Achieving
Financial Freedom*

MICHAEL BAKER · ERIC B. WATCHORN

Contact information for Blindpot Media– email info@financialblindspotsbook.com or visit financialblindspotsbook.com.

ISBN: 9781738221905 (paperback)
ISBN: 9781738221912 (ebook)
ISBN: 9781738221929 (hardcover)

Ordering Information:
Special discounts are available on quantity purchases by corporations, associations, and others. For details, email info@financialblindspotsbook.com or visit financialblindspotsbook.com.

Publisher's Cataloging-in-Publication Data
Names: Baker, Michael, 1965- . | Watchorn, Eric B., 1966- .
Title: Financial blindpot : insider secrets for achieving financial freedom / Michael Baker ; Eric B. Watchorn.
Description: [Canada] : Blindpot Media , 2024. | Includes bibliographic references. | Summary: Covers ten different blind spots consumers should be aware of when obtaining financial advice and products. Provides usable spotlights and solutions for financial consumers and clients in both Canada and the USA.
Identifiers: ISBN 9781738221929 (hardback) | ISBN 9781738221905 (pbk) | ISBN 9781738221912 (ebook)
Subjects: LCSH: Finance, Personal. | Finance, Personal – Canada. | Finance, Personal – United States. | BISAC: BUSINESS & ECONOMICS / Personal Finance / General. | BUSINESS & ECONOMICS / Personal Finance / Money Management.
Classification: LCC HG179.B35 2024 | DDC 332.024 B--dc23

TABLE OF CONTENTS

INTRODUCTION

Many people in Canada and the U.S. are overwhelmed by the number of options and the amount of *conflicting* professional opinions that exist about finances. To complicate matters, much of what people learn in the financial field is learned indirectly. *All debt is bad. Deferring taxes is always good. Banks are always safe, conservative places for your money.* Huge advertising dollars dominate print, audio, television, and the internet. Social media has crammed these subjects into people's smartphones, tablets, and computers.

There are certainly benefits to having information in the hands of those that need it, seek it, and want it. However, what some people fail to realize is that there is the other side of the coin, information and context that are hidden from view. We call these things *Blindpot*.

Most consumers experience some kind of blind spot in their financial experiences.

Kelly Keehn of the *Financial Post's Canada Consumer Advocate* completed a "Financial Blind Spots Survey" as commissioned by *FP Canada*. They evaluated the financial habits and behavior of Canadians and "found that a significant number are turning a blind eye to their personal finances due to confusion, lack of knowledge, or simply being overwhelmed."

Keehn adds rightly that "People can often get paralyzed by all the information available—to the extent that they just shut their minds off."[1]

In essence, a blind spot is what you don't know that you don't know, which makes it difficult to discover since it's truly hidden from sight.

No one can be an expert in all areas of finance and taxation. Even this book isn't an exhaustive collection of all the blind spots and spotlights out there today—not to mention the ones that may come into existence in the future as finance laws and tools change. (To keep up on evolving financial blind spots and spotlights, be sure to check out our YouTube channel at https://www.youtube.com/@FinancialBlindSpots.)

When providing financial services, most independent advisors have specific areas of competence and specialization. The most effective financial advisors are great communicators and are clear about their capabilities and how those skills relate to their clients. Great advisors welcome and seek professional collaboration for the purpose of achieving the best possible outcomes for

---

1   "Financial Blind Spots: Close to 40% of Canadians Feel Their Financial Futures Are Not Under Control," Newswire, October 17, 2017, https://www.newswire.ca/news-releases/financial-blind-spots-close-to-40-of-canadians-feel-their-financial-futures-are-not-under-control-651296543.html.

clients. The process of collaboration not only improves the client experience, but it is also an effective way to ensure that clients are not negatively impacted by blind spots specific to the advisors.

In this book, we'll show you how to identify your financial blind spots, and we'll provide ideas to navigate them. We'll show you how to judge what's good for you and your financial goals in the avalanche of information that all promises the best possible results for everyone including financial consumers like you.

We came into the financial services industry from different backgrounds, and like other industries, fresh eyes can identify challenges and disconnects that perhaps home-grown participants may not.

Mike is accomplished and enjoyed a successful career as a chartered professional accountant before becoming part of the financial services industry. Mike worked for PwC in the Cayman Islands for over 10 years auditing large financial institutions. When he returned to his hometown, Medicine Hat, Alberta, he was a partner with two local accounting firms that specialized in business consulting, taxation, and accounting for owner-managed businesses.

Eric had an entrepreneurial career as an owner of a trading floor in Canada and Vietnam that, in brief, included being an educator to hundreds of traders, business owners, financial analysts, traders, and hedge fund consultants before joining the financial services industry to assist clients with their financial journey.

Our intention is to share the practical and useful perspectives we've gained as financial professionals in the hope that you, the reader, can better navigate through times of volatility and uncertainty. One of the biggest mistakes we think people make is viewing the factors that affect personal finance, such as taxation, protection, and volatility of assets, as separate elements rather than as interrelated and connected. We believe that it is more useful to first understand these factors individually and then consider them holistically as part of your personal strategy.

Our aim is to make the journey to financial freedom less daunting and more attainable through the illumination of financial blind spots and spotlights. But before getting into the various financial subjects, we'll begin with YOU and your psychology. Your mindset and beliefs are paramount, and because of this importance we'll need you to consider and perhaps re-evaluate who you are, what you ascribe meaning to, and who you can be for yourself and others. One will never be more than what your mindset will allow.

Knowing enough about money to cover your bills is not enough financial literacy to provide long-term financial security. If you are in this situation, you might want to ask a simple question: *Is it possible that you have bought into financial myths that do not serve you?*

We feel that our discussion of financial blind spots will help you build your financial future on solid ground. The knowledge of the difference between investing and saving can make a big difference in the short and long term. Understanding when to consider structured and manufactured financial products versus when to consider unstructured solutions is also important. Let's face it—we have all invested when perhaps we should have simply saved. And, we have saved when we possibly would have been better off investing.

How do we allocate cash flow and capital toward different purposes? Are there options beyond the typical avenues offered to us? We believe the pathway is proven and established. However, the pathway is wide and covers lots of ground, and there are many ways to navigate the terrain. The chapters covering blind spots are meant to provide the reader with awareness, and the chapters covering spotlights will share and illuminate the paths we recommend.

It all starts with a teachable and open mind—a mind that can consider possibilities beyond the latest financial TV commercial or social media ad.

With that said, action is more important than awareness and knowledge. A significant number of men over 40 years of age experience some kind of lower back issue. And it's safe to say that most of those men are probably aware that 10 minutes of sit-ups and crunches to strengthen their core would go a long way to helping relieve most of these back issues. Yet, most do not act on something so simple, effective, and inexpensive that could easily solve their issue.

The same applies to succeeding with your financial strategy. Being a sponge to information and aware of concepts does little to implement positive outcomes in your life. One must act!

Most have heard the analogy of the frog in a pot of cold water. When the temperature is turned up, the frog misses the opportunity to jump out and escape before the water boils it to death. Why? Because the process is so gradual.

The years go by so gradually that you may miss starting to invest early. You may also miss out on locking in protective measures like disability, critical illness, and life insurance. These opportunities are real and at your fingertips, especially if you start early.

If used as intended, this book will illuminate many financial tools available and help you obtain the purpose and clarity necessary to achieve your financial dreams. This book's blind spot chapters and Spotlights are intended to allow you, the reader, to jump around without losing value.

Spotlights, as the name suggests, are highlighted strategies, concepts, and information on financial tools designed to provide a framework for immediate action. These insights will help you understand certain tools or strategies that may or may not have been presented to you in the past.

We appreciate you joining us on this journey. Here's to the financially successful YOU!

PART I
BLINDPOT

FINANCIAL BLIND$POT #1
YOUR MINDSET

Begin by thinking about your thinking.

Let's consider your health for a moment. Most experts would agree that optimal health includes a balanced diet, supplements, daily exercise, and quality sleep. Similarly, optimizing financial health includes earning an income, understanding the impact of taxes, navigating the dos and don'ts of financing, and other lifestyle factors—all of which culminate in earning a good return on free cash flow.

Now, if we know in theory what's required to have good physical and financial health, why are these things so hard to achieve in practice? Unfortunately, there are often many complex psychological and behavioral factors that can stop us from achieving optimal results.

This is why it's of vital importance to start with the mind. Believe it or not, the first financial blind spot is unrelated to money. Or, rather, it encompasses money but extends far beyond that.

Our first blind spot: *In our experience, most people don't spend enough time thinking.*

Often, we choose to not think much during our day because thinking is difficult. That's why many of us avoid thinking whenever we can.

You might be saying, "Wait a minute! I'm thinking all the time. Heck, it's almost impossible to stop thinking!"

Yes, you have thoughts. Some of them probably appear to be random, while others are aroused by a song, a smell, or a familiar place. But having thoughts is not the same as thinking. It helps to understand that the voice in your head is part of you but not all of you. Distinguishing yourself from the voice in your head can help to avoid common problems.

When we say "thinking" we're talking about actively using your mind to produce thoughts, rather than thoughts that arise without any action on your part. This type of thinking is something active rather than passive.

Too often people believe that when they *have* the things they want, they will *do* what they want, and they will become the person that they always wanted to *be*. The words *Have, Do, and Be* have become a mainstream prescription for a dream life, when in fact it's more of a fantasy.

If you want an example of this, look no further than advertisements for cars, jewelry, clothing, and other products. The messaging is essentially the same: When you have (fill in the blank), you will (fill in the blank), and you will be (fill in the blank).

For instance, picture Vin Diesel driving a supercharged Dodge coupe as he says, "We all have a choice to be sheep or shepherds (dramatic pause). And then there is the big bad wolf. He eats sheep (engines revved). Welcome to the brotherhood of muscle."[2]

Who knew you could become as cool as Vin Diesel, and even join his brotherhood, by simply purchasing a supercharged Dodge!

In reality, the formula for fulfillment works in a different way. When you're in a proper state of *being*, you will *do* what it takes, and you will *have* the things you want in life.

The true formula is *Be-Do-Have,* not *Have-Be-Do.* And *being* starts with thinking.

Where you are today is a result of your thoughts. Thoughts are translated into actions, and actions are then translated into what you have. What you have is what you perceive as bringing value to your life. In this way, you create meaning and value in your relationships, your physical environment, and your lifestyle.

A close friend of ours, Norm Trainor of the business training program Covenant Group, said that if you want to see what someone values, look at where they spend their time and their money.[3]

---

2   Test Drive, "Dodge Commercial 2017 - Vin Diesel - Brotherhood of Muscle Rally," YouTube, June 19, 2017, video, 2:10, https://www.youtube.com/watch?v=B8NdfuBStis.
3   Norm Trainor, "Expressing Your Values," LinkedIn, April 27, 2015, https://www.linkedin.com/pulse/expressing-your-values-norm-trainor/.

The Power of Where You Grew Up

Where you grew up is a big factor in determining income in the future. In a 2017 article in *The Globe and Mail* titled "A Tale of Two Canadas," reporters Doug Saunders and Tom Cardoso asserted that where you grew up affects your income in adulthood. The article was primarily based on the work of economist Miles Corak, who analyzed millions of Canadians' income data. The findings are startling, but not all that surprising from our view:

- The chances that a child with parents in the **bottom fifth** of income will have income in the *bottom* fifth when they become an adult ranged from 25.9 percent in Alberta to 41.4 percent in Manitoba.

- The chances that a child with parents in the **bottom fifth** of income will have income in the *top* fifth when they become an adult ranged from 18.5 percent in Alberta to 6.1 percent in Manitoba.

- The chances that a child with parents in the **top fifth** of income will have income in the *top* fifth when they become an adult ranged from 37.5 percent in Alberta to 25.6 percent in both British Columbia and Nova Scotia.[4]

Now we understand that it's natural to think about all the reasons why a child who grew up in a home with parents in the top fifth for income in Canada might be more likely to do the same or

---

4   Doug Saunders and Tom Cardoso, "A Tale of Two Canadas: Where You Grew Up Affects Your Income in Adulthood," The Globe and Mail, June 23, 2017, https://www.theglobeandmail.com/news/national/a-tale-of-two-canadas-where-you-grow-up-affects-your-adult-income/article35444594/.

better for their family. After all, we have all heard the benefits of children who were "born on third base."

However, does it make sense that the environment would have that significant of an impact if we all possessed the mental capability needed to think properly as we have just discussed? From this rationale, shouldn't we all be doing much better in general?

Why does our environment have such a dramatic influence on our future?

We cannot teach a baby the same way that we teach an adult. The infant is necessarily immersed in the experience rather than taught. And although there have been lots of studies, researchers cannot say exactly how children learn to speak. Eventually, though, the child utters their first words such as "mama" or "dada."

Similarly, young children continue to learn through immersion beyond that first year. There are many writers, educators, medical doctors, and other professionals who have indicated that this immersive period lasts until we reach the age of five or six years old.[5] Thereafter, we all relate our "new" experiences (those after the age of six) to the context we gained during the immersive period. This feedback loop becomes one of the primary ways we learn to move through the world.

It may be shocking to realize that at times we're looking at the world and reacting to our experiences from the viewpoint of

---

5   Jeff Suchan, "Immersive Learning: What It Is and How To Use It," Roundtable Learning, April 3, 2023, https://roundtablelearning.com/immersive-learning-what-it-is-and-how-to-use-it/.

a six-year-old. For instance, have you ever wondered why we continue to question whether we are good enough, whether people like us, and whether people care—even into middle age?

Immersed in Money

Now let's apply this to how a person might come to view money. If scarcity of money, fear of money, or fear of the loss of money are hardwired into our subconscious through immersion, the stats we cited earlier start to make more sense.

If much of our context around money and finances is wired into the subconscious during our childhood years, the next logical step is to look back and see what those limits or barriers might be—and, more importantly, to see how those limits or barriers might be affecting your life in the present.

For instance, in our experience it's not uncommon to find that if a client feels a lack of control surrounding money, it could be a result of early experiences that included the lack of control or access to money or savings. Here are examples of how our thinking about our finances are shaped—for better or for worse—at a young age.

When Mike was about six years old, he developed a positive association with life insurance. His family lived in a large apartment complex during the early 1970s. The units in the complex backed onto a large, fenced-in green space the size of two football fields. All the kids would gather and play for hours after school and on weekends.

One day a kid told all the other kids that he had $100 in his bank account. This would be the equivalent of around $600 today. All the kids gasped. Mike remembers running back to his apartment to ask his parents what he had in his bank account.

His parents laughed and told him he did not have a bank account. Mike was dejected until they told him he did have approximately $400 of cash value in a life insurance policy they had started funding for him after he was born.

Mike ran out to tell all his friends how much was in his bank account. To this day he puts almost six figures into cash-value life insurance every year.

———◦◉◦———

This story comes from one of Eric's clients, who we will call Daniel. When he was a teenager, Daniel worked a part-time job to earn money, as a lot of kids do. Most of what he earned went into a savings account for his plans to go to university.

Daniel watched as the money slowly accumulated. He says he enjoyed always knowing his balance and loved the excitement of watching his money grow.

Rarely did he splurge on things, and most of the time when he needed to go somewhere he borrowed his parents' car. Daniel figures he must have borrowed it one too many times without asking, because one day he came home to find a red Ford Pinto out in front of their house.

"It's yours," his father said.

Being a teenager at the time and not really knowing how banks and accounts worked, Daniel didn't realize that because he'd opened up the account with his father, his father could access the account—which is exactly what his father did. He'd gone down to the bank, cleaned out Daniel's saving account, and bought the Pinto so his son wouldn't need to borrow their car anymore.

Daniel told Eric he'd made the best of the situation and drove the car. His father most likely thought he was teaching his son a valuable lesson. He was, in fact, but it was not the lesson he thought he was imparting.

For a long time after that "lesson," Daniel says his view on saving was, "What's the point?"

Social Conditioning

In working with clients, we've noticed how the large-scale impact of social conditioning by major financial institutions also influences how people feel about money. When we break it down, almost everyone's relationship with money changed the first day they opened a bank account.

Up until that point you had probably saved some of your birthday money or a few dollars left by the tooth fairy. You may still be able to remember when your parents finally let you purchase something from a store.

What a feeling that was when you could hand over physical money and receive an item that you valued and chose. We remember the look of amazement that our children had and the feeling of power they exuded. We never lose that exhilarating and powerful feeling experienced when we can control our money.

However, the first lesson you were taught at the bank was that you don't completely control your money. After all, at that point, you are hardly the expert. As such, for your own best interests, it's appropriate and customary for you to defer to authority, which in this case is the bank. After that day, the lessons come along quickly.

You get your first debit card, for it is right and good that you have immediate and almost universal access to your accounts at the bank. Then, you're approved for a credit card after the bank determines how much of your future cash flow you can expend in the service of debt.

After that, you apply for your first loan. The process is a bit daunting and can feel like an interrogation as they ask for all your financial information. You might be surprised to learn that if the loan is approved, your reward is that the bank will lend you someone else's money. *That's right, you heard correctly: Banks do not carry and are not required to have reserves to match dollar for dollar the loans issued daily. You are essentially borrowing money that others have deposited in the bank.*[6]

These lessons are reinforced over and over again throughout our lives because the need for financing increases at an accelerated pace.

For better or worse, our parents were not our only teachers when it comes to money. At an early age, there are a whole host of characters involved in developing your financial intelligence. Banking is big business, and your bank manager, the credit officer, and investment advisors reinforce a lot of the negative and disempowering thoughts, feelings, and emotions around money you may have experienced over the years.

Why? Because it's profitable to do so.

Some may think after reading the commentary above that we are being a bit hard on the banks. The truth is that we're simply pointing out that a big machine (financial services) has a huge number of long tentacles reaching into every household. And like any well-run organization, it uses its tools, branding, and narrative to move people toward products that improve shareholder value. But the interests of the shareholders of a large financial institution and their customers are *not* the same.

---

6   Abha Bhattarai, Talia Trackim, and Martin Tognola, "What Banks Do With Your Money," Washington Post, July 6, 2023, https://www.washingtonpost.com/business/interactive/2023/what-banks-do-with-your-money/.

So, What Does This Mean?

Financial institutions have taught us that we do not control our money. To a certain extent, they're right. Try to go to the bank and withdraw $10,000 in cash. Other than being told that you'll have to fill out a form used to identify *money laundering,* you'll have to come back to pick up the money, which can take up to three days from the date of your request.

Or, consider how easy it is to make purchases with debit and credit cards. The use of cash has gone down significantly. If you use a card, computer, or smartphone to move money, the transaction is recorded in the banking system to the delight of the bankers and the government. Have you noticed the increased advertising and discussion of a central bank digital currency in Canada?

The ultimate irony is this: Financial institutions could easily provide more value to people. They have powerful systems and access to many of your transactions. Sure, your financial institution sends you a statement every month. But if there is any organization capable of printing a monthly report that categorizes your income, how much you spent, what you spent it on (clothes, restaurants, bills, etc.), and then compared the current month to months prior on an absolute and percentage basis, it's your financial institution.

Yet they don't. Remarkably, so much financial information is in the background. Consider transaction fees on debit and credit cards. The more you spend, the more fees the institutions earn. Though the information is available to you, it's not put front and center so that it's easily found. Instead, you're forced to search for answers and solutions that will help you move toward your financial goals. This is a blind spot you will see consistently throughout this book.

Yes, we may be disempowered in our actions toward our financial situation and in dealing with financial service providers. But we also want to be clear that the answer isn't to develop a deep negative association with the bank and other financial institutions. That will only guide your decisions in yet another unproductive direction. It's the other side of the same coin.

Instead, our goal is for you to be able to look at financial institutions simply as service organizations that *may* be able to assist you in your journey to have your finances support the life that you want to live.

Pulling It All Together

The lightbulb moment for most of us is when we hear that little voice in the back of our head for what it is—a survival mechanism. When you recognize that voice is not "you," and you look at a situation from a different perspective, you'll probably see that there are lots of different meanings that you could take from any one situation. Odds are you haven't chosen the story that empowers you, and that's okay—it's human nature. Knowing this, hopefully you're better able to see the impact of your environment and your social network (i.e., referrals from people you know, the desire to keep pace with your peers, etc.) on your mindset.

Another useful exercise is to look at your complaints. Examine them to see what benefit you gain from holding on to your complaints. For example, maybe you have too much debt. It's important to examine what, if anything, all that debt is doing for you. Perhaps your debt is why you're able to have a large home or luxury car that gives you a feeling of social status, and that status is important to you. Maybe your debt is due to starting a business.

Another complaint might be that your investment portfolio is not performing. What could be a benefit of an underperforming portfolio? Maybe that portfolio is managed by a friend or someone you were referred to by a friend. By *not* moving your money to a different advisor, you kept an important friendship intact, and that's something you value more than financial profit.

An additional benefit of poor performance may be holding yourself accountable by facing the fact you did not spend enough time finding a qualified advisor. Now you recognize you need to put in your due diligence as you seek a new advisor.

When you understand that most of our complaints can serve us in some way, you're one step closer to having the ability to take real action in your life.

This is why "thinking about our thinking" is critical. Just be aware that it can feel unnatural or unusual, which is why most of us do not do it. Maybe it's because we do not realize it's a blind spot, or because we think it's too hard. Though it's tempting to give up, don't. We have one major advantage built into our brains: *We become what we think about.*

So, let's start thinking about money in a way that works for you. As Dr. Joe Dispenza says, "be defined by a vision of the future instead of the memory of the past ... become conscious and stop making the same unconscious choices."[7]

---

7   Timothy Lafortune (thetruthseeker33), "Dr. Joe Dispenza Speech," TikTok, March 20, 2023, video, 2:01, https://www.tiktok.com/@thetruthseeker33/video/7212836094147087662.

FINANCIAL BLIND$POT #2
BIASES AND TENDENCIES

Now that you are aware of thinking about your thinking, let's examine how your biases and tendencies—some of which you probably aren't even aware of—can influence your financial actions.

A client (we'll call him Jim) came to us looking for financial advice, and through the course of our conversations, it became evident he was protective of his relationship with a specific bank.

Brand loyalty is common, and our clients have their reasons for being true to their bank. It could be that our clients have friends who work at the bank, or that the client's family has a long history of banking with the institution, as Jim's did. Sometimes the client is simply averse to change.

When our clients are intent on continuing their financial relationship with "their" bank, most often that's fine with us, too.

More than anything, we want our clients to feel secure in knowing their finances are in hands they trust.

But when our clients' trust in any institution, bank or otherwise, turns into unquestioning commitment, we recognize that for the red flag it is. This sort of trust often switches our clients to "autopilot" when it comes to the details of their finances, and that's not a good thing.

This is the type of unquestioning commitment Jim had in his bank. He was so comfortable, in fact, that he didn't bother paying close attention to the terms of a loan he took out. Why should he? He could trust "his" bank, right?

It wasn't until Jim started working with us that he discovered that he'd signed a loan document that happened to include a break fee of over $100,000. In other words, if Jim wanted to pay off the loan early, it would be viewed as breaking the contract. The penalty for doing so would cost him an additional $100K.

Now, Jim is a smart person. But even smart people can be fooled, and more often than not they're fooled by themselves. In his case, Jim fooled himself into thinking he could trust his bank so completely that he didn't need to pay attention to the details of what he was signing.

Unfortunately, Jim is not alone. We all succumb to certain psychological biases and tendencies that we carry around in our heads. These biases and tendencies are neither good nor bad. They're simply predictive, shorthand ways our brains make sense of the world. For Jim, his tendency was what's called "consistency and commitment tendency."

In his case, Jim had inherited a family commitment to a particular bank. Like most of us, he wanted to act consistently with that commitment because we tend to view that kind of behavior as a positive trait.

We regularly see all sorts of biases and tendencies in our clients. Though these are mental rather than financial blind spots, it pays to be aware of the tricks your mind can play on you when dealing with your financial well-being. The only real way to make sure you don't fall victim is to be aware of them.

When you learn to think about your thinking, it'll be easier to see the other blind spots that we'll get to a bit later on.

Denial

Most of us are probably familiar with *denial*. In psychological terms, it's when we choose to deny the reality of a situation so we can avoid an uncomfortable truth and the way it makes us feel.[8] The key word here is "choose."

Examples of this might be someone refusing to believe an unwelcome diagnosis from their doctor or, say, holding onto a stock long after it's lost its value and shows no signs of rebounding.

---

8   "Denial," Psychology Today, accessed August 31, 2023, https://www.psychologytoday.com/us/basics/denial.

Consistency and Commitment Tendencies

Like Jim in the story above, most people have the desire to be consistent in their behavior, choices, and commitments.[9] That is, once we commit to a course of action, we tend to limit the amount of additional thinking related to that particular action.

It's like that old parable of the baby elephant tied with a rope the thickness of two fingers. Years later you see the same elephant as an adult held in waiting with the same rope tied to its leg even though as an adult it possesses the strength to easily snap it.[10]

Other examples of our bias toward consistency and commitment are all around us. As already discussed, many people seldom question their relationship with their bank. For instance, according to a 2013 article from the *Guardian*, "account holders are more likely to stay with their bank—typically for 17 years—than remain loyal to their husband or wife, with the average British marriage lasting just 11 years and six months." [11]

Pavlovian

Most of us have heard about Pavlov's dog. For those who haven't, Pavlov would ring a bell before he fed the dog. Over time,

---

9   Patrick Hunt, "Commitment and Consistency – Lirio Bias Brief," Lirio, December 18, 2018, https://lirio.com/blog/commitment-consistency-lirio-bias-brief/.

10   Thanh_min, "The Elephant Rope," Medium, April 8, 2017, https://medium.com/motivationapp/the-elephant-rope-c22ee790a226.

11   Patrick Collinson, "Switching Banks: Why Are We More Loyal to Our Banks than to a Partner?" Guardian (U.S. edition), September 7, 2013, https://www.theguardian.com/money/2013/sep/07/switching-banks-seven-day.

Pavlov found that the dog would salivate when he rang the bell. The experiment found that conditioning could create a response that would not be normally associated with that particular act or event.[12]

Ever wonder why companies like Coke, Pepsi, and McDonald's continue to spend huge amounts of money on advertising even though they've captured a large market share? Well, it's because if they don't, we'll stop thinking (i.e., salivating) about them.

Just like the canine salivating in its cage, we form strong associations with fast food franchises. Strangely enough, this phenomenon also creates a connection with major banks and other financial institutions.

Reciprocation

Another significant tendency comes from reciprocation. That is, if someone does something for you, you feel the need to do something for them.

If you look at your own experiences, you're probably familiar with that uneasy feeling when you might believe you *owe* somebody. Reciprocation is hardwired into all of us.

For example, in his book *Influence: The Psychology of Persuasion*, psychologist Robert B. Cialdini outlined how a religious group

---

12 Kendra Cherry, "Pavlov's Dogs and the Discovery of Classical Conditioning," Verywell Mind, last updated November 20, 2022, https://www.verywellmind.com/pavlovs-dogs-2794989.

called the Hare Krishna received significant donations after offering people in passing a flower, which was then followed with a request for a donation.[13]

This trend extends to financial institutions too, only they offer to provide a financial plan at no charge. It could also be something as slick as handing you documents in a leather-bound portfolio that's yours to keep or taking you to lunch. These gestures, whether well-intentioned or not, work. We all should be aware of those instances when they may be used contrary to our best interest.

Social Proof

Social proof is another powerful influence on the choices we make. We can't know everything about everything. So, we've evolved to use shortcuts to establish trust. Paying attention to how and what others are doing is one of the ways we all navigate the world. Client testimonials are great examples of powerful social proof at work.

So too are celebrity endorsements like Samuel L. Jackson for Capital One, Morgan Freeman (that voice!) for Visa, or Aaron Rogers and Patrick Mahomes for State Farm Insurance. Heck, the celebrity doesn't even have to be a person to convince us. When the animated, lovable Groot from *Guardians of the Galaxy* teamed up with Geico, we were essentially taking financial advice from a cartoon character.

---

13   Robert B. Cialdini, *Influence: The Psychology of Persuasion* (New York: HarperCollins, 2009), 32.

There's nothing wrong with looking to others for input. However, you must recognize when you're putting too much emphasis on what the crowd—and marketing dollars—are doing.

Distortion of Perception

This bias is rooted in perception. It occurs when you're presented with a contrast between two or more things, and it changes the way you view those things if they were instead presented to you without any comparison. Distortion of perception by contrast has a *huge* impact on logical thinking.

Think of the real estate agent showing either a run-down property (or an extremely overpriced one) before going to the home that they really wanted to show the potential buyer. The potential buyer is so affected by seeing a run-down property (or a house so out of their price range) that the buyer develops a stronger attraction to the next home shown to them.

Or how, after spending $60,000 on a vehicle, we are "conveniently" shown a $3,000 detailing package. Three grand for the package suddenly appears inexpensive relative to the big purchase you just made.

Bias against Math

We regularly see clients exhibit a bias against math. This stems from the non-mathematical nature of the human brain.[14] Clients are often confused by the improper application of numbers to a particular situation.

Here's a head-scratching example to illustrate what we mean. Three men go into a hotel and are told a room will cost $30 for the night. They each pay $10. Later that day, the manager looks over the details for the room and she figures out that basically the men should only have been charged $25 total. The manager gives five $1 bills to the bell captain and asks him to give $5 back to the men.

But on his way to their room, the bell captain figures out that there's no way he can split the $5 evenly between the three men. So, the bell captain pockets $2 and gives the men back $3.

Each man received a $1 refund for their individual cost of the room for the night, meaning each man paid $9. So, $9 x $3 = $27.

Add to that the $2 the bellman kept. That brings the total to $29. But wait, the men originally paid $30. Where's the missing dollar?

No idea, right? It's logical fallacy.

---

14   "Bias from the Non-Mathematical Nature of the Human Brain," MOI Global, December 13, 2017, https://moiglobal.com/bias-from-the-non-mathematical-nature -of-the-human-brain/.

We've given you a whole bunch of information. We inserted the numbers "$27" and "$2" and now you're adding that up to $29 and looking for a missing dollar that's not missing. The hotel got $25. The bell captain kept $2. The three men got $1 each, accounting for the full $30.

Incentive-Cause Bias

The good news is these next two aren't on you. They have more to do with the motivations of the person you're dealing with.

Have you ever noticed that the investment advisor suggests that your money should be placed in investments? Or that the insurance advisor suggests whole life insurance?

Meanwhile, the real estate agent suggests, surprise, rental properties and the—well, you get the drift.

These professionals are biased by incentives. They are incentivized through their compensation models to sell their products to people like you. Don't get us wrong—we believe incentives are great when the incentives are aligned with the needs of the customer. However, it's less so when those incentives are the primary driving force behind the advice your advisor is giving you.

Persian Messenger Syndrome

This can be described as "there's usually a sad ending for the bearer of bad news."

For example, your investment advisor is always excited to review your portfolio after a year with double-digit returns. But that enthusiasm and excitement seem to vanish during severe market downturns.

This is despite the irony that more opportunity and wealth can be created in market downturns than has ever been created during a market run-up.[15] You should require your professional advisors to communicate with you during all market cycles.

The Antidote: Ask

As this list of biases shows, our human nature can be hijacked fairly easily—especially if we're not aware of it. The simple antidote for many of these biases is to simply ask questions of your advisors. And you do not have to become an expert to do it.

For example, if your advisor is using a simple example that causes contrast distortion, ask them to illustrate the point on a whiteboard. Or when your advisor offers services without a fee, politely ask the advisor how they are compensated. Understanding the compensation will allow you to avoid the tendency to commit to a plan due to the power of reciprocity. We have included several questions at the end of this chapter that can help you.

---

15   Adam Hayes, "Investing in Crisis: A High-Risk, High-Reward Strategy," Investopedia, last updated August 9, 2023, https://www.investopedia.com/articles/investing/041415/investing-crisis-high-riskhigh-reward-strategy.asp.

Also, if you employ some of the strategies covered in the Spotlights section of this book, we believe you'll be better equipped to deal with whatever life throws at you. Awareness of our ability to think about our thinking, and the impact that social conditioning and programming can have on us, is a powerful force that will help you in all areas of your life and not just in all things financial.

Here are a few questions you might consider asking your advisor to help spot and guard against any biases or tendencies (yours or theirs) influencing your decisions.

Questions for Advisors

- Can you tell me a bit about your experience and how you became a financial advisor?

- What products or services do you typically recommend or specialize in?

- Are there certain products or services that you never recommend, and can you explain why?

- What licenses do you have and how are you regulated?

- How do you get compensated? (Incentive Clause Bias)

- What do you enjoy most about your business?

- Do you have any staff or strategic relationships you use to provide your services?

- What has been the most significant challenge you've faced in your business?

- Who is your ideal client?
- What is your view of the current market and prospects for the future?

Questions for Yourself When Coming to a Decision

- Am I leaning a certain way on a decision because I would like to avoid an uncomfortable truth? (Denial)

- Am I choosing this only because it's what I've done in the past? (Consistency/Commitment)

- Am I choosing out of some sense of loyalty to a company or brand? (Pavlovian)

- Is my decision based on an obligation I feel because I received a small gift, perk, or deal to get me to this point? (Reciprocation)

- Is my only reason for making this decision simply because celebrities endorse it? Or is it because this seems to be what everyone else is doing? (Social Proof)

- Does one option seem better than the other because of the way they were presented to me? Would I feel this way if I had been presented with only the option I'm leaning toward? (Distortion of Perception)

- Am I procrastinating or following an advisor's suggestion without really breaking it down just because I don't like math? (Bias against Math)

Note: If you want to know more about biases and tendencies toward money and other areas of life, try Robert B. Cialdini's

Influence: The Psychology of Persuasion[16] and the speech "The Psychology of Human Misjudgment" given by Charlie Munger that's printed in the book *Poor Charlie's Almanack.*[17]

> *"The important thing is not to stop questioning. Curiosity has its own reason for existence… Never lose a holy curiosity…. Don't stop to marvel."*
>
> -Albert Einstein[18]

---

16   Cialdini, Influence.

17   "The Revised Psychology of Human Misjudgment, by Charlie Munger," Farnam Street Articles, accessed August 30, 2023, https://fs.blog/great-talks/psychology-human-misjudgment/.

18   "Old Man's Advice to Youth: 'Never Lose a Holy Curiosity'," Life Magazine, May 2, 1955, 64, https://books.google.com/books?id=dlYEAAAAMBAJ&lpg=PP1&dq =Life%2C%202%20May%201955&pg=PA61#v=onepage&q=Life%2C%202%20 May%201955&f=false.

FINANCIAL BLIND$POT #3
YOUR PROCRASTINATION

Procrastination isn't a weakness; it is a signal you need to evaluate, ask questions, and even ask for help.

> *"Bravely overcoming one small fear gives you the courage to take on the next."*
> -The Way of Youth: Buddhist Common Sense for Handling Life's Questions

We want you to embrace procrastination.

Yes, we realize it's highly unusual for someone to ask you to get excited or feel positive about being called a procrastinator. It's a label not generally thrown around as a compliment.

Procrastination is, of course, the act of delaying or postponing something. It's inaction as action; not making a choice is still making a choice.

True, procrastination can cost you. As you will come to

understand, time is *the* most significant factor in wealth creation. If you're procrastinating, then you're stopped and not taking advantage of your time. And if you aren't taking advantage of your time, there's a real cost for your inaction.

So, why the heck are we asking you to embrace your procrastination?

An Impulse and an Opportunity

First, know that procrastination isn't your fault.

As it turns out, the urge not to do something is truly an urge. There's research evidence showing a biological evolutionary root to procrastination. It's tied to our species' survival, and the need to conserve energy during downtime to save energy for hunting or gathering food.[19]

Of course, our culture evolved and our food supply stabilized, leaving that unconscious biological urge to conserve energy through inaction to find some other way to manifest itself. In part, this is what's behind your procrastination.

That said, it's also not *not* your fault. Once you become aware you're procrastinating, it's your responsibility to deal with what's causing you to procrastinate.

---

19   Daniel E. Gustavson et al., ""Genetic Relations Among Procrastination, Impulsivity, and Goal-Management Ability: Implications for the Evolutionary Origin of Procrastination," *Psychological Science* 25 no. 6 (2014): 1178—88, https://journals.sagepub.com/doi/10.1177/0956797614526260?url_ver=Z39.88-2003&rfr _id=ori:rid:crossref.org&rfr_dat=cr_pub.

A biological root impulse doesn't mean you should let yourself off the hook for procrastination. Remember, procrastination costs you time—the most precious resource when it comes to building wealth. With that said, when you can identify and accept procrastination for what it is, you can learn to use it as a powerful tool for action.

Procrastination should be a signal that something's not right with your situation. Use it as a sign pointing you in the right direction. The catch, of course, is that direction isn't one you're crazy about going; otherwise, you wouldn't have hesitated and would already be well on your way.

Still, there's power in recognizing procrastination as an opportunity to assess the situation rather than avoid it.

Over the years, we've both had many clients who procrastinate. While they won't come out and say they're procrastinating, we know it when we see it. They're not returning phone calls. They're not getting us the information we need to help them. They're late for meetings, postpone meetings, or simply don't show up.

They've engaged us to help them with their financial strategy. They've already basically said, "I don't know enough about what I'm doing. I need help."

So why after they've taken that step to reach out to us do they procrastinate? What makes them put off doing the thing they've come to us for help in doing?

Scary Reasons

When someone asks you about your financial situation, "I don't know" is an acceptable answer. But only once. After that, the responsibility is on you to know where you stand. Too often, people leave their situation at "I don't know" rather than recognizing "I don't know" as a signal to find the answer. To be fair, there are many good reasons why people put off finding the answer.

First, finances are a personal subject with a whole host of personal issues that come with it. The truth is, financial matters scare people. It's not fun wondering if you have enough money for the future. For some, it's so scary that as long as they have a good-paying job and can meet their bills every month, they would rather not know the answer.

Often people are overwhelmed by all the information. They're inundated with information, options, terms, slogans, and sagacious sayings, and that overload can lead to a kind of paralysis by analysis. They think it's complicated. And at times, it can be complex. Of course, this is why they sought us out in the first place.

Let's also remember the mental programming from our childhood that covers everything from our health, intellect, and weight to our finances and social skills. How is anyone supposed to make good decisions, even if they're working with an advisor, with so much coming at them?

Perfection is another problem. Everyone wants to choose the absolute best course for themselves, their loved ones, and their wealth. But this need for perfection can stifle action due to the fear of making the wrong choice.

Another reason might be that they feel they don't have enough time to deal with any of it. Though we would argue that if you don't have time for someone to help you, you probably need to make time so they can.

Clients sometimes offer up some version of, "I didn't send you that information because I was embarrassed about my financial situation."

To which we reply with some version of, "We've seen how many people's financial situations? More than we can count. It's like somebody getting naked in front of the doctor. It's no big deal to us."

Then we ask a simple question: "What choices do you have?"

A. You can continue to be embarrassed and do nothing.

B. You can take action and change your situation.

The hope is that they choose option B because we've seen many people turn around their financial lives in a matter of a few years, with some going from nothing to millions of dollars.

These reasons, of course, tie back to fear. Fear of looking bad, of not understanding, and of ignoring the truth about your financial situation.

So, when you find yourself procrastinating, turn that procrastination into something positive. Know that fear is causing you to avoid taking control of your financial situation.

Recognize your procrastination as a red flag that's signaling a problem that needs to be addressed. Do you need more information? Do you need less, or maybe better, information? Or perhaps you need another meeting to re-explain the information.

If you haven't addressed your finances the way you know you probably should, it could be your embedded limiting beliefs causing havoc with your intended actions. Knowing that you should change your autopilot thinking would be a solid step in the right direction.

If not, maybe you're not seeing the bigger picture.

———— ◆ ————

Mike had a situation with a client that was a farmer (we'll call him Dave) and was procrastinating with a financial strategy Mike had put together for him.

When Mike first suggested an insurance strategy that uses discounted dollars to provide for his family, Dave insisted he could just save the money. He has an amazing farming operation and was conscious of his situation and where the money was going. This is a common mindset among farmers. They are accustomed to dealing with the ups and downs in their seed prices, crop yields, market prices for their crops, and, of course, the weather.

Mike told him, yes, absolutely he could just save the money and have it sitting there for his daughter in the future.

But knowing his goals to expand his operation, Mike asked him what if he started saving the money today and then three or four years down the road, a piece of land he's been waiting to purchase was listed for sale? What would he do then?

Dave was going to buy it, of course! He was going to spend the money he intended to save for his daughter, even though he thought she may not want to farm someday. He wasn't seeing the full picture.

He was not thinking about the land he was looking to acquire, his non-farming daughter, and the money he wanted to have for her. He was only thinking of accumulating money for a specific purpose and not what may happen down the road. As in "This bucket of money goes to my daughter so I will put it over there."

Mike finally got him to see that the strategy suggested would allow him to provide for his daughter's future AND expand his operation.

Situations aren't solved in isolation. The only certainty in life is uncertainty. Life will come at us, and when it does, we all need to be prepared to deal with it.

Nothing happens in a vacuum. Procrastination affects your timing as well as your big financial plans. Two examples are your will and end-of-life taxation. You could wind up paying much more than you need to, all because you didn't take action that could target end-of-life taxation or asset transfers from investment accounts and personal corporations.

It can also affect the smaller stuff, too. For instance, when trading stock, options, futures, and currencies, many investors have discovered that *knowing* when to buy does not yield any result whatsoever. It's the action of buying that yields a result, positive or negative, on the trade. Too many investors and traders hesitate. Their continued hesitation translates into *late* execution and unnecessary losses.

Getting You Started

Whatever it is that's causing you to procrastinate means you need more support. When it comes to your financial advisor, you'll find the support you need by simply asking one of the questions for advisors that we listed in the previous chapter.

If you're not getting the right answers, our advice would be to go to someone else. To be clear, that doesn't mean your other advisors are bad people or poor at their job. We all have our strengths and weaknesses. Your questions may be outside the advisor's competence or they may not feel comfortable in your relationship. And that's okay!

This is the start of building your education and taking control of your finances. You don't have to be an expert, but you are responsible for your finances. By asking questions you'll find people you trust and support you as you work toward reaching your goals. They will be in sync with the things you're feeling and allow you to communicate in a way that allows you to move forward.

Again, this is about changing your mindset. Recognize that many of your thoughts and reactions around your finances have been programmed into you. Accept that those thoughts and reactions aren't going away. Fortunately, now you have the tools to recognize them for what they are, which empowers you to take command of your response rather than simply reacting out of programming.

Shift your perspective so you come to see procrastination as a waving flag yelling, "Go, go, go!"

FINANCIAL BLIND$POT #4
YOUR ECONOMIC UNIVERSE

You can create your own successful economic universe regardless of what's happening in the larger economic universe around you.

There's a lot going on in the world. As of this writing, we've had three years of COVID, a war in Ukraine, and, after low interest rates for almost a decade, we've seen an increase in rates by roughly 2.5% to 5.00% within 16 months, according to the Bank of Canada. This represents a 100% increase in the policy interest rate that is regularly reviewed and set by the Bank of Canada. The situation is similar for the United States.[20]

We all tend to let what's going on in the world impact us personally. But believe it or not, when you understand the drivers of wealth (as discussed in the next chapter on maximum potential)

---

20 "Canadian Interest Rates and Monetary Policy Variables: 10-Year Lookup," Bank of Canada, accessed August 31, 2023, https://www.bankofcanada.ca/rates/interest-rates/canadian-interest-rates/.

you will have the master key to succeeding in any environment. We believe that as individuals, we have never been in a better position to create opportunity and prosperity.

One of our favorite books on economics is actually a comic book. *How an Economy Grows and Why It Doesn't* by Irwin Schiff is a parable that explains in clear, simple language how individuals can create an economy from scratch.[21]

Schiff, an anti-tax activist and father of stockbroker and radio personality Peter Schiff, uses a light-hearted "fish" story to teach basic economic principles in such a clear way that we encourage you to read the original comic for yourself.

In brief, *How an Economy Grows and Why It Doesn't* tells the story of three people living on an island and fishing for food every day. The men, named Able, Baker, and Charlie, dive into the nearby waters and, unaided by tools, fish by hand. Day after day it's the same challenging work, and the result is one fish per day for each person.

Then one evening after a long day of fishing, Able starts to wonder if there isn't more to life than *catch*, *eat*, and *catch* again. The mere question that there might be other possibilities ignites Able, who soon comes up with an idea for a "fish-catcher."

Having dared to dream, Able trusts himself, and with this idea he decides to take action. The next day he goes to work in a different way. He begins gathering material for a net.

---

21   Peter D. Schiff and Andrew J. Schiff, *How an Economy Grows and Why It Crashes* (New York: Wiley, 2010).

Meanwhile, the other two men, Baker and Charlie, are skeptical. This is not how we do things! They warn Able that if he does not go fishing, he will go hungry that day. And it's true: Able is taking a huge risk. He's sacrificing catching a fish—and possibly going hungry—so he can build his net. He's investing his time and energy to make the net and at the same time he's going hungry. He's sacrificing a fish today for the idea that he can gather more fish with a net. He's betting on a better life once he's constructed it.

We believe Able's important step forward is a result of questioning his programming, biases, and tendencies. Dramatic improvements in life, in your economic universe, can be created through seemingly simple yet very important steps.

At the end of the day, Able completes his net. The next day, as Baker and Charlie struggle for their one hand-caught fish, Able's net catches two fish with relative ease. This ingenious cartoon illustrates so clearly that each of us can create our economic independence from the world around us. But to do so, it requires a different mentality, effort, ideas, and strategy gained through new sources of information.

All this is in a cartoon to get across the idea. But what does it look like in real life?

⌐●⌐

Alex Hormozi, the founder of Acquisition.com, is a great example of what's possible when you create your own economic universe. Alex's father immigrated to the U.S. from Iran. Following his father's plans for him, Alex went to college and graduated Magna Cum Laude from Vanderbilt University with a bachelor's degree in corporate strategy.

After college, Alex stuck to his father's plans for his son, accepting a job as a management consultant. But after two years there, Alex decided to venture out on his own.

Alex had developed a passion for fitness and wanted to start a gym. He saved $50,000 to get his venture off the ground. He quickly learned that to be successful he needed to have clients for his gym. Alex said in his videos it was that in 2013 he spent $3,000 to attend a weekend workshop on Facebook Ads.

In his first two weeks of running Facebook Ads, 27 people signed up for gym memberships. He'd spent $1,000 on ads and earned over $8,000 in membership fees.

Alex continued to use his new digital advertising skills to obtain clients and build his gym business. He worked hard and grew his gym operations, opening five more gyms with plans for more.

Then, Alex went to an event where he received career changing advice.

He was one of the only people at the event running a brick-and-mortar operation. When he told everyone what he did to open and fill his gyms, the facilitator told Alex he had a Level 10 skill set with a Level 1 opportunity. The group advised him to change his business from running gyms to showing other gym owners how to fill and operate their gyms.

This changed everything for Alex. It led to him developing a Gym Launch and supplement business called Prestige Labs. It offered a licensing model for gym owners and other related businesses. Eventually, he sold these businesses for $46.2M, with Alex receiving an undisclosed amount for a software company that he also owned.

He now manages his family office Acquisition.com that invests in private businesses. Alex and his wife's net worth crossed $100 million as of 2021.

As we've laid out in the previous chapters, subtle mental programming, and the ever-present urge to procrastinate influence your mindset. In turn, this mindset determines your actions, and ultimately, your results. Influencers often suggest that when you're sick and tired of being sick and tired, that's when you're finally ready to change.

This is when you're most open to changing your behavior despite how uncomfortable it may be to do something about your situation. The key is to not allow your procrastination to take over your nature and desires. After all, we live only once, and failure is better than regrets. We would argue that there's no such thing as failure, and if such a thing does exist, it would only manifest if you quit.

You can choose to steer your financial decisions and create an economic universe that, if not impervious to outside economic forces, can withstand the predictably unpredictable twists and turns of the economic world at large. In essence, you may be surprised by what you can create, especially when you trust yourself, and perhaps even others.

Creating Your Economic Universe

First and foremost, creating your economic universe requires that you adjust the time frame in which you hope to realize your plans. People tend to overestimate what they can do in a year and severely underestimate what they can accomplish in a decade. Think of your willingness to alter the time frame in which you expect to see results as a necessary precursor to the Big Bang that you will experience as you develop and expand your economic universe. It's the power that sets your economic universe in motion and then keeps it expanding for your benefit.

Of course, adjusting the time frame in which you expect results is much easier said than done. Luckily, some foundational elements can help you create and shape your economic universe.

Commitment

As we said above, creating your own economic universe is a choice you make. Because it's an active pursuit that requires consistent commitment over time, it's always helpful to know your motivation for making the choice. It could range from "I want to be rich" to "I don't want to be poor" (truly not the same thing). Your motivation might be something as grand as making the world a better place to the humbler, but no less noble, desire to provide for your family. However, your commitment will ground you in your belief and actions toward the future.

It's important to know and understand what's driving you to create your personal economic reality for a few reasons. First, knowing why you're doing something can often help you make choices when you're trying to figure out how to do something. Second, there are times when reminding yourself why you're pursuing your financial dream can help you persist in those moments when things aren't going exactly as you envisioned.

Imagination and Vision

If knowing why you're doing something is your starting point, then it's just as important to have an idea of where you want to go. What do you imagine success looking like? Once you have that broad vision, you can then begin to set short- and long-term goals tailored toward helping you realize the fantastic success you've imagined.

It truly is a privilege to dream and then be able to work to achieve that dream. So, dream big! Get creative! Be the innovator in your own life! Have daily gratitude for the options you see before you. Many people on this earth today do not have the same opportunities and/or financial options we enjoy. Just like Able in the comic, your efforts can turn out to be rewarding for both you and your community.

Education

Once you know why you're creating your own economic universe and what you want it to look like, you'll want to explore the ideas that can help you make it a reality. Luckily, when it comes to access to information, you live in the best time in history. You don't need to be an expert with every tool or concept at your disposal. In fact, no one has it all figured out. But you do need to educate yourself enough so that you can ask pertinent questions, and the answers will help you determine if a particular tool or concept can help you build the economic universe you envision.

Educating yourself will also give you the confidence to fend off the inevitable moments of self-doubt—not to mention the doubt of others who, for whatever reason (programming-based fear, lack of imagination, envy, etc.), fail to see your vision for your economic universe.

Action

There's no replacement for action. Action is the most important factor in determining your future. You can only read about things for so long before you have to be in motion. We truly do not learn without trying. The context gained during action reinforces and informs your education. It's an absolutely necessary cycle that course corrects as you move through time. Without action, everything else is academic.

Persistence

When you come face-to-face with hardship (and you will), you'll have to answer a simple question: *Are you willing to grind for what you want?* The only way you fail is if you quit. As some of our closest colleagues say, 90% of success in life is just showing up.

Once you've identified why you want to create your own economic universe, what you want it to look like, and have some sense of the tools available to help you create it, you're more likely to opt for the latter. Where once you might have viewed the grind as a painful sacrifice, you now embrace the effort as a powerful tool.

By committing today to creating your economic universe, you're putting yourself in the position to reap economic benefits tomorrow. Remember Able from the comic book? He created his personal economic universe by sacrificing a day of hand fishing and risking hunger in order to pursue an easier and more lucrative form of fishing for the future. Not only that, but his effort benefited everyone around him. They too could use nets to catch fish, making their work more efficient and productive. This simple cartoon underlines that through your vision and efforts, your savings and capital have the potential to benefit everyone—from your own family to the community and families around you.

For instance, when you save, the bank turns around and loans that money to other people and businesses who are using debt as a tool to create their own economic universe often based on innovative ideas. Today, people make incomes in ways that weren't even imagined 10 or 20 years ago.

Make Your Move

All that's left is for you to make your first move. Start by asking questions about your own desires, preferences, and why you're even asking these questions.

Realize that any change requires action and effort. We often think that a delay in enjoyment or gratification is required;

however, that is not the case. What you have done by going through the process above will redefine what you enjoy and what gives you meaning in your life.

Outside Forces

We're not pretending outside forces don't exist. These forces can exert some influence over your personal economic universe and can range from the state of the economy or the job market to your personal business. Economic booms and busts come and go, taxes are levied and taken, and governments adjust interest rates to influence the larger economy.

What happens, though, is that all too often an awareness of these forces creates perceived limitations that hamper your creativity and ingenuity. The truth is your awareness of these forces should empower you! Let's take a look at an example. A business owner we know named Larry has built a large, successful landscaping company, and if you ask him what he thinks allowed him to be successful (regardless of outside forces), he'll tell you a profound story from his childhood.

When he was a young kid in Calgary, he had a job delivering newspapers. One day the newspaper announced a contest for their paper carriers. The person who signed up the most subscriptions would win a trip to Disneyland. Excited by the prospect of a trip to The Magic Kingdom, Larry did a little math. Based on his delivery experience, he figured out that if he knocked on one hundred doors in an evening, he could get a certain number of subscriptions. And if he continued to knock on one hundred doors per evening, he could probably win that trip to Disneyland.

So, he had his mother drop him off in various neighborhoods around Calgary, where he proceeded to knock on the required number of doors a night. Unfortunately, he wasn't always met with a warm welcome. He got responses ranging from unanswered doors and "Get out of here, twerp!" to the odd person that invited him in to hear his sales pitch. Larry told us that from time to time, an older woman would say "Come in, dear" and offer him a cookie and would of course buy a subscription. He would not quit, and yes, he won the contest.

But more than the trip to see Mickey Mouse, the valuable part of the experience was Larry's personal lesson in the rewards of relentlessness. He credits that lesson with making a huge difference in his life. He's been spit on, punched, and kicked out of people's homes. When that happened, what did he do? Larry just moved on to the next door.

It's that tenacity, Larry says, that's allowed him to build a successful business despite outside factors like economic ups and downs, changing technology, and shifting customer demands. None of it affects him that much. He may react to events and prepare for changes in the outside world, but it's not stopping him from reaching his goal. Larry is now a multimillionaire and has reported that his daughter, who is a Realtor in Arizona, has also reaped the rewards of his teaching and has built a business that even he could not imagine.

As these forces unfold, you'll come to see, as Larry did, that your actions to build your own economic universe supersede the bigger economic picture, no matter what state it's in. You are more than a match for these forces because you're taking action with understanding and purpose. That, too, is a formidable force. And when you feel overwhelmed, remember that it's not a unique place to be. Rest, dust yourself off, and continue on.

The lesson here is to trust yourself. Get busy producing, creating, saving, and investing in the long term. Your economic universe is as limitless as your imagination.

FINANCIAL BLIND$POT #5
YOUR MAXIMUM POTENTIAL

Applying your new mindset to understand—and reach—your maximum financial potential.

So far, you've been urged to shift your mindset around wealth, because thinking differently will help you recognize some strategies that, at first, might not be so obvious. This new mindset is going to help you now, because this chapter requires practical application to allow yourself to see a huge blind spot for many people. And by huge, we mean it costs people with even modest incomes significant time, opportunities, and, literally, millions of dollars.

First, we're going to take a general look at the total wealth you generate throughout your lifetime. To be clear, this chapter lays the foundation for everything else remaining in this book. Once you're aware of your potential wealth and the factors positively and negatively affecting it, you'll be better suited to maximize it.

To track the amount of money that passes through your hands during your life, it would be nice to have a calculator in hand to tally your maximum potential. Well, thanks to Kim Butler and Todd Langford, we have one of those. Kim and Todd are at the forefront of the Prosperity Economics Movement, which is about examining the whole truth about wealth and how everyone can apply those insights to create a thriving economic foundation for their lives.[22]

The calculator they've come up with—called a Maximum Potential Calculator—helps people to see data differently. Often the result reveals patterns, actions, and ramifications most of us normally might not see.[23] It also allows people not well-versed in numbers and finances to gain clarity around a few paradigms concerning the accumulation of assets, investing, and wealth.

As an example, let's look at the wealth potential over a 30-year period. Let's say your family has an annual income of $150,000. Over this 30-year period, the potential income you will accumulate is $4.5 million. Of course, this is a gross amount rather than a net amount. Though we haven't accounted for several other variables yet, it's important to pause here and let that sink in. Most people don't realize how much money passes through their hands during their lifetime (Figure 5.1).

Here's another wrinkle: Is your family going to earn a flat $150,000 per year for the next 30 years? Or is it reasonable to expect some increase in yearly earnings? If we're truly going to talk

---

22 "Learn Online," Truth Concepts, accessed August 31, 2023, https://truthconcepts. com/learn-online/.

23 "Maximum Potential," Truth Concepts, accessed August 31, 2023, https://truthconcepts.com/buy-now-old/maximum-potential/.

FIGURE 5.1

CURRENT AGE:	30			TOTAL INCOME	
CURRENT ASSETS:	0		FIRST YEAR:	150,000	
ANNUAL INCOME:	150,000		AVERAGE:	150,000	
			LAST YEAR:	150,000	
			CUMULATIVE:	4,500,000	
			COMPOUND:	4,500,000	
				100.0% INCOME TO SAVINGS	
			FIRST YEAR:	150,000	
			AVERAGE:	150,000	
			LAST YEAR:	150,000	
			CUMULATIVE:	4,500,000	
			COMPOUND:	4,500,000	

MAXIMUM POTENTIAL

100% SAVINGS @ 0.0%

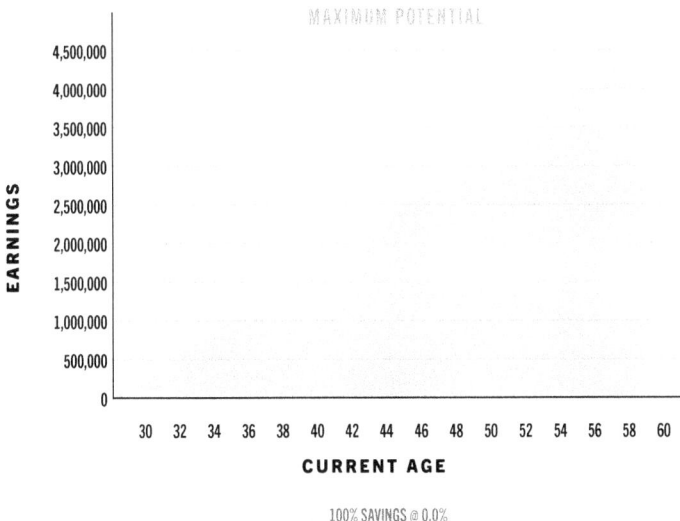

A family earning 150k/year for 30 years is going to accumulate 4.5million dollars

about your maximum potential, we should include a conservative increase of 4% per year. As you see, this mere 4% increase significantly changes the game. Now, over this 30-year period, you've gone from $4.5 million to almost $8.5 million (Appendix, 5.2).

For simplicity's sake, let's say you're able to save every dollar. That's not practical, of course, but it will help shift your mindset. Let's pretend you have no expenses. All your living expenses, housing, transportation, travel, etc. are covered for you. (Again, we know this isn't realistic, but please bear with us for our purposes in this chapter.) If your family could save and invest every dollar they make for the next 30 years and get a rate of return of 5%, what would that look like?

With a few simple changes, your family has gone from $4.5 million to $8.5 million, and now you're at almost $17 million (Figure 5.3). You can see from a gross income perspective how your family has potentially millions of dollars flowing through their hands. This is what your maximum potential might look like.

The True Costs of Taxes

Okay, it's time to talk about taxes. There are so many varying taxes that there's no way to know exactly what taxes you may encounter down the line. To make things easy, we've chosen a rate of 40% (Figure 5.4).

The result is you've lost almost $7 million off your total from

FIGURE 5.3

YEARS TO ILLUSTRATE:	30

CURRENT AGE:	30	**INCOME INCREASE:**	4.00%		
CURRENT ASSETS:	0	**NET EARNING RATE:**	5.00%		
ANNUAL INCOME:	150,000				

	TOTAL INCOME
FIRST YEAR:	150,000
AVERAGE:	280,425
LAST YEAR:	467,798
CUMULATIVE:	8,412,741
COMPOUND:	16,987,082

	100.0% INCOME TO SAVINGS
FIRST YEAR:	150,000
AVERAGE:	280,425
LAST YEAR:	467,798
CUMULATIVE:	8,412,741
COMPOUND:	16,987,082

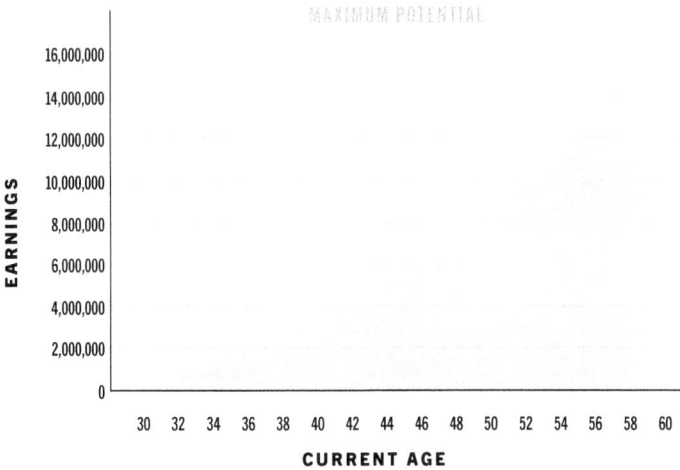

100% SAVINGS @ 5.0%

Continuing above scenario, adding investing 5%

FIGURE 5.4

YEARS TO ILLUSTRATE:	30				— □ X

				TOTAL INCOME	
CURRENT AGE:	30	INCOME INCREASE:	4.00%		
CURRENT ASSETS:	0	NET EARNING RATE:	5.00%	FIRST YEAR:	150,000
ANNUAL INCOME:	150,000			AVERAGE:	280,425
				LAST YEAR:	467,798
	TOTAL TAXES			CUMULATIVE:	8,412,741
% OF INCOME:	40.00%			COMPOUND:	16,987,082

			60.0% INCOME TO SAVINGS	
TOTAL COSTS:	(3,365,096)		FIRST YEAR:	90,000
ACTUAL LOSS:	(6,794,833)		AVERAGE:	168,255
			LAST YEAR:	280,679
			CUMULATIVE:	5,047,644
			COMPOUND:	10,192,249

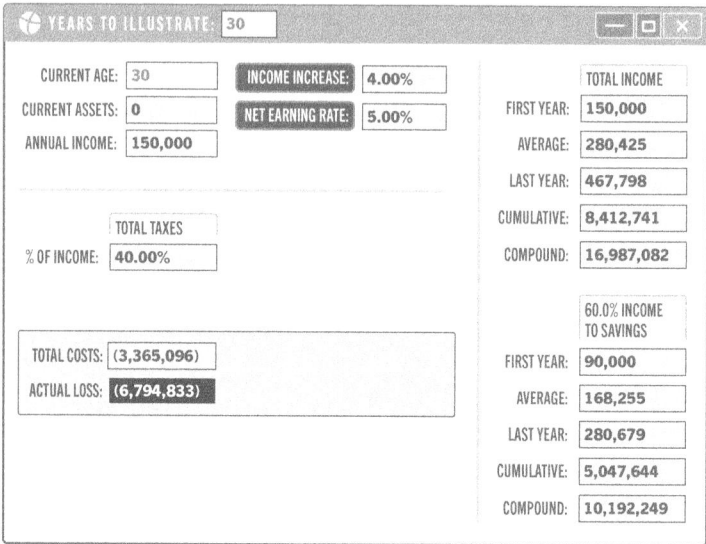

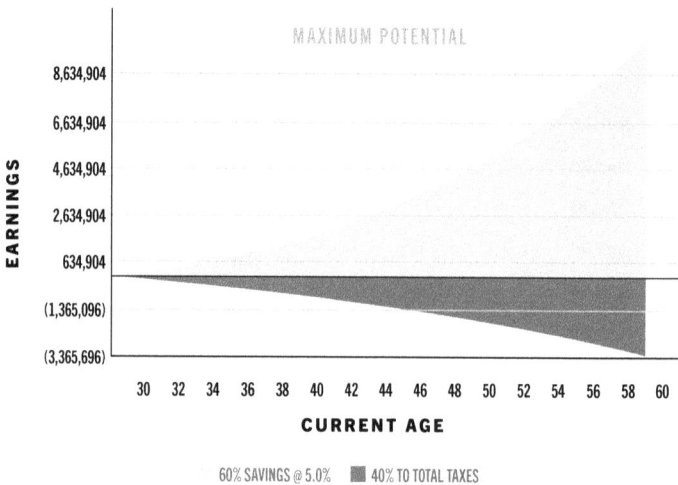

Continuing above scenario, 40% in taxes

a 40% tax alone. Looking at the chart, you can see the cost of the tax is listed at $3.3 million. But in fact, it's more than double that. Why? Because our taxation system requires us to file and remit the taxes owing each year. In fact, for those of us who earn a salary or paycheque, the taxes are withheld at source or, in other words, the tax is deducted from your cheque and sent to the Canada Revenue Agency by your business or employer.

Over a lifetime we never see a significant portion of the wealth we earn because it never reaches our hands. We cannot wait until the end to pay the tax, so those dollars are taken and do not have the opportunity to help grow our wealth over time. This is an example of lost opportunity costs.

Here's another simple example of opportunity costs. Let's say every day for five years you get a coffee at Tim Hortons, but you suddenly decide to stop. The combined amount that you paid for those cups of coffee is an example of lost opportunity costs. Now you have the opportunity to spend that money on other things. We understand that there is value in those warm cups of java that you chose to spend your money on; however, there is value in understanding that there is a cost represented by lost opportunity to put that money to work elsewhere.

Looking at these examples of opportunity costs might cause you mental pain, and we don't blame you. But trust us, we simply want you to fully comprehend your true wealth potential. Why? Because that awareness is the first step that leads to all the other steps if you want to maximize your wealth. The purpose here is to give you a contextual mind shift so you can see exactly how much wealth you're generating.

Notice that the biggest factor in all of this is time. Time is so influential because of its relationship to opportunity costs. The more time you have, or the more "runway" we have, the more possibilities and opportunities there are to build wealth. Realize, too, that each spending event may or may not have an opportunity cost. Surely, we need to live and enjoy life along the way, but the opportunity cost awareness creates habitual use of capital in the next most productive way.

Too bad we can't wait until the end of our earning lives to pay all our taxes and instead put the money to work for us.

Financing Costs—They Are in Effect Like the Unlikable Cousin of Taxes

There's still another major factor in your maximum wealth potential: *debt service.*

Simply put, debt service refers to the money that is required to cover the payment of interest and principal you pay on things like loans, payment plans, credit cards, and so on. And just as your wealth accumulates from day one, taxes and debt service payments cut into your wealth in terms of lost opportunity costs from day one.

Nelson Nash, a mentor of ours, wrote in his iconic book *Becoming Your Own Banker* that on average about 34.5% of people's money goes toward some type of debt service—whether it's credit cards, mortgages, auto loans, consumer loans, or lines of credit.[24] Not everyone has a debt service level of 34.5%. For some people it will be higher. For others, it will be lower. But for our purposes, we're going to use it as a gauge for measuring debt service (Appendix, 5.5).

Like our discussion regarding taxes, the financing costs in terms of payments were almost $3 million. When you factor in the lost opportunity cost, the total cost is almost $5.9 million. As we pointed out with taxes, you can't wait on your debt repayments. In the case of debt, nonpayment means that you lose the things you purchased with that debt, such as your vehicle or your home if the situation gets bad enough. Those dollars that are used to repay the debt cannot be put to work to build wealth, and as such the opportunity cost is real. Ignore this concept at your peril.

Lifestyle

Of course, you have to live your life too, right? That means lifestyle expenses. The good news is that these tend to be more in your control. To that end, let's factor in lifestyle expenses making up 23.5% of your wealth over a 30-year time frame (Figure 5.6). In this example, the actual costs are almost $2 million and a true cost (including opportunity cost) of almost $4 million. We might point out here that, unfortunately, the percentage we get to spend on lifestyle is the *smallest* amount of the main factors that impact wealth.

---

24   R. Nelson Nash, *Becoming Your Own Banker* (Infinite Banking Concepts, 2009), 17.

FIGURE 5.6

				TOTAL INCOME
CURRENT AGE: 30	INCOME INCREASE: 4.00%			
CURRENT ASSETS: 0	NET EARNING RATE: 5.00%	FIRST YEAR:	150,000
ANNUAL INCOME: 150,000		AVERAGE:	280,425
		LAST YEAR:	467,798

YEARS TO ILLUSTRATE: 30

	TOTAL TAXES	DEBT PAYMENTS	LIFESTYLE
% OF INCOME:	40.00%	34.50%	23.50%
ANNUAL COST INCREASE:	4.00%	4.00%	
TOTAL COSTS:	(3,365,096)	(2,902,396)	(1,976,994)
ACTUAL LOSS:	(6,794,833)	(5,860,543)	(3,991,964)

CUMULATIVE:	8,412,741
COMPOUND:	16,987,082

2.0% INCOME TO SAVINGS

FIRST YEAR:	3,000
AVERAGE:	5,608
LAST YEAR:	9,356
CUMULATIVE:	168,255
COMPOUND:	339,742

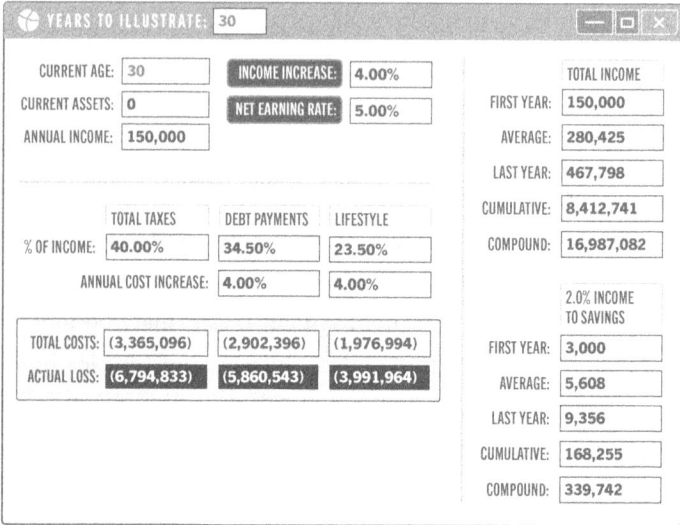

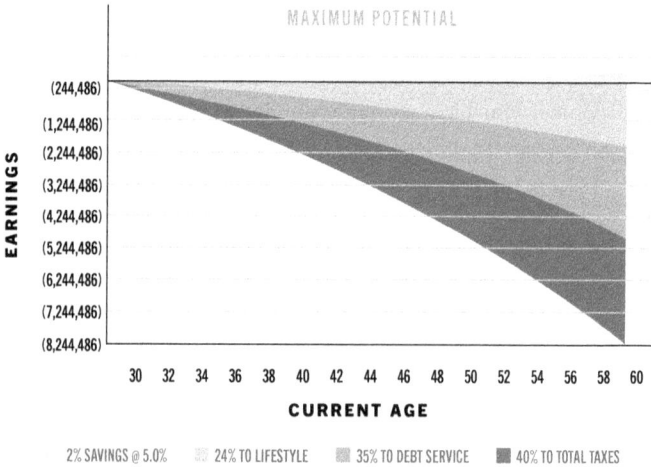

Continuing above scenario, adding 23% of income is lifestyle income
(what you have to live on)

Drum Roll Please

Remember, we established from the above example that your maximum potential wealth over 30 years could be roughly $17 million. But once you account for taxes, debt service, lifestyle, and the associated opportunity costs, you would have about $339,000 left over by the time you get to the end of those 30 years.

To give this a bit more context, you may remember when we said that your family may expect an increase in their family income over time and that we would include a 4% increase. Well, at the end of that 30-year period, family income would have grown from $150,000 per year to $467,798. That means that the amount left over of $339,742 represents less than one year of income, or 0.73 of a year, to be exact!

That is correct: The amount left over is *not even a full year.*

People often wonder why so few Canadians or Americans in general can save money even when they're making a respectable paycheque. It's not because we're failing to save. We have trouble saving because all of us are constantly battling several headwinds at once as we try to get ahead and turn income into wealth. So, what can we do?

Most people assume the most direct way to increase wealth is to get better rates on their savings. If we could only invest and do better than the 5% figure that we used in our example, we'd have more money, right?

Now let's look at what happens to the numbers when we increase your annual earnings rate to 10%, up from 5% (Appendix, 5.7). As you can see, with those additional earnings over 30 years, you can move from 0.73 years of income to 1.7 years of income or from $339,742 to $781,330. You may also notice that the strategy of "increase my rate of return" doesn't even begin to address the issue. Yet that's where so many people focus their efforts. Whether it's your own mindset or your advisor's, what we seem to be searching for is this: *How can I get a couple more points on my return?*

The problem with this thinking is that they're looking in the wrong place. Over time, earning more on the small amount that's left over doesn't have the impact people think it does. When you take a look at the figures we used, including the 40% taxes, the 34.5% financing cost, and the 23.5% lifestyle expenses, our family is left with 2% of their income to provide for their future.

So, the question remains: *What can you do to reach your maximum potential?* Many people go immediately to lifestyle. We say STOP! There may be some holes in the bucket as they say when it comes to lifestyle expenses. However, it's not the first place to start.

Remember the 40% tax rate we looked at above? We will often look at somebody's financial affairs and work with their accountants to reduce taxes. Let's see what might happen if there were 10% savings to be had in the area of taxation. That would mean a change from 40% to 36%. So what happens when we move the tax rate down to 36% over 30 years (Appendix, 5.8)?

You've gone from around $400,000 to just over a million dollars. That's not huge, but it demonstrates that reducing the tax rate by even a small amount can have a significant impact. Also, it's proof that time can be your worst enemy or your best friend, depending on how you make it work for you. We should point out that those gains are accumulated *without* increasing the client's risk by investing their savings in places where they might lose value due to market whims and fluctuations.

The next step might be a conversation about how you're using your money, or more specifically, how one can manage the use of debt and finance more efficiently and effectively. For instance, let's just say we can get debt service down from over 34% to 18% (Appendix, 5.9). Now we've helped you build almost $4 million, which represents 19 years of income. That makes a massive difference in retirement, and we haven't even touched on lifestyle expenses—and for good reason. Most people don't want to touch lifestyle expenses. Who can blame them? We all want to live in abundance throughout our lives, not just at the end.

The point here is that you must understand your tax situation and have conversations about financing and opportunity costs. Then you'll be wired and in tune with your financial situation. You'll have more capital and cash flow during your lifetime. As Nelson Nash always said, "When you have cash, opportunity hunts you down!" What if you used your additional capital and cash flow on other opportunities, like alternative investments or real estate, that provided a return larger than 5%?

As you can see, the possibilities are nearly endless.

To truly build your wealth you must see these *blind spots* and understand them from a holistic perspective. Once you have a clear-eyed view of the whole picture, you and your financial advisor will be able to pursue a range of strategies to ensure you realize your true wealth potential.

Be aware of taxes, as they are wealth destroyers. Nothing will have a larger impact on your wealth than how you use debt and financing. And finally, you need to understand and be intentional regarding your lifestyle. We'll go into each one of these areas in the next three chapters.

FINANCIAL BLIND$POT #6
TAXES, YOUR GREATEST EXPENSE

Taxes are likely the greatest expense in your lifetime—ignore them at your own risk.

Taxes are everywhere in our lives. A list of the many taxes that are assessed and levied throughout the world include:

- Payroll tax
- Gift tax
- Resort tax
- Fuel tax
- Excise tax
- Goods and services tax
- Personal tax
- Corporate tax
- Property tax
- Carbon tax
- Sales tax

We could fill another page with other examples of taxes that aren't described as such, including tariffs, duty, tolls, license fees, and probate fees, among others. The point is we all pay a lot of taxes.

In this chapter, we'll only discuss personal and corporate income taxes. The other taxes, tariffs, and charges listed above will be considered lifestyle expenses in the remaining chapters and Spotlights.

The first possible blind spot in this chapter: We all pay more taxes than we might think. But a more significant blind spot is how taxes can impact wealth accumulation, making them argu-ably the biggest expense over your lifetime.

At this point, it's important to make it clear that *we are not commenting on the morality of taxes*. Nor are we expressing our opinion on how taxes should be imposed or implemented. We are simply commenting on how taxes play a role in finances and impact your overall wealth. Having said all of that, there is a lot of emotion that necessarily comes with discussing taxation, and there is no doubt you will see some of this reflected in our commentary on this subject.

An Interesting Exercise

Let's take $100 with 10% interest compounded annually without tax for 105 years. (Canada instituted a federal income tax in 1917—105 years ago as of this writing—to help finance the

First World War.[25] We thought it would be fun to see how taxes would affect $100 if we started at that date.)

After those 105 years, you will have $2,017,619. Not bad.

Now let's say the government imposes a 50% tax. What do you think the ending value is going to be at the end of those 105 years with a 50% tax? A likely answer: $1,000,000 (roughly half of that $2,017,619, right?).

Wrong.

The actual amount you have is $15,984.

Why? Because the annual tax not only cuts into the interest your money earns, it also lowers the amount on which the interest earned is based—each year, over and over.

Bigger amount = more interest earned.

Lower amount = less interest earned.

Each year the tax cuts into the interest you earned. More than that, though, it also lowered next year's amount in the account. This means the next year you earned less interest because the amount is smaller than it would have been without a tax.

Then the next year, that amount in the account (smaller than it potentially could have been without the tax) earns less

---

25   Maya Bilbao, "Income Tax in Canada," The Canadian Encyclopedia, last updated January 28, 2022, https://www.thecanadianencyclopedia.ca/en/article/income-tax.

than it could have without the tax. Then the year after that ... and so on.

Ultimately, you not only pay the annual tax but also hampered your money's opportunity to grow your wealth. The taxes you pay along the way cut into the amount of your money available for compounding growth. In other words, the money you pay in taxes doesn't have the opportunity to grow through compounding. Again, this is what we like to refer to as opportunity cost.

Lost opportunity costs are the real reason why taxes are a wealth destroyer.

Let's look at various scenarios using again our 105 years and 10% earnings rate:

Interest Earned	Tax Rate	Tax Payment	Ending Value
2,017,519	0%	0	2,017,519
31,668	50%	15,884	15,884
71,127	40%	28,491	42,836
106,199	30%	48,703	113,740
277,007	20%	74,794	299,275
866,977	10%	86,708	780,469
1,322,140	5%	66,112	1,256,228

As you can see from the chart above, reducing the tax rate is increasing both the tax payment to the government and the ending value. Only when the tax payment starts to get below 10% in the table above does the tax payment start to go down. At a 10% earnings rate, the payment to the government is the highest at around

12.5%. However, being purely practical, the government lowering tax rates isn't likely. That's why you need to understand how you can lower the amount of taxes you pay by using the rules in your favor.

Many people believe that the purpose of government plans is to optimize the taxes they pay. After all, RRSPs and 401(k)s (U.S. equivalent to the Canadian Registered Retirement Savings Account Plan), are often promoted as legitimate tax breaks offered to everyone. In truth, these plans do not offer a permanent tax deduction, but rather a deduction today and taxes tomorrow when you withdraw the funds—in other words, a tax deferral.

Let's take a look at the difference between the two.

Deductions, Deferrals, and Deception

Pamela Yellen's Hayward-Yellen 100 Ltd Partnership and Strategic Education Technologies, LLC has formulated a spreadsheet showing the comparison between paying taxes upfront versus deferring them through government-promoted retirement savings plans like the ones mentioned above.

As Yellen explains it, "The Society of Actuaries says that if the tax rates are the same, *it doesn't make any difference* whether [the taxes] are taken away from you at the beginning (tax-exempt) or at the end (tax-deferred). It's the same fraction of your money that's left to you."[26]

---

26 Pamela Yellen, "Tax Deferral is a Scam and Here's Proof," Bank on Yourself, July 16, 2021, https://www.bankonyourself.com/tax-deferral-con-exposed.html.

In other words, it doesn't matter if you pay now or defer and pay later. Either way, you're still left with the same amount after taxes.

We can illustrate what Yellen was saying through a simple example. In the analysis, Yellen is comparing a 401(k) to a Roth IRA, which is like comparing an RRSP to a TFSA. RRSPs and TFSAs are called registered plans because these programs are registered and tracked by the Canadian federal government for tax purposes.

If we assume a 40% tax rate and a contribution of $100,000 ($60,000 for the TFSA because it's after tax) earning at 5% over 25 years, you would get the following balances in the account:

RRSP: $338,635

TFSA: $203,181

If you removed all the funds from each registered account the following year, then the funds you would have left after paying taxes at a 40% rate would be:

RRSP: $203,181

TFSA: $203,181

<hr/>

Assuming the tax rates you paid when you put the money in are the same as when you take the money out, at the end of 25 years, the outcome is the same. The government gives you a break on the seed short term and then taxes you on the harvest.

We may think that all the money in the deferred vehicle is ours, but it's not. We owe the government—our partner for life— the taxes it allowed us to defer. Or to put it another way:

- You put up all the money.
- You take all the risks.
- You pay all the fees.

Meanwhile, the government controls the process of the taxes and, thus, your partnership.

What's more, these funds are locked up with little or no ability for you to take advantage of other "outside" opportunities such as real estate, investing, etc.

Oh, and if you're in Canada or the U.S. and saved successfully to the point where your retirement income is over $86,912 (as of 2023), you get to experience an Old Age Security (OAS) "claw back," which is *another* tax based on your higher income tax bracket.

Is it even possible to come out ahead with a deferred plan in this comparison?

Possibly. *If* the tax rates decrease over the long term or if you are in a lower tax bracket in retirement. This leads us to a couple of our favorite questions. First question: Who really wants to plan to have less money in retirement? Second question: Do you think that tax rates will increase or decrease in the future?

We think that, after COVID-19 and all the additional expenses incurred by most governments, tax rates in the future are more likely to increase. In fact, the stress on the system from an aging population, along with the required infrastructure, will force most governments to keep increasing taxes.

A Somewhat Exciting Addition

It would be remiss for us to not talk about Tax-Free Savings Accounts (TFSA) and Registered Education Savings Plans (RESP). Our commentary on RESPs would be similar to RRSPs except that there's government matching. The recommendation is simple: Put the funds into the plan up to the amount the government will match.

Yes, there's another potential deferral inside RESPs, but there are complications created by significant unknowns. For instance, do your children intend to go on to post-secondary education? There are other tools, such as whole life insurance, that can serve as an education fund for children and that are much more flexible and provide much more control than TFSAs and RESPs.

A TFSA is a good tool. There's often a debate about whether to put money into an RRSP versus a TFSA. We answer that with another question: If the government made two plans that offered tax incentives, but Plan A has a limit of 18% of your earned income up to a maximum of $27,830 per year (currently) and Plan B has a limit of $6,000 per year (currently), which do you think is the better deal for the government? Refer to the Spotlights for a further discussion on RRSPs and 401(k)s.

Death and Taxes

If you're a Canadian resident, your last moment alive on earth is shared with the Canada Revenue Agency (CRA).

CRA deems that an individual disposes of all their assets at that moment immediately *before* they die. Even *death and time*, it seems, are no match for the almighty power of taxes.[27]

This has led to a common misconception that there's no estate tax in Canada. Technically that is true, as the taxation levers are pulled right before you pass on, making it possible for the government to collect a share of taxes on those assets. Of course, the tax system in almost every country is built to ensure that there are regularly occurring tax "events." These can include transactions, sales, yearly reporting of income, and the unfortunate passing of a loved one to ensure more money is continually added to the public coffers.

We would argue that the deemed disposition under the Canadian scheme is somewhat punitive. But no matter where you live (and die), death comes with some obvious financial impacts. All too often we've witnessed how big of an impact those financial concerns (taxes, unpaid debts, inheritances, etc.) can have on family harmony.

---

27 "What Taxes are Payable at Death in Canada?" National Bank, May 30, 2023, https://www.nbc.ca/personal/advice/succession/canada-estate-taxes.html.

Death can significantly impact your family financially, and that impact can extend far beyond finances to the heart of your family.

Fortunately, that doesn't have to be the case. The more you know about financial issues, taxes, and the rules you might face when a loved one dies, the better equipped you'll be to work with your financial advisor and make the financial landscape surrounding death and taxes easier to navigate. Even more importantly, you'll be able to maintain family harmony with those who share your grief.

Issues, Taxes, and Rules

It should come as no surprise that there are special tax rules in both Canada and the U.S. for certain assets in the event of a death. One such asset is the family home. In Canada, the family home is known to the CRA as your "principal residence." The increase in value of your home is not included in your income upon death. Nonetheless, the disposition must be reported or there are penalties.

Tax on Personal Property

Other assets such as personal property are not taxed unless there's a gain. But if the fair market value of that property and the adjusted cost basis (which is a fancy way of saying cost) is over $1,000, then it technically should be reported.

To further complicate matters, there is a special type of personal property called "listed personal property," which includes items such as jewelry, artwork, etc., that also should be reported. In other words, technically speaking, the CRA would like its share of the increase in the value of your deceased mother's engagement ring. Simply put, most people don't understand taxes on personal property.

Financial Assets

Taxes on financial assets are generally more straightforward than taxes on personal property, as we're used to seeing the balances on account statements. For instance, we pay taxes on financial assets each year, if only because the banks and other financial institutions file and send us tax slips on the income earned. But nothing is ever as simple as we might prefer.

Certain financial assets, such as those in registered plans, have special tax rules. Let's say you have registered assets like RRSPs and RRIFs. Now let's say you chose to withdraw some money from these accounts. Or, in the case of a RRIF, you were required to withdraw money from the account. In either case, the money you withdrew is considered income. You will pay tax on that income. CRA is patient with the money in RRSPs until you turn 71. That's when they make you convert the account to a Registered Retirement Income Fund ("RRIF") and start paying them back for the "tax loan" (remember, the money they gave you to put into the plan) made to you years earlier.

The tax paid on deemed dispositions on registered plans—including 401(k)s and RRSPs—can be a real disaster. This is because in general, the full amount of the account is taxable and must be paid by the estate. However, the funds held in the account may be paid to a specific beneficiary who is not responsible for paying the tax. This can lead to situations where an adult child or relative receives all the money from one of these plans while the rest of the family is left to pay the tax bill from the other assets remaining in the estate.

Real Estate

Real estate assets can also bring up significant issues when settling an estate. The first issue is determining a value for the asset, though this may not pose a significant issue if there's a well-established market in the area.

The next and generally most significant issue concerns liquidity. It can be difficult to pay the taxes on the deemed disposition of real estate unless there is cash available or some or all of the real estate assets are sold. This can get complicated if the real estate asset is a family cottage or some other property where family ties and emotions are involved.

To compound matters, some income-producing real estate may have been depreciated in earlier years to save on taxes. When the depreciated real estate is sold, all the previous amounts deducted as depreciation must be repaid on the final return. Even worse, this amount is usually subject to tax at the highest rate!

Family Business

Another area that requires significant planning is family businesses—specifically private company shares. Many books have been written about family businesses as it relates to transition or succession. What most people don't know is that there's the potential for double taxation on the deemed disposition of private company shares.

Most people understand that there's a tax on the increase in the value of private company shares left as part of the estate. But many are surprised to learn there's also tax to pay when distributing the assets from the company now that you own the shares. There are tax plans that deal with these issues to help reduce the tax paid to either the dividend rate or the capital gains rate, which, thankfully, are lower. However, to do so will require the assistance of a tax professional.

Family Matters

Up to this point, we've hinted at underlying issues related to family harmony. More than any of the financial issues, it's the relationships within the family that are affected the most when settling an estate. This point cannot be understated.

We have seen families fall apart after a parent passes away despite the parent's best efforts to make things "fair." Unfortunately, in this context, the concept of fairness rests with the individuals that have been left with the estate, and their views of what's fair can be very different from those of the deceased.

In one situation we're aware of, there were two brothers. Let's call them Sam and Dave. Sam borrowed $50,000 from their mother to purchase a home. The home Sam purchased was located in a resort town and, over 30 years, appreciated substantially. That $50,000 used to purchase the home had grown by over 10 times and was worth $500,000 at the time of the mother's passing.

The other brother, Dave, did not borrow anything from his mother. He received his share of the borrowed money ($50,000) when the estate was settled some 30 years later, at which point the value of that money had greatly diminished due to inflation. In addition, Sam never paid any interest back to the mother. After he sold the house, Sam paid $50,000 back to their mother's estate.

Good for Sam. Not so good for Dave, who harbored some ill will toward his brother for not paying interest. After all, by not paying interest, Sam prevented their mother's assets (and, thus, her boys' inheritance) from growing. This means Dave lost the benefit of the money that could have grown had Sam never borrowed the money.

This was a difficult situation for everyone involved, though we're happy to report that ultimately this situation was resolved amicably as Dave, valuing his relationship with his brother over monetary gain, found a way to make peace with the situation. Unfortunately, many similar situations are not resolved and become painful wounds that impair family bonds and relationships at a time when families need each other most.

The takeaway here is to have awareness of the laws and rules surrounding estate planning. Work with a financial planner and learn to communicate with loved ones about your estate plans so that expectations are set before you die. This will ensure that those you've left behind are taken care of and can depend on each other for the support they need.

Hidden from Sight

Remember our list of taxes at the beginning of this chapter? Despite that lengthy list, the amount we pay has been almost eliminated from our sight. Another blind spot: Whatever you think you make, your paycheque says different.

Here's a way to illustrate our point.

First, write down your gross salary per year. Now take your paycheque and multiply it by 12 (months), 24 (bimonthly), 26 (biweekly), or 52 (weekly) depending on how often you're paid. That number will not be equal to your gross salary. Let's look at how that happens without us noticing.

Let's say you make $120,000 per year. Of course, your T4 slip will agree with you. Your bank account, however, says differently. Now say that $120,000 per year (or $10,000 per month) is subject to a 30% marginal tax rate. That means you wind up paying $3,000 per month in tax ($10,000 X .30 tax rate = $3,000). And you would receive a net amount of $7,000 as a deposit it your account with the bank.

Now imagine the following entries on your bank statement:

ABC BANK

123 River Road
Anywhere, Canada

CHEQUING ACCOUNT

Description	Debit	Credit
Payroll	–	$10,000
Canada Revenue Agency	$3,000	

If your bank statement looks like the one above, we would almost guarantee that there would be a significant and profound change in how we view personal income taxes. That $3,000, or whatever it might be for you, is eliminated from your sight.

What to Do

Some of you may have read the book *Rich Dad Poor Dad* by Robert Kiyosaki[28] (and if you haven't read it, you should).

---

28   Robert T. Kiyosaki, *Rich Dad Poor Dad: What the Rich Teach Their Kids About Money That the Poor and Middle Class Do Not!* (Scottsdale, AZ: Plaza Publishing, 2022; self-pub, 1997).

Someone who is also famous is his accountant, Tom Wheelwright, whom we are lucky to say is a friend of ours.

Tom has written a number of best-selling books, one of which is called *Tax-Free Wealth*.[29] In his book, Tom does a wonderful job at describing the various tax rules and associated regulations in a number of different countries. What surprised us is how consistent the tax rules are around the world. One of the blind spots he points out is that *taxes are essentially rules of a game that the government wants us to play*. If we play the game and deploy our resources consistent with the government's wishes, we pay less tax. It's that simple.

In Tom's book, there is a diagram called the "Cashflow Quadrant" which illustrates how people should move from being employees and self employed (small business) towards being investors and big business owners. The recommended flow is shown in the following diagram:

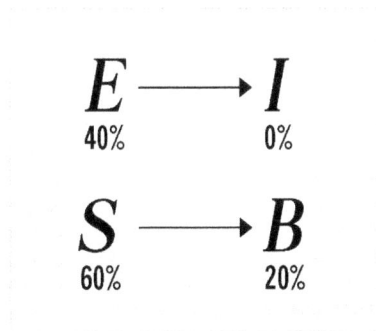

$$E \longrightarrow I$$
40%   0%

$$S \longrightarrow B$$
60%   20%

- *E* represents an employee

---

29   Tom Wheelwright, *Tax-Free Wealth* (BZK Press, LLC, 2015).

- *S* represents self employed (small business)
- *B* represents big business
- And *I* represents the investor

The percentages in the table are a rough estimate of the average tax rates paid by people or entities on income earned in any of these categories. Throughout his book, Tom emphasizes that employees (E) should move toward the investor (I) quadrant and small businesses (S) should move toward the big business (B) quadrant to significantly lower their taxes.

The reason for the 60% tax rate for the self-employed small business owners is that these entities in the U.S. pay Social Security and Medicare taxes. Also, in Canada, self-employed individuals may have less deductions and pay the employer and employee portion of Canada Pension Plan contributions.

Some of the strategies mentioned in Tom's book include the following:

- Employee to Investor: Invest in real estate, insurance strategies, unincorporated businesses (i.e., side hustle).
- Small Business to Big Business: Build your team (lawyer, accountant, financial advisor) and improve your records so that they can be audited.

If you want more, please read the book. We couldn't agree more with Tom's outlook and mindset when it comes to approaching taxes. Now that we see them, we can act.

Here is an example of a business owner who used the need for tax efficiency to expand his professional teams, grow his business, and move from the S (small business) to B (big business) quadrant, as referred to above.

Mike has a client named Daryl. He started working with Daryl, who had a small commercial construction drywall company, more than 10 years ago. The commercial construction market is very competitive in the city where Daryl's company is based.

When he started his company, Daryl had contacts from a previous job working for a large construction company in a major centre. He used those contacts to meet with the large construction builders in his new city. Once he started landing jobs in his new location and built a reputation as a dependable and high-quality construction company, he landed bigger and bigger jobs.

Meanwhile, as Daryl built up capital and cash flow, he started to develop relationships with other sub-trades. He made connections with other companies who provided framing, painting, and electrical work. Through these relationships, he was able to build his team and add these trades to his offerings.

Over time, he's developed his service offerings, and now he has a solid network. Now the people he works with know he's responsible, does good work, and sticks to his word. Because of this, he continues to get bigger and bigger jobs.

Daryl also saw the benefit of building his network on the financial, legal, and planning side of his business. When Mike started working with Daryl, he was the accountant. Later, Mike introduced him to a great lawyer. As Daryl's personal wealth grew, Mike went from being his accountant to his financial advisor.

When they met, Daryl had a $5 million company. He's set a goal to create a $100 million company and he's well on his way to getting there. Right now, he's running a $30–$40 million business. But he'll be the first to tell you he isn't doing it alone. His success is due in large part to his ability to nurture relationships and build his team.

The Cumulative Effect of Taxes

With the constant changes in tax policy and tax rates, not to mention the confusion caused with registered plans, we understand why most people may get overwhelmed and choose not to consider additional options that could reduce their taxes.

However, it is critical that you do the work to find someone who can help you understand how taxes affect your maximum potential.

FINANCIAL BLIND$POT #7
UNDERSTANDING FINANCING AND OPPORTUNITY COSTS

Interest can become a massive financial drag over your lifetime. Reducing its costs requires both awareness and new processes.

It's difficult to understate the impact that access to credit and debt financing has on our everyday lives. It can be the difference between living a life you dream about or living in crisis and despair.

There are pundits like Dave Ramsey and Suze Orman who preach against debt altogether. We believe that's a big mistake. The truth is the price of many goods and services has already factored in the cost of credit financing and debt. We often say at our seminars, "Why does a Ford F-150 cost over $100,000?"

The answer: "Because Ford finance will give you a $100,000 loan to buy it."

Whether you use the loan or not, to get that truck you are going to have to hand over the funds or sign the loan application. It bears repeating: the price of certain goods and services, especially houses and cars, has already factored in access to credit. It goes without saying that we like our houses and cars. And not surprisingly, most of the financing costs incurred by the average household are related to housing and car purchases. Other significant contributors to financing costs include credit cards and lines of credit provided by banks and other financial institutions.

As indicated in the chapter "Your Maximum Potential," it is our aim to reduce the impact of financing in our lives. Let's take a step back and consider how we use debt and money.

It's Stuck Around So Long for a Reason

Financing is not a new thing. Lending in one form or another has been around since 3000 B.C. and originated in Mesopotamia. The ancient Sumerians, Babylonians, Assyrians, and Persians first used food to repay their debts. Debt was used to finance seeds and animals for farms. In a real sense, financing was a tool that allowed people to survive tough times. If you were trustworthy, you received credit and were able to access the items needed to continue with your farm.

Eventually, rather than trading goods or services, exchanges were arranged using a fiat currency. Interestingly, the ancient Code of Hammurabi laid out a maximum interest rate a lender could charge, which was 33% per year. Failures of repayment often resulted in forced labor for the borrower or for a spouse and/ or child. Since the consequences were so dramatic, one can understand why many avoided debt as much as possible. Nevertheless, when it comes to life and death outcomes, the act of borrowing could often become the lesser of two evils.[30]

Today, loans, mortgages, credit cards, and other lines of credit can be obtained from banking institutions, private organizations, and other less traditional sources like loans on cash-value life insurance. Sure, great credit and assets usually secure loan requests easily. Yet, what happens when things go wrong?

Often the fine print leaves the lender the right to make the loan a "demand loan." This demand feature can create extreme stress and economic fallouts at the worst time. During the period between 2008 and 2022, governments around the world have aggressively kept interest rates unusually low, but have also continued to print money at an unprecedented rate.[31] This significant increase in the supply of money has caused strong inflationary pressures. Incurring debt became extremely easy as payments were low compared to the amount of funds borrowed. Every time the cost of money drops closer to zero, the prices of goods start to rise dramatically due to the significant increase in the amount of money that's being fueled by borrowing.

The significant increase in the supply of money is the cause of

---

30 Paige Smith, "A Brief History of Lending," Funding Circle, last updated May 1, 2023, https://www.fundingcircle.com/us/resources/history-of-lending/.

31 James McBride, Anshu Siripurapu, and Noah Berman, "What Is the U.S. Federal Reserve?" Council on Foreign Relations, last updated November 8, 2022, https://www.cfr.org/backgrounder/what-us-federal-reserve.

today's inflation. The government's attempt to solve matters thus far has been an abrupt change in the opposite direction, aggressively increasing interest rates. Ironically, this also perpetuates inflation, as financing costs rise and this in turn creates a domino effect on many goods and services.

Yet should this reality cause us to ignore debt, denounce it, and avoid it at all costs?

It doesn't matter what your answer is to the question of ignoring, denouncing, or avoiding debt. The reason is that governments, businesses, and individuals will not be able to function in the world we have created without the use of credit.

Our approach is to gain control and reduce the financing costs in your life. Let's say we could cut financing costs in half and reduce the burden on families. This would make a massive short- and long-term difference on your ability to accumulate wealth. We may not be able to control macroeconomic decision-making, but we can learn to control and use debt and financing in a smarter way.

We would encourage you to move the needle and seek to understand how financing works and how it's impacting your financial situation. No matter how you finance your life (i.e., cash, credit cards, lines of credit or continuous refinancing of assets such as homes, investment assets, or even cash-value life insurance), it's best done with purpose and intention rather than unconsciously based on patterns that you learned through your life experience.

Easy Money

Credit cards and lines of credit are easy and high-cost sources of borrowing.

Credit cards are a convenience, and they should be viewed as such. The issue with credit cards and even debit cards for that matter is they psychologically separate us from the process of paying cash for our purchases. Most of us feel much more comfortable tapping our plastic cards against the payment terminal than taking a $100 bill from our wallet to pay for groceries.

Lines of credit have become popular in the last decade of low-interest rates, and people use them for all sorts of reasons including house renovations, vacations, and for a source of emergency funds.

Again, these facilities should be used very cautiously, as they can work against asset accumulation and appreciation.

Mortgages, aka "The Death Pledge"

You may have heard that the term "mortgage" means "a pledge until death," or something of that sort. It's as if buying a home wasn't daunting enough. We don't necessarily agree with the "death pledge" sentiment; however, mortgages are serious stuff.

The purchase of a home is a dream for many of us and owning a home can provide us with an extreme amount of joy. We must always remember emotion is a big driver of action and inaction.

And we need to be prepared to give up a lot of future income to purchase a home.

Banks and other financial institutions have guidelines under which they evaluate and price a mortgage. The calculation used by the lender can change dramatically depending on where we are at in the economic cycle. The reason for this is interest rates.

For instance, a $400,000 loan amortized over 30 years at an interest rate of 2.7% (which was the prime rate in March 2022) would require monthly payments of $1,622.39 (Appendix, 7.1). Whereas another loan for the same amount over the same period at an annual interest rate of 6.7% (which is the prime rate in March 2023) would require monthly payments of $2,581.11. This represents an almost 60% increase in your monthly payment (Appendix, 7.2).

When we enter the housing market, we should intend to stay in that home for a long time. However, in practice that's not what's done.

A 2023 article written by Alyssa Davies for Zolo, a popular Canadian real estate online marketplace, mentions that the average Canadian will own between 4.5 and 5.5 properties in their lifetime, and the real estate commissions alone for these purchases could total as much as $180,000.[32] What many people don't understand is that although the commission is technically paid by the seller, the amount of commission is usually factored into the price.

---

32 Alyssa Davies, "How Many Homes Will You Buy in Your Lifetime?" Zolo, April 14, 2023, https://www.zolo.ca/blog/how-many-homes-will-you-buy.

In other words, the buyer pays the commission and not the seller.

Let's say we are intentional and have found the right house at the right price and intend to make this a real home for at least 10 years. That's a perfect start. Conventional wisdom would say, let's get to work and pay the house off as fast as possible.

We would say that paying off your house as fast as possible might not be the right strategy for most people. There are several reasons for this point of view. Remember that the price of that house has factored in the use of credit, whether we like it or not. You're not likely going to get a discount for paying cash.

The second point is a bit more subtle but just as important. If after reading this chapter we accept that we must play the "*game*" of credit and debt financing to accumulate and grow our wealth, then on what assets might we get the best terms for that credit and debt financing?

We believe that your home would be at the top of that list. Most of us are going to get the best financing rates that we will ever get on a home. This is because there's a well-developed and established market for residential housing. The asset is long-lived (which means it can be used for decades and even for a century or more) and there's a lot of demand for houses. It's well established that the banks love the collateral security afforded by home mortgages.

Another point to be considered is that you get to benefit from the greatest economic game in town: inflation. Housing moves with inflation, and as such protects the value stored up in the asset. To make things even better, the value of liabilities goes down with inflation, which means you're paying the liability with cheaper dollars. To give you a more tangible example of the impact of inflation on debt, we regularly point out that if you take our advice *and* pay back your mortgage loan using a 25- or 30-year amortization, your utility payment will likely be higher than your mortgage payment at the end of those 30 years.

There's absolutely nothing new with what we are saying concerning using a long-term perspective on the repayment of your home mortgage. Then why is there so much confusion around this point?

One place to look might be the financial institutions themselves. The banks love the security of home mortgages; however, they hate to tie up their capital for that long. They will do almost anything to get their money back as fast as possible.

How does this confusion manifest in the general public? The answer to this question lies in the confusion regarding how interest rates work.

A 30-Year Mortgage is More Expensive Than a 15-Year Mortgage, Right?

We cringe when we have to debunk this statement. However, it's so important to the fundamental message of this chapter.

As with most things, it's better to illustrate our point with an example.[33]

Let's begin with the $400,000 mortgage we mentioned earlier and use an annual rate of 6.7%. The payment for the 30-year mortgage is $2,581.11 per month and the payment for the 15-year mortgage is $3,528.56. In looking at the total interest over both periods the interest paid over 30 years is $529,200.29 and the interest paid over 15 years is $235,140.57. Accordingly, the person that amortized their loan over 30 years did pay more interest (Figure 7.3). However, is that the whole story?

Let's just say we had $400,000 sitting in the bank and we decided to buy the house outright. If we did not buy the house and we could invest the money at 6.7% for 30 years, what would that look like (Figure 7.4)? Would it be inappropriate for us to say that using that $400,000 from our savings to purchase the house cost us almost $3 million in savings in the future?

To make an appropriate comparison, let's see what the mortgage payment of $2,581.11 over 30 years would look like (Figure 7.5).

Wait a minute. The future value of a payment of $2,581.11 per month at 6.7% over 30 years is almost $3 million.

That can't be right, could it?

FIGURE 7.3

30 YEAR VS 15 YEAR

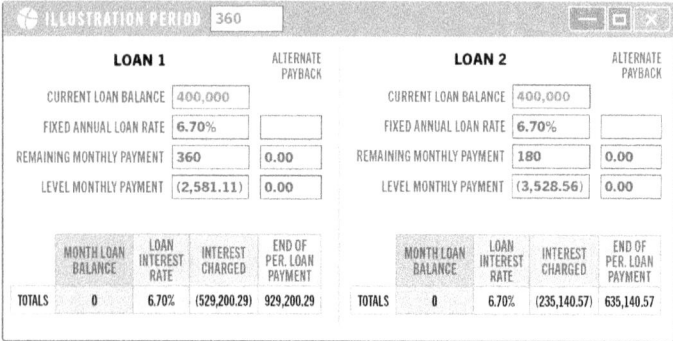

FIGURE 7.4

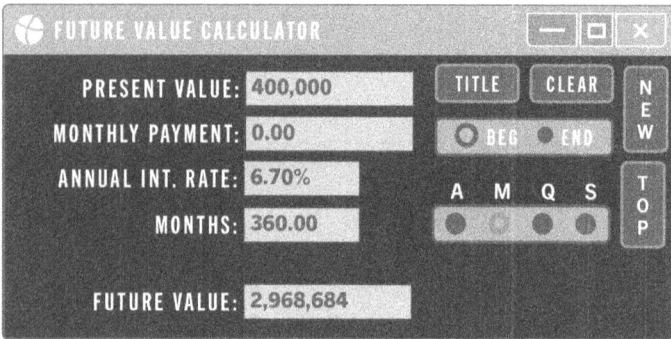

FIGURE 7.5

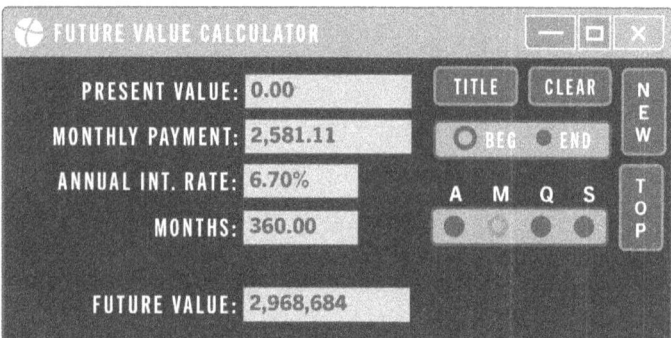

Yes, it is correct. We have done the math and, excluding the impact of taxes, there's no difference between the choice to pay for the house upfront and save and invest $2,581.11 per month for 30 years at 6.7% and investing the same house payment and paying a mortgage payment of $2,581.11 per month for 30 years at an interest rate of 6.7% per annum.

When looking at these two choices, are they the same? What would having access to $400,000 growing at 6.7% per annum during that 30-year time frame do for you? Let's leave that thought for a moment.

How about the 15-year monthly payment of $3,528.56?

Ah hah! The proof is finally here, as the future value of the payment over 15 years at 6.7% is only just over $1 million (Appendix 7.6)! The issue with this calculation is that we're only looking at this choice over 15 years. To make a true comparison we would have to look at the full 30 years. Accordingly, taking the value at 15 years of $1,089,713 and calculating the future value over another 15 years at the same 6.7% interest rate, we get a figure of almost $3 million (Appendix, 7.7).

If you're a bit perplexed right now, we don't blame you. This is a huge blind spot. From an opportunity cost perspective, using the same rates over the same time period of analysis, there's no difference between a 30-year and a 15-year mortgage.

Somebody might say, "Wait a minute. After 15 years there would be no payment. What about saving payments of

$3,528.56 per month for 180 months? That should be worth something."

And you would be correct, the payments would be worth something: Exactly the other half of the calculation we have done for the 15-year mortgage, which equals $1,089,713.

What people often forget is that the person with the lower payment and the 30-year mortgage can start saving the difference in their lower payment right away. What is that worth? You guessed it: The future value of the difference of $947.45 at 6.7% over 30 years is the same $1,089,713 (Appendix, 7.8).

Banks and other financial institutions throw out 25 basis points or a quarter point for a shorter mortgage payment. Who does that benefit? Yes, you would pay less interest. However, the accelerated repayment significantly reduces the risk to the bank, as you're repaying the mortgage over a shorter period of time.

We understand the feeling of not being tied to the bank. We all want freedom in our lives and for some people having the mortgage paid off is a huge relief. What happens if you have had an accident, lose your job, and you need access to your equity. Will the bank give it to you?

It's important to distinguish between method and desire. The method people are using to achieve their desire of having freedom is to pay off their house mortgage. What if they could get to that desire another way?

If your house is paid for and you're still worried about loss of job, disability, or disease, does it matter? Without other resources, you're probably going to lose your home. Do you think the banks are more likely to work with you if you get into trouble if you have 99% of your home paid for or if you have nothing paid on your house?

What would happen if you took the difference in payments on a 30-year mortgage and a 15-year mortgage and had it sitting somewhere? Now you would have a source of money to make those payments. Now you have options.

This illustrates the illusion of equity. Where does equity exist? You can't touch it and you can't see it other than a number on a piece of paper. And the only way you can access it is to get a loan from a bank. If there are two identical houses side by side on the same street and they have both been well taken care of and repaired, is there any difference in the selling price of those houses if one has a mortgage and the other doesn't?

The answer to that question is a resounding NO!

Continuing with this thread: Can repaying my house provide me an increase in my equity from the appreciation of the home that might be, say, 3% or 4%?

Again, the answer is NO!

The house is appreciating irrespective of the loan repayments. The key to living your life is being conscious of the choices you're making and understanding the implications for both now and for the long term. In fact, we want you to live your life. By living we mean being intentional, setting goals, and having dreams for the future.

In fact, let's cut to the chase and focus on another huge topic: how we finance automobiles.

0% Is Not Zero

Up until COVID, auto dealer lots were filled with cars in every city in every province in Canada and every state in the U.S. When considering the size and scope of the automobile industry, you start to realize there's a problem.

Think about automobile manufacturing for a second. Do you think they make more money from the manufacturing of automobiles or from the financing of those automobiles?

If you said financing, you are correct.[34]

But how do they make all that money by offering 0% financing?

You can't say it's volume, as a million multiplied by zero is still zero. It just does not make any sense. When you really look at what the deal is with the 0% financing or 1.9% or whatever the gimmick is, there's always a rebate somewhere. It may be unpublished, but it most likely exists.

---

34   J.B. Maverick, "Key Financial Ratios to Analyze the Auto Industry," Investopedia, last updated August 21, 2023, https://www.investopedia.com/articles/active-trad-ing/082015/key-financial-ratios-analyze-automotive-industry.asp.

If there's a published rebate, then we can do the math. Your choice is a $35,000 car with a $4,000 rebate or 0% financing. To do the math, we need to use $35,000 for our loan and divide it by the payment period of 48 months to get a monthly payment of $729.17 (Appendix, 7.9).

Now if we decide to take door number two and go to my banker, how much do we have to borrow? We have to borrow $31,000 because we received a $4,000 rebate. To understand how this works, we really have to think about this for a minute. The car manufacturers who make all their money from financing are going to pay you to take your loan somewhere else. Does that seem logical? Are they going to pay you $4,000 to not use their financing? Something is really not quite right there, don't you think?

To illustrate more clearly, if my bank asked me to make the same payment of $729.17 on the $31,000 loan over the same 48-month term, then the rate is 6.08% (Appendix, 7.10). As you may have guessed, all they've done is added the interest to the price of the car and called it 0% interest. It's all smoke and mirrors. They added the interest upfront.[35] This is confusing to so many people that some have talked to their banker, found out that the payment with their banker is going to be slightly less, and still opted to finance it with the dealership due to the magic attraction of zero.

The best thing for you to do is find the cash price first and then do the math. It's very hard to do after the fact, as one can

---

35   "How to Protect Yourself from the Latest Scams," Consumer Reports, October 2012, https://www.consumerreports.org/cro/magazine/2012/10/protect-yourself-from-the-latest-scams/index.htm.

imagine. The best thing to do is to say, "I'm going down the street and I'm going to talk to your competition. Tell me what the bottom-line cash walkout price is." Once you get that information from them you can then say, well, what would it look like if I took the financing?

The Real Cost of Automobiles

As we have seen earlier, there's a significant cost incurred to finance a mortgage. It might be hard to believe, but the impact of financing cars might be even more significant. For example, let's say a family has $100,000 in savings and is saving another $20,000 per year. They're increasing their savings rate by 4% a year and earning a net of 5% on their savings, which is very good. Using these factors over 35 years, you will see that a whopping $3,848,447 in savings will be accumulated at the end of this time frame (Appendix, 7.11).

We're talking with these friends, and they say, "Why are you paying all that interest to your banker to buy your cars at 8% when you have all this cash? Everybody knows if you pay cash, you eliminate the interest cost." You might think that this is very sound advice and decide to try it and see what happens.

Going forward, you decide to buy your cars with cash. You buy a car for $35,000 every four years, and in doing so your account went from $3,848,447 down to $2,947,548. This is a difference of about $900,000, yet you only bought $315,000 worth of cars (Appendix, 7.12). When you look at our analysis, you might be confused. Why did eliminating an interest payment on $315,000 result in a $900,000 reduction in your assets?

The answer is due to the lost opportunity. You're financing your cars with your future assets. You can either finance it directly with a financial institution in the form of a loan or finance it with your future by paying cash. We may eliminate an interest payment but not a cost. Those are two entirely different things that have been incorrectly bundled together to mean the same thing, and they're not. We still have an interest cost even though we don't have an interest payment.

In the above example, at what interest rate did this individual finance his automobiles by paying cash? The account was earning 5% so the choice of taking money out of that account means it was financed at 5%. Would it be better to finance it at 5% instead of 8% with his banker? Maybe. However, many of us do not have the education to complete the process and make it worthwhile.

The message is that if a person couldn't use their savings, would they have found the money to pay for their cars? In our experience, the answer to that question is almost always yes. Even if financing the cars at 8% wasn't the most efficient way to do it at the end of the time frame, the individual in our example would have had the $3,848,447 if they left the cash in the savings account alone.

Unfortunately, it's possible to make this situation even worse. Are those automobiles going to increase in price? To complete the illustration, we will increase the price by 4% inflation, add 5%

sales tax, and add $1,000 for insurance premiums (which will also increase with inflation of 4%).

After all of the above, the true cost of a car purchase is *$1.7 million* (Appendix, 7.13).

Unfortunately, most people figure all of this out at the end. It's like suddenly waking up in your 50s or 60s and something is not right. We don't have the amount of money that we thought we going to have for the future, and by that time, it may be too late.

There's no other way to say it, and this realization can be devastating.

You can now see that even without an interest payment you can still have an interest cost. We believe that we have an obligation to educate others to understand how to use their money at its highest efficiency. Additionally, it's important to understand that when we take money from our assets to pay cash, we are giving out the interest that we were receiving.

Reducing the Role of Banks

As with taxes, the chapter on "Maximum Potential" clearly showed that for most of us, the costs of banking and financing will end up becoming a huge portion of your overall spending. Nelson Nash, one of our mentors who created a way to reduce the banks' role in his life, determined the amount that the average household spends on some form of financing cost is an average of 34.5%.[36] This figure includes the financing of several cars over a lifetime, the interest on depreciating assets, mortgages, credit cards, banking fees, lines of credit, etc. In the end, he concluded that even in low-interest-rate environments the habitual utilization of credit will create a massive drag on your financial health.

For example, paying minimum payments on a toaster bought with your credit card may result in that $30 toaster costing you $400. Just because you can finance something doesn't mean you should.

Some people consider debt economic slavery. Yet for others it can be the solution to many day-to-day business matters, as well as an accelerator of asset and wealth growth. We discussed the initial indoctrination experienced opening up our first bank account, then the offer of our first credit card, and so on. Realistically it's almost impossible to function financially in this world without good credit. And of course, good credit is obtained by building credit with small loans and credit cards.

This eventually enables opportunities for larger loans, mortgages, and lines of credit. Our surroundings also include constant reminders of credit, debt, loans, mortgages, and even government-related debt issues. None of these, taken at face value, are good or bad per se. It's the context for the debt. Does the debt you're incurring help you build your wealth? If so, it's good debt. If not, it's bad debt.

---

36   R. Nelson Nash, *Becoming Your Own Banker* (Infinite Banking Concepts, 2009), 17.

Unfortunately, many of us haven't had the benefit of being coached on how to distinguish between good and bad debt. Robert Kiyosaki paved a great road of enlightenment with his *Rich Dad, Poor Dad* books.[37] His differentiation of debt, income, and behaviors surrounding these tools have helped many people progress forward financially. We very much recommend reading his materials.

One way the wealthy utilize credit and debt to their advantage is that they *make the debt a productive element of their wealth accumulation and continued growth*. As Kiyosaki taught many of us, good debt is what you want to utilize. This debt helps create assets that grow more than the net cost of the debt, and that occurs with the help of being able to write the interest cost off on your taxes.[38]

When debt and credit are used as a productive tool to earn business income or income from property, then the cost is often reduced also by being able to deduct the interest cost on your taxes. Naturally this would be optimized with the assistance of your tax professional, so be sure to seek his or her advice on this topic.

Lastly—A Closer Look at Opportunity Costs

To repeat within the context of finance, the blind spot of opportunity cost is often overlooked. And although many people believe debt is something that should be avoided at any cost, they

---

37 "Robert T. Kiyosaki," Rich Dad, accessed August 31, 2023, https://www.richdad.com/about/robert-t-kiyosaki.

38 "How Debt Can Generate Income – Robert Kiyosaki," The Rich Dad Channel, February 16, 2018, video, 15:30, https://www.youtube.com/watch?v=dN5qHjnd_xk.

may realize all too late that paying cash for items is an indirect form of financing when they consider alternative uses of the same monies.

For example, maybe you're the type of person who says, "I'm not going to borrow to pay for my car. I'm going to save $1,000 a year for 10 years, and then buy a car for $10,000." Like a lot of people, you think there's no financing cost if you're paying cash. Yes, you're saving the car loan interest, but there's an embedded opportunity cost. Not to mention you are trying to get around without a car! The cost to you is the lost opportunity for that same $10,000 to do something else.

The reality is that we finance everything we buy. Sometimes that financing takes the form of interest payment through a bank. But other times, financing takes the form of opportunity costs. To be clear, the notion of opportunity cost can be taken too far. Yes, collecting lump sums for investment or other opportunities makes a lot of sense. Using a payment plan to pay off an obligation is often easier than completing the saving toward an item.

But labeling opportunity costs on daily items for living makes little sense, especially when interest rate is attached. Calculating the opportunity cost of a hamburger over a period of 30 years is probably an example of taking this idea too far. Just enjoy your hamburger! Think of financing this way: It's what it costs you to use money, whether you borrow it, use credit, or use your own money.

How Many Times Can You Spend the Same Dollar?

We have all been taught that you can only spend your money once, so do it wisely. When you use money one way, you lose the opportunity to use it in another way. While opportunity costs may seem abstract, they're very real costs that come with a dollar amount attached.

⊷◉⊷

To make matters worse, every time you save a bunch of money and then pull it out of savings to buy something, you stop that money from earning **compound interest**. Once you understand the exponential power of compounding interest, the question around the blind spot of opportunity cost becomes, *how can I save and spend my money without interrupting its compounding growth?*

To accomplish this, we would need to create two accounts. The first account, we'll call it Account A, would be used to accumulate money—using the funds you deposit and the uninterrupted compound interest earned on the amount you have in the account. That account would also have to have liquidity, which is financial advisor-speak for "any time you need some money, you can take it from your account."

Now comes the other fun part: To be able to take out money *without interrupting the compound interest*, you would need to create a separate but related account that tracks how much money you've taken out. We'll call this Account B. Account B would need to come with some special features. You will need to define the terms under which you will pay yourself back. That's right, you're paying yourself. Remember, you borrowed the money from yourself rather than a bank or other financial institution. This type of loan is generally referred to as an unstructured loan because there are no specific repayment terms in the contract. Even though there are no specific repayment terms, interest is charged on this loan at a rate that is higher than the rate that you are receiving from Account A. You might ask at this point, how does this all work?

Let's be clear: *This is where your discipline and awareness have to come in.*

⸺◈⸺

The amount accumulating in Account A is relatively simple. Funds are deposited regularly into the account, and the interest on the account is continually growing uninterrupted without tax.

Account B would act in the exact same fashion as Account A unless you set repayment terms on the unstructured loan. The act of setting repayment terms and making the payments interrupts the compound interest that would otherwise accumulate in Account B.

Money taken needs to be accounted for. Even if the loan format is open and flexible it does not mean it should be ignored. While Account A is where you save, you can borrow some portion of your money and track it in Account B while the money in Account A continues to grow without interrupting your compounding interest.

The question now is how to use the funds in Account B. Ideally, the funds in Account B would be used as an emergency and opportunity fund. However, you could use the funds in Account B for other purposes such as a renovation on your home or for a long-awaited vacation. However, if you are using the funds in Account B for lifestyle purchases, some caution needs to be exercised, especially if the amounts borrowed are not repaid on a regular basis. As mentioned earlier, there is a cost to borrowing from Account B, and this can erode the value of your asset in Account A.

The good news is this all lies within your control. Ideally, you repay these unstructured loans as responsibly as you would conventional structured debt, but with the knowledge that the unstructured loan provides you certain liberties that a conventional loan does not. Simply treat these types of unstructured loans responsibly, and you will be able to see some real positive results financially.

Hopefully, you can see how valuable this would be. Instead of putting that money in a bank or in a portfolio with a stockbroker—that is, places where your money is either in and making money or out and *not* making money (unless you use margin, which can be very risky, especially when markets are volatile)—you could save for retirement while still being able to purchase the things today that make life more fun and comfortable or take advantage of an opportunity that comes along.

And you could do all this *without interrupting growth through compound interest.*

That can't be real, right? There's no way you can save money, make money, *and* still use the cash at the same time, right? After all, when it comes to money it's a "use it and lose it" world.

Wrong.

This is where we actually can do more than one thing with our money. The wealthy have figured out exactly how to do this using several tools. Many use deep lines of credit that they know the bank will never challenge because of their creditworthiness or repayment capability—regardless of overall economic factors. Yet these are never really guaranteed. How often have you heard about credit facilities being changed or removed, or loans demanded back when times are tough? However, many people—and not only the wealthy—have leaned on another more flexible tool and process. It's called *participating whole life insurance*, which we'll delve into more in the Spotlight section.

It's unlikely any of us will avoid some kind of financing in our lives. The goal should be increasing your awareness of how financing and interest rates work, remaining cognizant of finance options, and being able to implement a place for emergency funds, a fund for opportunities, and lifelong retirement. This will allow you to benefit from compounding interest while creating a source of liquidity for yourself, your family, and your business.

FINANCIAL BLIND$POT #8
LIFE AS A VENTURE

It pays to view your life as a venture—and yourself as its owner. Such a life is lived with more intention and awareness, and it will cause you to rethink certain financial assumptions.

Many people who work as employees do not see themselves as business owners. They might work as employees in public service or in the private sector. They go to work, do a job, and come home with a paycheque that more or less meets their desire to make a living. To an employee, it may seem incomprehensible to even consider oneself as a business owner.

Yet, when you get right down to it, a business is simply making your living by engaging in commerce. In reality, isn't that true for anyone with a job like the one described above? That person is selling their time for money in the form of an hourly wage, piecework, or a salary. They're engaging in commerce by selling something—in this case, their skills, labor, and time.

Having a venture mindset and being in the business of "you" is one of the most important things you can do to transform your life. This change will create courage and desire to learn and understand what makes up your financial world. It will put you in a position to make your life better, which will result in more security and help you to develop a keen eye for income growth and protection opportunities.

This mindset and approach will create within you the urge to be more aware and discerning of your financial choices and options. You'll start to see life as a journey, which can create excitement and help you embrace life's unpredictable nature.

Who's the Boss?

The notion of pure employment by another, or the action of giving work to another for money, is not old. Even laborers in centuries past would hire their labor out to several farmers and land barons with nothing regular promised or guaranteed. People were opportunistic and most were clever enough to survive, possibly even prosper. If not, life often became limited and desperate.

Employment today has arguably made things easier and more comfortable—perhaps even too comfortable for employees. To paraphrase businessman Kevin O'Leary, a.k.a. "Mr. Wonderful" from the TV show Shark Tank, a salary is a drug your employer gives you so that you forget your dreams.[39]

---

39   Kevin O'Leary a.k.a. Mr. Wonderful (@kevinolearytv), "A salary is the drug they give you to forget your dreams," Twitter, November 2, 2022, 1:40 p.m., https://twitter.com/kevinolearytv/status/1587862105600016387?lang=en.

If we continue to operate on autopilot, creativity likely shows up as researching our next two-week vacation. The blind spots that we have discussed in the earlier chapters remain hidden from sight. We continue to ignore bills and our spending patterns. We fail to put structure around sound financial practices such as savings, investing, and debt management. We become unable to shift or change our mindset because we've learned through experience that making true and lasting change is unrealistic.

When it comes to long-term planning, unfortunately "32% of Canadians are nearing retirement without any savings."[40] In the United States, according to the U.S. Bureau of Labor Statistics, only 40% of workers in the private sector earning wages in the lowest quarter of earners have access to retirement programs through their employers or unions.[41] And only 56% of Americans would be able to cover an unexpected $1,000 bill with savings, according to a telephone survey of more than 1,000 adults conducted in early January of 2022.[42] Our experience tells us the numbers in Canada are similar. Unfortunately, the days of counting on job security for decades and a generous pension that follows seem to be long gone today.

It doesn't appear that continuing with the "I am taken care of as an employee" mentality is benefiting us, especially from a long-term financial perspective.

---

40   Pattie Lovett-Reid, "32% of Canadians Are Nearing Retirement Without Any Savings: Poll," BNN Bloomberg, February 8, 2018, https://www.bnnbloomberg.ca/32-of-canadians-are-nearing-retirement-without-any-savings-poll-1.991680.

41   "Employee Benefits in the United States – March 2022," Bureau of Labor Statistics, accessed August 31, 2023, https://www.bls.gov/news.release/pdf/ebs2.pdf.

42   Carmen Reinicke, "56% of Americans Can't Cover a $1,000 Emergency Expense with Savings," CNBC, January 19, 2022, https://www.cnbc.com/2022/01/19/56percent-of-americans-cant-cover-a-1000-emergency-expense-with-savings.html.

Get Assertive

When you think of yourself as being in the business of YOU, things change. You begin to be more assertive when it comes to finances. After all, revenues created (what we call a wage or a salary) and put into our bank account are no different than revenues received by any other business owner. Metaphorically, you go from signing the back of the cheque to signing the front, just like an owner of a business.

You begin to see that the goals that you have for the future MUST be aligned with the goals and objectives of your employer. You will see that to grow personally, you MUST acquire new skills and experience. You will come to see how it could be disastrous to your financial future to assume that focusing solely and completely on the success of your employer's company goals will result in you being taken care of. Your employer's success is independent of your own. When it comes to your financial well-being, it's good to remember that things change over time and the overriding consideration must always be alignment between your goals for the future and the role that the company has asked you to play in their business.

The way we manage our minds, our thoughts, and, subsequently, our money, influences and affects every aspect of our lives. Once people accept that at the core, we are in fact business owners in one form or another, one begins to see more clearly that one's destiny is one's own. Greater clarity of personal and family goals develop. The meaning of one's occupation, job, or business becomes more and more important, and both short- and long-term considerations develop independently.

Just reading this chapter and accepting that you are in charge of a business called *My Life Inc.* will improve your financial outlook. You will realize that purpose, intent, and intelligent money allocation can consistently create results and take you in the direction you want to go. Perhaps you will pay greater attention to taxes and start to question if there are better ways to improve your tax situation. You may focus on the need to protect your income or health to make sure that you will reach your goals and provide for your family no matter what life throws at you.

If your life is a business and you have a family, then you have a family business. You may set out to guide your family toward financial goals, awareness, and a lifelong pursuit of knowledge. Time spent together on these topics will only enrich your family dynamics and financial acumen. It all starts with a mindset of believing that you can empower yourself to take control. With the first dollar you save, your commitment toward financial freedom has begun. If you stop to ponder this for a quiet moment, we think you might find a small sense of peace and accomplishment in just this choice alone.

This feeling will only get stronger as you continue to commit and build more momentum toward your future. Soon, you'll be armed with the information to make choices for yourself on how to invest, learning more about the tools at your disposal while building your comfort level as you go. "Know thyself" is the key not only to financial freedom, but to financial peace of mind.

It's important to learn to see debt for what it truly is—a tool to be used—and understand when debt is a good idea and when it's not. You will learn to be wary of get-rich-quick schemes dangling promises that are really too good to be true. Instead, you will take the time to recognize the true nature of any given opportunity.

Recently, a gig economy has emerged, seemingly eroding the traditional job opportunity with its unfulfilled promise of security, benefits, and stability. Now you may choose to contract out to employers. Creating a consulting service that may serve multiple clients is quickly becoming the norm, thereby creating stability through an expanded network along with independence and, possibly, more income than you would have made at a "job."

Ownership of yourself will out of necessity spur your creativity, boost awareness, and increase your thirst to understand not just your financial environment, but your life in its entirety. Lack of certainty will make you question everything. Now that you have the awareness that you're in the business of you, you'll see that the next step is to focus on what all successful businesses require: cash flow and capital.

Saving and Investing Are NOT the Same Things

It seems obvious, right? No way anyone could confuse saving with investing or vice versa. But let us ask you this: How are you saving for retirement? Many would say they are saving by using some investment retirement account ("IRA"), an RRSP, 401(k) or a TFSA. Would one of those choices be your answer?

Gotcha! In general, those are all investment buckets. They—and, by extension, your "savings"—are invested in them and are by definition subject to shifts in the market. Good market, your assets go up. Bad market, your assets go down. In contrast, true savings are safe from the whims of the market. Yes, interest rates affect how much or how little you earn in the form of interest. But if the money is for savings, the amount you put in the account or the asset that grows over time goes untouched no matter what the market does.

Some people might say something like, "I'm going to save 10 percent of my monthly earnings." For the sake of keeping things simple, let's say that's $1,000 per month. For the most part, people don't separate that $1,000 by putting $200 in a savings account and $800 in the markets, or vice versa. They put the whole $1,000 in a RRSP, TFSA, 401(k), or IRA.

Why do people do this?

Well, for one, there are tax incentives.

Second (and this may be more to the point), so much of the confusion over investing and savings can be attributed to the relatively good markets we've experienced, with few notable exceptions, over the last 50 years. The combination of our collective short memories and the almost uninterrupted bull market we've seen since 2009 alone has reinforced the notion that markets only grow. When the markets dip, eventually they will bounce back to greater heights than before they stumbled.

This extended bull market has promoted the idea of placing saved funds into these seemingly buoyant markets. After all, why would you want to experience a return of 1% to 2% safely when you can experience 10%-plus annually? But is "saving" by investing benefiting people? Again, it could be argued. "*Yes, it is! Just look at the markets! Look at the returns!*"

In 2021 and years prior, the answer would be a resounding *yes*. Yet, this positive track record did not stop many people from panicking during COVID and in 2022. And what does the long-term picture look like? Will you be able to time the market so you profit now? Next month? Ten years from now?

As investments fluctuate, you never know how long a downturn will last. During these times investments decrease while many jobs and businesses disappear. Will your finances and income sources survive this? Will you need cash? Or will you cut your losses at the worst possible time by selling low? Is it wise to have all your investments be your savings too?

It's only when the market goes through downturns that people instinctually become aware of the differences between *saving* and *investing*. Being venture-minded about your life drives your understanding of capital and cash flow as they relate to both your household and, if you're a business owner, your company.

The business of you, like many other businesses, is a cash eating machine. Because of this we highly recommend that you pay yourself first. This requires that you separate your cash into a savings vehicle that ensures low volatility and full liquidity and is preferably tax advantaged. Ideally, you should separate these funds by putting them with another financial institution if possible.

During 2022 many of our clients realized the need to have separate savings—that is, savings separate from the markets. It seems the down markets are helping people realize that using savings for a *safe* allocation of funds with respectable returns is key. Another key is the importance of liquidity. Being able to access these funds without a major tax consequence and having the ability to participate in growth is also important. Some of our smartest clients were able to utilize savings (what we like to call dry powder) and allocate them when they saw the markets bottom (for now) in October 2022.

Risk, Volatility, and You

Knowing your "risk tolerance" is important when it comes to managing your money, especially as it relates to savings versus investing. This is true for both individual or family household assets, and for a professional fund.

Here's another way to ask the question: How comfortable are you with volatility when it comes to your money?

⸺⊷◈⊶⸺

Eric gained some practical psychological insights while teaching investment strategies to hundreds of traders around the world. With a few exceptions, most of his students were young males in their early 20s. In general, they were full of testosterone and hungry to get rich fast. So it was interesting to watch these "aggressive" traders' personal risk profiles evolve from being risk-happy to risk-averse in a relatively short amount of time. They would start as extreme and very active traders. But before long most of them invariably began to mellow and prefer less risk. Eric's take on the reason for this is that the human mind is not built for non-stop stress.

What's more, most traders were unable to retrain themselves from one strategy to another. They may have done well when the markets behaved in a way that suited their strategy, yet when the markets changed, even some of the best traders could not adapt. This is why some portfolio managers shine during some periods and not in other environments.

An example of volatility that's been in the news in the past few years is Bitcoin. Its massive volatility, which includes wild swings in prices that offer speculators the chance to make and lose great sums of wealth, is the element that excites investors. Other every-day examples of volatility can be fuel prices and even real estate, to some extent, depending on area and nature of the property.

There are all sorts of arcane calculations to measure and quantify volatility and risk. A good rule of thumb for spotting volatility and risk is that the greater the fluctuation in prices, the greater the risk. For example, Bitcoin has a huge standard deviation (that is, fluctuation and thus high risk), whereas a savings bond or GIC has a low standard deviation (low fluctuation and thus low risk).

It may be obvious, yet it's still worthwhile to point out that for the long-term portfolio, volatility can destroy wealth by creating fear and uncertainty. This has a strong psychological effect causing some investors to make poor investment decisions. Maybe they're getting into a growing market too late and chasing prices. Or it could cause them to get out at the bottom of a price and lose money, only to watch that price bounce back and generate wealth for others that they're missing out on.

Good portfolio managers know how to manage this reality to align with your age, risk profile, retirement, and withdrawal goals. As we age and want less fluctuation in our portfolio, we will drift toward assets with lower volatility. This begs the question if investors are truly making the needed efforts to balance overall portfolio volatility. It's said that the best way to mitigate your portfolio risk is to diversify it.

Traditionally, this meant with both stocks and bonds, or a set of funds. Our approach to diversification would be to expand the scope of assets and investments beyond conventional stocks to include several assets such as participating whole life insurance policies (PAR), precious metals, and real estate investment trusts (REITs), among others. Spotlight B will elaborate more on asset diversification.

Savings in Simple Terms

Let's go back to explain these terms by their simplest definitions. *Saving* is to save money (or something else perhaps) for safekeeping. You may plan to use it in the future on a "rainy day." Or maybe you're saving so you'll have the ability to act quickly when a financial opportunity arrives. Whatever the reason for saving, the main idea of saving is that *saved funds should not be at risk.*

In contrast, investing by definition involves a degree of risk. To invest is to aim for a return on your investment with the understanding that you're risking your investment. Even conservative, guaranteed investments that seek to minimize risk carry the potential for negative returns or even failure. It should be noted that risk means the likeliness of loss. This bears repeating: the higher the risk, the higher the likelihood of loss. Many believe that the higher the risk, the higher likelihood of significant gain, and that is emphatically not true. We have met some seriously wealthy people who basically never take on great risks. They take careful steps forward with acute purpose and design.

So, yes, saving and investing are not the same, and not all forms of saving are the same.

There's more to this financial blind spot than the differences in risk between saving and investing.

Banks Are Safe ... Right?

As we pointed out in the first chapter, most of us are conditioned from childhood to think of banks as the safest place to keep our money. Generally, banks are a safe place to keep our money. The bank accounts where you deposit your money has insurance for eligible deposits up to a certain limit from the Canada Deposit Insurance Corporation, or CDIC, in case anything goes wrong.

Heck, most banks even have a big room where they keep money called a "safe." So, yes, generally speaking, banks are a safe place to keep your money.

Until they aren't.

We're not trying to scare you, but we'd be doing you a disservice if we didn't tell you about a little-known but significant blind spot involving banks. It's called a "bail-in," and if you're unaware of it, this blind spot could (under certain circumstances) potentially cost you much of your savings.

As you might suspect, a "bail-in" is the opposite of a "bailout." A bailout is when an external party, usually the government, rescues a company or institution on the brink of financial failure. It does this by using taxpayer dollars to fund the institution's financial shortcomings. This means bailing the institution out of trouble and ensuring the institution's creditors don't lose much, if any, of the money they're owed by the institution. A bailout also helps ensure customers saving money with the bank won't lose much, if any, of their savings they have deposited there. Many of us first became aware of the concept of bailouts during the 2008 financial crisis.

In contrast, a bail-in requires a financial institution on the brink of failure to cancel the debts it owes to creditors and depositors. There's no money coming in to help save the bank. Instead, a bail-in mandates that you, the depositor, support the bank with the financial difficulty. It's as if the bank says to people it owes, "Sorry, but we had to use your money to help us keep our business afloat."

You won't walk away empty-handed, of course. Most often the bank issues you stock certificates in the bank. The idea is that you can sell that stock to recoup your deposits. Um, stock in a failing bank? You don't have to be an expert in money to make a good guess about how much that's worth. Certainly nowhere near what you had deposited in the bank.

There are a few circumstances in which the government may implement a bail-in (and more scenarios could develop):

- The collapse of the financial institution isn't likely to create a systemic problem (in other words, it isn't "too big to fail").

- The government doesn't have the financial resources necessary to cover a bailout.

- The government wants to limit the amount of taxpayers' money used to resolve the situation.

Bail-ins don't happen often, but they have happened. In 2013, the customers of the Bank of Cyprus lost a substantial portion of their deposits. In return, these depositors received bank stock. However, the value of these stocks did not equate to most depositors' losses. In a July 29, 2013 article *USA Today* noted that overall depositors lost approximately 47.5% of their savings.[43]

Not much has been written on this event since a 2018 Reuters article about the depositors' compensation claim in a European court.[44] That's when an EU court rejected a petition for compensation filed by bank depositors whose funds were confiscated in Cyprus' financial crisis of 2013. During the crisis, depositors lost billions of dollars in two Cypriot banks when people's savings were confiscated to protect the country's banking system.

But could it happen here? The answer is an unequivocal "yes." In the 2013 budget, Canada announced that it will introduce a Cyprus-style bail-in regime for systematically important banks .[45] Then in March 2023, we again learned that a bank failure isn't a concern without cause. The bank run on Silicon Valley Bank marked the second largest bank failure in U.S. history after Washington Mutual in 2008. [46]

In addition to our savings, many of us have retirement plans through banks and credit unions. This makes it vital for you to recognize the existence of bail-ins, to keep an eye on the health

43 Menelaos Hadjicostis, "Bank of Cyprus Depositors Lose 47.5% of Savings," USA Today, July 29, 2013, https://www.usatoday.com/story/money/business/2013/07/29/bank-of-cyprus-depositors-lose-savings/2595837/.

44 "European Court Dismisses Compensation Claim in Cyprus 2013 Deposit-Grab," Reuters, July 13, 2018, https://www.reuters.com/article/us-cyprus-banks-idUKKBN1K3242.

45 "Bail-In: Coming to Canada," Fasken, December 18, 2013, https://www.fasken.com/en/knowledge/2013/12/financialinstitutionsbulletin-20131218.

46 "The Silicon Valley Bank Collapse Explained," University of Washington School of Law, March 24, 2023, https://www.law.uw.edu/news-events/news/2023/svb-collapse#:~:text=Over%20a%20period%20of%20just,after%20Washington%20Mutual's%20in%202008.

of any institution to whom you've entrusted your money, and to diversify where and how you use your wealth. It's worthwhile to ask yourself and your advisor if you have too many assets in a banking environment. There are well established financial alternatives to help you save money in a diversified, and very importantly, accessible manner.

Don't Interrupt

It's a mathematical fact that the opportunity to have uninterrupted compounded growth can create more wealth over time. If you want to make money, one of the easiest and surest ways is to create an asset—monetary or otherwise—that experiences a constant progressive rate of growth for as long as possible. But life has a way of making this easier said than done.

Emergencies occur and opportunities arise. When these events present themselves, they often need to be addressed in one way or another with money. Often that money needs to be pulled from savings or investments.

Let's say you have a situation where you need cash quickly because you have the chance to buy a condo for your daughter who's going to university in another city. You can get the property for an unbelievable price ... but you need $20,000 for the down payment, like, right now.

If you pull your money out of your RRSP, IRA, or 401(k), or even your traditional savings account, your earnings on that "saved" money will stop as soon as you pull the money out of the account. You can use that money for the down payment on the condo, but you've interrupted your compounding growth. This is key to understanding this blind spot: Most people think they're getting ahead by saving and then spending, saving, and spending, versus going into debt and paying it off. *But the result, either way, is still zero.*

Why? Because you're spending the money you pulled out of your savings, RRSP, 401(k), or IRA *and* you're not making any return on that money.

So how do you balance life's predictable costs with the unpredictable events of life with the desire to maintain uninterrupted compound growth to build your wealth? The good news is you've started that process by grasping the difference between savings and investments. Now you need to implement a better way to save. By better, we mean one that affords you the capital to deal with life's unexpected financial needs while protecting your uninterrupted compound growth.

What if You Could Have It All?

There are ways to save and have access to cash for investing without interrupting your compound growth.

One tool we've come to value more and more is participating whole life insurance, or PAR. (To be clear, PAR doesn't stand for anything and isn't an acronym. It's simply a shortening of the word "participating.")

Many people have not heard of PAR, and of those who have, many don't fully understand it. They think of it as just life insurance. But the truth is, it's built more for the living benefit than for its death benefit. More than an insurance policy, PAR is a financial tool, an asset you own that experiences compound growth over time while also giving you access to cash for emergencies and opportunities without interrupting that compounding growth.

We'll go into PAR and how you can use it as part of your wealth-building strategy in Spotlight E. But briefly put, when you borrow against the PAR policy, the account continues to grow without interruption as if you haven't taken money out. It's similar to the way your home still appreciates despite taking out a line of credit against equity.

Insurance companies track the loans against your PAR policy and charge interest on the amounts borrowed. When you pay back the loan amount, the amount available for future loans increases. Not only are you repaying the balance, but you're also reducing the interest charge and refilling your pool of available capital.

Another benefit is that often policyholders will borrow against a PAR policy to invest in business opportunities that will also allow them to write off the interest cost against their taxes. But what about the obvious purpose of the PAR life insurance policy—the death benefit? The death benefit also continues to grow even as you extract and replenish the balance.

When it comes to building wealth, life is a marathon, not a sprint. Saving and investing are long-term endeavors, and the sooner you can set yourself up for compounding growth, the better off you'll be. Saving better with PAR policies makes a lot of sense. Think of it as a safe haven for cash, like a modern-day vault. You can access cash without interrupting compound growth, it's a reliable long-term wealth asset with low volatility that's unaffected by the highs and lows of the market, it offers the peace of mind of a built-in death benefit and, honestly, the performance of a PAR policy is hard to beat.

The Empowerment of Responsibility

At first, coming to terms with the fact that we're responsible for our own lives, happiness, income, and how we spend and save is a little scary. But soon you'll find it's so empowering when you accept the reality that you're the owner of the business of your life.

Don't worry—you're not alone. We are in the midst of an incredible transformation in the way we work and the way we do business. We've witnessed many new young millionaires, and that trend will continue. In contrast to the conventional path of college and university—a path many of us over the age of 30 enjoyed—the new generations using the power of the internet can easily obtain their education online from various websites and other quality platforms. This new path cannot be followed whilst on autopilot. It takes courage to set course on a less conventional path.

Embracing your life from a business perspective empowers

you well beyond your immediate financial concerns. It seeps into every area of your life. It clears the way for having dreams, gives you courage, and helps you find the resources to act on making those dreams a reality.

FINANCIAL BLIND$POT #9
WHY STRATEGY IS IMPORTANT

"Would you tell me, please, which
way I ought to go from here?"
"That depends a good deal on where
you want to get to," said the Cat.
"I don't much care where—" said Alice.
"Then it doesn't matter which
way you go," said the Cat.
"—so long as I get somewhere,"
Alice added as an explanation.
"Oh, you're sure to do that," said the
Cat, "if you only walk long enough."

–Lewis Carroll, Alice in Wonderland[47]

Most of us loathe the word "plan." Like so many other words in the English language, the power of the word "plan" has been muted because of how it's used. We show up at our friend's house and we say, "So, what is the plan?"

---

47   Lewis Carroll, *Alice in Wonderland* (London: Macmillan, 1865).

Or when someone does not come to a meeting they say, "I was planning on attending but something came up." To most of us, a plan is a wish, a hopeful idea, or a *someday*. Unfortunately, that usually results in a *probably not*.

The real meaning of the word "plan" is to design, plot, project, and scheme, and the word implies a method devised for making, doing something, or achieving an end. In the mindset chapter, we told you that we become what we think about. Those words are, in our view, the most powerful words ever spoken. But the saying is misunderstood.

Take for instance the person who is in their early 50s, sitting on their well-worn couch wearing a T-shirt slightly big enough to hide their "Molson muscle." After reading that sentence you might say, "Are you telling me I thought about becoming an overweight 50-year-old on a vintage couch?"

Of course, you didn't envision that exact picture. But we can say with certainty that you didn't envision yourself being a middle-aged person full of vitality sitting in a leather armchair in front of a fire in your country cottage on a cold winter evening. That mental picture requires creation, intention, and action.

A proper strategy (our word for *plan*) demands the specific inputs of creation, intention, and action. You have probably heard this before, but that makes it no less true: It may seem simple, but it's not easy. We remember the first time an insurance professional asked us what the future looked like for us and our families. Our responses were some versions of "I don't know."

Ironically, we wish we could count on only one hand the number of times we've heard that answer from prospects and new clients. In hindsight we have realized that asking someone what the future looks like is a big question. However, when we start asking questions about the future of your family, career, or business, and we get the same response, it's clear to us that many of us have not set an intentional path for our future.

In early meetings as new financial advisors, the response "I don't know" from a client had us experience a certain amount of fear, anxiety, and frustration. We would try to ask clarifying questions, but the clients could sense what we were feeling. This only created more confusion as they sought to give us the "right" answer. We've since learned to meet people where they are. It's our job to create a space where our clients can clearly articulate where they want to go. That means a commitment to discover what is important to the client and in turn help them see and create a future that excites and energizes them.

During the creation phase, it's important to be as clear as possible in outlining your future. There's a psychological basis for being clear in what you want. The subconscious mind has no choice but to accept our suggestions, no matter how extreme they may seem.[48] You might make another choice in the future and that's okay. We almost guarantee you will. The process of creation will continue throughout your lifetime. It's like climbing a mountain that has no top.

---

48   Brian Tracy, "Subconscious Mind Power Explained," Brian Tracy International, accessed August 31, 2023, https://www.briantracy.com/blog/personal-success/understanding-your-subconscious-mind/.

There are lots of useful methods to create your financial values and set goals for the future. One method is detailed by Bill Bachrach in his book *Values-Based Financial Planning*. He suggests asking questions designed to discover your financial values.[49]

For instance, if in conversation a person says that freedom is important to them, the process is to ask what about freedom is important to them. If the person responds that freedom will allow them to travel for a month at a time, the process suggests asking what about travel is important to them.

The next phase of this discovery process may uncover adventure, childhood memories, charity, happiness, and serenity. The result is anchoring a value to an emotion. This is critical. In our experience with clients, people do not move unless there's emotion in the background. We think of it as "energy in motion."

If we ask you what you want for your financial future and you say, "I want a great life," that's not specific enough.

So, we might ask a follow-up question along the lines of, "So tell us more about that. What does have a great life mean to you?"

And you respond, "Oh, well, I want to be happy."

That's a step closer, but there are a lot of things that can make a person happy. At some point you have to bring that picture of your future into something tangible that you can aim for.

---

49   Bill Bachrach, *Values-Based Financial Planning: The Art of Creating and Inspiring Financial Strategy* (Aim High Publishing, 2000).

You've probably heard of SMART goals. These are goals that are specific, measurable, achievable, relevant, and time-bound. Anyone can apply this framework in their own financial goal setting. We all need to have a "North Star" to aim toward in our lives as it is the journey toward that vision of the future that gives your life meaning. It's also good to have multiple stars to aim at as it relates to the different components of your life such as romantic relationships, family, and career, to name a few.

Here's the hardest part of strategy: *setting your intention.* Understand that intention can be fleeting. For it to be effective, you must link your intention and emotion with action. Know that the process of linking your intentions and emotions to actions will not be an exact science. There will be lots of course corrections along the way as you discover new information and actions to take. Every step along the path toward your goal will either take you closer or further away. However, it does not matter what direction your actions take you as long as you take the time to consistently reassess where you are.

Notice that in this chapter, we haven't described what most people might consider a financial plan or a strategy prepared by a financial planner. The typical financial plan takes a person's finances and applies a somewhat arbitrary inflation and growth rate against the individual's estimate of expenses for periods of up to 30 to 40 years. Although there's a use for this type of plan from time to time, it's not what we're talking about here. The type of strategy discussed here causes an individual to stretch themselves in ways they're not used to.

We have one client named Becky who owns a beauty salon.

The salon has been successful for several years and has even allowed Becky to rent chairs from time to time. But in a recent discussion, Becky said she was considering getting out of the salon business and selling real estate. She felt that the salon was an exercise in trading dollars rather than growing her wealth. *Trading dollars means cash in equals cash out.* She indicated she saw limited upside in the future of her business and wanted more. Her business skills have helped her develop her confidence and grown her network. She's excited for her next challenge.

But Becky's next challenge wasn't in real estate after all. It turns out Becky's next challenge was taking her salon to a new level of growth. Rather than change her situation, she changed her *view* of her situation with her salon. With her sharpened business skills, Becky was able to identify possibilities for growth in her business that at one point didn't seem possible to her.

There's a saying: *When the student is ready, the teacher appears.* The act of linking your actions to your intent will align and fit elements into your life—elements that you could not have predicted. Once your awareness of relevant finance matters increases, the financial opportunities to help you go where you want to go will also increase.

That's what we mean by strategy. An individual needs to continually evaluate and tally their inventory of skills, network, market growth, industry, and technological trends. We have witnessed individuals become millionaires in a matter of a few years by constantly evaluating and creating possibilities.

If that's what you want, you can too.

FINANCIAL BLIND$POT #10
BUILD YOUR TEAM

You improve your chances for financial success with a team around you. Here's how you build a winner.

§tatistics show that investors who work with financial advisors have over four times more in financial assets than those who go it alone.[50]

As we mentioned in the first chapter, most people choose their financial advisor within two degrees of separation. In other words, a friend or a friend of a friend. Conventional wisdom tells you that word of mouth is a great method for choosing an advisor to team up with. After all, we take referrals from friends for all sorts of services—everything from dentists to roofers to house painters. So why not a financial advisor or another professional like an accountant or lawyer?

---

50   "2012 Quantitative Analysis of Investor Behavior," Dalbar, Inc., April 2012, https://static.fmgsuite.com/media/documents/c96b3ccc-953d-4f2a-9761-5aa3c3489df2.pdf.

The world of finance can be complex. On one level, this complexity requires specialists with a deep understanding of a specific subject matter, such as rules and regulations. But the sheer volume of information also leads to the development of generalists. The world needs both generalists and specialists, but the devil is often in the details. Does your situation require a generalist or a specialist? And, following from that, do you have the knowledge or understanding of your situation to be able to make that determination? Will you ask the questions necessary of this person who has been referred to you? Will you overlook signs and signals because the person you have been referred to has the benefit of the trust that comes with the referral from a friend?

That's why as a financial consumer, you first must know what's important for you and those closest to you. It will help you to keep that self-knowledge front and center evaluating the information any advisor presents to you. So, if referrals aren't always ideal, what's the best way for you to build your financial planning team? First of all, you need to understand what a financial advisor is, and more importantly, what services should be provided.

Picking Your Team Leader

There have been several initiatives like those in Ontario where government regulators decided to require credentials to use the title "financial planner" or "financial advisor." Whilst we would never say that these types of rules are not important to inform the public, at the very least, and punish bad actors at the most, we believe the responsibility for the financial advice sought still rests with you, the consumer.

As the consumer, you need to establish the support you require. Once you know your needs and goals using the awareness you've gained through these pages, your first action step is building your team. This is critical to stack the deck in *your* favor. There may be many players on your team, including the investment advisor, the insurance agent, the banker, the accountant, and the lawyer. Depending on the nature of your financial activities, that list might expand to include a fee-only financial planner, a real estate agent, and a mortgage broker.

With so many professionals involved in your financial affairs, you can see how easily advice can become fragmented and how easily critical information and process gaps can go unnoticed. To limit fragmented advice and to make sure nothing is missed, you should designate one of these professionals to take the lead in developing, communicating, and maintaining your strategy. If you decide not to engage a fee-only financial planner, then you will have to evaluate the players with the most resources and capability to take on this role.

Next, let's dive into the usual activities of the investment advisor, the insurance agent, the banker, the accountant, and the lawyer. To be clear, our objective is not to diminish any one profession, product, or advisor. Rather, we want to help you understand the potential roles these individuals play, putting you in the position to choose these roles as they relate to your financial life.

Investment Advisors

It's important to know that most of the time, the investment advisor is really a relationship manager. The person often does not have much, if any, responsibility for investment decisions and generally does not trade the portfolio. Trading the investment portfolio is highly specialized and the best of the best have lots of training. One of the first documents they usually give you is an investment policy statement, which is designed to gauge your risk tolerance and highlight the goals for the funds you're investing. The investment advisor generally gets paid based on a percentage of your assets under management (AUM). As such, the advisor has an incentive to move your assets into the portfolio.

Over the years there have been many changes in disclosures related to the exact amount of fees that investment advisors get paid for their services. Increased transparency through disclosure has led to significant reductions in costs to the customer, which we see as a positive development. However, there are still financial tools deployed inside certain strategies (such as mutual funds and segregated funds) that carry fees that often range from 2% to 3% per year.

Given that the prime lending rate in both Canada and the United States has been in the range of 2% to 3% for almost a decade until late in 2022, this should give people more context as to how much in fees that they may be paying.

But be careful you're not penny-wise and pound-foolish. Certain products may carry a slightly higher fee than lower-priced options. For example, some segregated funds may have a higher fee than an exchange-traded fund (ETF) or a mutual fund. Yet they offer the benefits of bypassing probate, deposit guarantees, and annual performance bonuses toward retirement that show continuous growth even in negative market conditions. These insulating guarantees and bonuses may justify a higher fee. It's still less than the experiences of hard losses and volatility that may affect your psyche.

All investments are subject to risk, of course, and risk means exposure to loss. If you invest, your advisor must use investment management tools. You as the consumer need to understand the purpose, cost, and advantage of such tools. Remember you do not have to become an expert, but you do need to ask good questions.

If you're involved and asking questions, you will begin to notice that, for the most part, many investment professionals continually suggest you put more money into investments for the long run. The idea behind this strategy is to have your assets under their management for as long as possible.

In contrast, an insurance professional will usually suggest that the first steps to your financial well-being are protection and risk management with the use of insurance products. We contend you need both protection and an investment portfolio—but insurance is a must. Protection is always step one. We suggest you steer clear of any financial advisor who doesn't start with limiting your risk.

Insurance Professionals

As insurance professionals, we feel we are well qualified to say there are not many barriers to entry to becoming an insurance agent. You do not need to have any post-secondary education. Four tests need to be completed as part of the life license qualification program (LLQP) and all four tests can be written on the same day.[51] We don't share this as a criticism of the industry or the agents. Many insurance professionals are some of the most educated and highly qualified financial experts in existence. We point out the low barriers to becoming an insurance professional to illustrate that there can be lots of agents in the insurance space and that has created some confusion for the public around products and methods. There's a reason that an Image of Professions survey completed by Roy Morgan listed insurance agents at or near the bottom of the list for trusted advisors.[52]

Insurance agents get compensated by commissions, and the amount of these commissions can vary significantly depending on the product. The first goal of the insurance agent should be to conduct a needs analysis and communicate with the client. This conversation should include the amount of protection available to clients to provide for their family, their estate, their business, and often their community. The amount, type, and positioning of that protection will make all the difference in helping people

---

51 "Life Licence Qualification Program (LLQP)," Financial Services Regulatory Authority of Ontario, accessed August 31, 2023, https://www.fsrao.ca/licensing/life-and-accident-sickness-agent/life-licence-qualification-program-llqp.

52 "Insurance Brokers Among Nation's Least Trusted Workers, Survey Says," Insurance Business, May 12, 2016, https://www.insurancebusinessmag.com/au/news/breaking-news/insurance-brokers-among-nations-least-trusted-workers-survey-says-57485.aspx.

ensure they'll be able to reach their wealth target no matter what life brings their way.

While the investment advisor recommends investment funds, the insurance agent is going to suggest insurance products. Here's where it can get interesting. The amount of cash required to fund the insurance strategy suggested by your insurance professional may dig into assets under management by the investment advisor. It's when financial professionals start to compete for cash flow that the client gets confused by mixed messages and nobody wins when that happens.

Bankers

A bank is geared to provide as many services to their customers as they can. The idea is that the more services it offers to a client (you), the more likely the client will be to continue to use the bank's services. The term for this is "sticky."[53]

This "stickiness" creates a consistent stream of cash flow for the bank. After all, money begets money and what follows are more fees and service charges.

Our advice is to use the bank for what it's best at—providing credit. We had a financial advisor colleague once point out to us that they could generally tell which bank their customer did business with from just a cursory review of the portfolio statement. If their portfolio was invested in the Royal Bank Bond Fund or the

---

53   Ron Daly, "Is Your Bank Good Sticky…Or Bad Sticky?" Virtual StrongBox, January 7, 2023, https://www.virtualstrongbox.com/articles/is-your-bank-good-sticky-or-bad-sticky/.

BMO Bond Fund, there would be a high chance that the portfolio manager was either with the Royal Bank or with BMO. Kind of obvious when he put it that way.

Other Team Members

Now it's time to deal with the professionals behind the scenes: your accountant and your lawyer. The behind-the-scenes characterization may not be fair, as there are certainly accountants and lawyers who are out in front and doing a great job for their clients. Again, you need to choose the relationship that you want from these professionals.

Accountants

The accountant will generally be a chartered professional accountant (CPA). Once upon a time there were other designations such as certified management accountant (CMA) and certified general accountant (CGA). However, in Canada these organizations came together under one banner in 2014.[54] You should know the distinction between a professional with a designation and one without.

The CPA profession is well established with a disciplinary body that monitors and addresses public complaints. In addition, there are requirements for liability insurance and practice inspections

---

54 "Chartered Professional Accountants of Canada (CPA Canada)," Thomas Reuters Practical Law, accessed August 31, 2023, https://ca.practicallaw. thomsonreuters.com/0-595-6006?transitionType=Default&contextData=(sc. Default)&firstPage=true.

that make sure that the procedures, processes, and recordkeeping requirements are there to protect the public interest.

In contrast, if you have a bookkeeper that files your taxes, those safeguards are not in place. That's not to say that all accountants with a designation are created equal, which might be an obvious statement.

To say what a professional accountant does is complex is an understatement. The tax rules and regulations change each year to accommodate new initiatives put in place by the government to either incentivize or discourage certain activities by taxpayers. This level of complexity requires specialization, and as we discussed earlier, specialization narrows the focus and can create gaps.

Most financial planning strategies are not well understood by a professional accountant who is a general practitioner. An open mind is critical for working effectively with your accountant. In most cases, there will be a certain level of conservatism that may be warranted. It's our view that when it comes to tax rules and regulations, the most successful professional accountants understand where the line is, and they are skilled at determining how close to the line the client wants to get. It really is that simple. Tax rules and regulations are written in legal terms and, as such, are open to interpretation.

In our view the focus of the professional accountant should be to file accurate reports with the government that withstand scrutiny and to reduce the payment of tax to the lowest amount allowable under the prevailing rules and regulations. If you read the taxpayer bill of rights guide on the Canada Revenue Agency website, the first right listed is as follows: "You have the right to receive entitlements and to pay no more and no less than what is required by law."[55]

If your accountant is not actively discussing and looking at ways to reduce the taxes you pay, then we recommend you look elsewhere.

Lawyers

Having a good lawyer is just as important as having a good accountant.

The lawyer is responsible for documenting legal agreements and instructions and keeping them on file for the time that these agreements may be needed. The mandate of the lawyer is even broader than the accountant in that they must be able to handle the crossover between personal and business activities.

No legal agreement can protect someone from a "fight" if the other individual is set on taking a matter in that direction. Having said that, legal agreements are designed for those what-if scenarios, and having a well-drafted agreement is always preferable. Just because an agreement is legal does not make it a good agreement. The issue we see most when choosing lawyers is that most people do not understand the depth and breadth of some of these practices.

For instance, a lawyer may not have any training in estate and

---

55   "Your Rights as a Taxpayer," Tax Tips Canada, last updated July 31, 2023, https://www.taxtips.ca/personaltax/taxpayers-ombudsperson.htm.

tax matters, or in certain business and commercial transactions. A lawyer who mostly engages in residential real estate transactions is probably not the best choice for drafting a family trust. Know your lawyer's strengths and weaknesses and don't be afraid to speak up when you suspect they're out of their area of expertise.

Ask, Ask, Ask

We live in a world that is transactional by nature. We have become so accustomed to transactional dealings that we often confuse these dealings with those that are relationship driven. This can cause people to fail to recognize or understand the underlying incentive for the party they're working with. This can often lead to poor results.

With new ways of looking at your mindset, programming, and procrastination, you're now able to ask new and better questions as you build your team. We've provided a basic framework along with a solid understanding as to which will allow you to take control of your financial future. However, as we have already said, the devil is always in the details. Look back to the end of Chapter 2 to see some sample questions you should ask your advisors, whether they were referred to you or not.

In the next Spotlights section we would like to make you aware of several practical tactics you might consider implementing. With regard to implementation, awareness, and ultimately, action, these spotlights address some options and actions many people do not consider for various reasons.

PART II
$POTLIGHT$

FINANCIAL $POTLIGHT$
AN INTRODUCTION

"Insanity: doing the same thing over and over again and expecting different results."
–Popular saying widely misattributed to Albert Einstein[56]

The following Spotlights are, for the most part, broad practical strokes to further illuminate the financial landscape. To reiterate, the scope of this book is not to be a financial encyclopedia, but instead to be a resource you can refer to for financial empowerment, perspective, and alternative considerations.

These Spotlights will review a range of topics, including the protection and accumulation of assets, including an array of financial tools and capital allocations, as well as the journey of distribution during retirement—in other words, we will discuss many areas on the path up and then down the mountain of financial well-being. (It's worth noting, to extend the metaphor, that

---

56   "Insanity Is Doing the Same Thing Over and Over Again and Expecting Different Results," Quote Investigator, March 23, 2017, https://quoteinvestigator.com/2017/03/23/same/.

more climbers die on the way down Mount Everest than on the way up.[57] Knowing how to navigate the distribution years is just as important as the years of accumulation, which in many ways can be a much more forgiving part of your journey.)

To that end, our Blind Spots and our Spotlights sections are meant to inform and guide financial understanding and empower you, the reader, to go further on your journey *without* hesitation.

---

57 Jordan Lite, "Death on Mount Everest: The Perils of the Descent," Scientific American, December 10, 2008, https://blogs.scientificamerican.com/news-blog/death-on-mount-everest-the-perils-o-2008-12-10/.

FINANCIAL $POTLIGHT A
FINANCIAL PROTECTION AND SAFETY FOR YOU AND YOUR FAMILY

Because neither time or health are guaranteed, understanding financial priorities and creating a solid base for your financial well-being are vital.

There are four traditional pillars to the finance industry: banks, trusts, insurance companies, and investment brokerage houses. They're regulated separately, and there has also been some convergence over the years. Interestingly, the insurance industry still stands on its own. It's a financial staple that has not been given enough credence in financial planning.

It's surprising to us that insurance companies have not been as recognized and utilized in planning given the strong regulation, guarantees, and protection that has been proven to be effective. There may be other reasons for this lack of recognition; however, times are clearly changing. Insurance companies are establishing themselves in their rightful place in the market—especially given the weakness seen in the banking sector. Another fundamental reason for the underutilization of insurance can best be explained by an analogy.

When someone buys a power drill, they aren't really buying a drill. They're buying the hole the drill will make. After all, no one needs a drill unless they need a hole. This reframing of the situation by focusing not on the method but rather on the benefit can help to build valuable financial results.

No one grows up thinking, "I can't wait to have some Microsoft stock in my portfolio!" Well maybe Warren Buffett did; however, he is an exception to the general rule.

What you want are financial tools that provide for financial protection and growth. Much like with the drill, you want the end result and what the money can do for you and your family.

If you're like most people, what you want is freedom in your life. You want to be able to do what you want, with who you want, when you want, and how you want. It's about a lifestyle, now and in retirement, coupled with the peace of mind that enough money can bring you. Of course, what's important to each of us when creating our future is not the same. For instance, what's important could include:

- Financial protection of your wealth no matter what life throws at you.

- The necessary funds to obtain the best care wherever it exists anywhere in the world.

- Funds to make sure your children have the very best start in life.

- The security of knowing that, should something happen, you have all the necessary resources to pay off all your debts and be allowed the time to prepare and grieve.

- A pool of money to provide education funds for your children.

- Funds that provide consistent, guaranteed, and steady progress of wealth independent of market conditions whilst keeping up with the rate of inflation.

- The financial security and achievement in having arrived at a state of mind about money, wealth, retirement, and spending that's sensible and yet full of joy as the years go by—all because you understand the financial services industry more fully and are aware of what is available.

- The confidence that your finances are insulated from certain risks that you and your family could be exposed to now and in the future.

- Knowing that the tools you use to accomplish this are tax efficient and favored.

- The peace of mind from having control, transparency, and liquidity in the short and long term for things such as emergencies, education, travel, a business start-up or expansion, real estate, and retirement.

- Understanding that saved funds for security are actually secure, liquid, and accessible.

When it comes to money, always stop and ask yourself: "Do I want the actual financial tools my financial advisor presents to me? Or do I want the end result?"

Is It Enough to Ask This?

When most people meet with their financial advisor, they have questions like:

- What's the rate of return on this mutual fund?
- What's the rate of return on the stock?
- What has your portfolio provided in net returns over the last five years?

Then based on the answers, they choose this one or that one. The problem is, only focusing on investments and investment returns is like furnishing your entire home with three-seat sofas. When you're considering the financial furniture that will provide you the ability to live the life you always dreamed about, would it serve you to fill your living room full of three-seat sofas? How about an armchair, a lamp, and an area rug? For that matter, do you have a foundation for your home or is it built on uneven ground?

If you're sitting in a room full of sofas, nothing will bring your situation into focus like market volatility. Being solely dependent on positive market upswings is a narrow way to approach your finances and can lead to inadequate outcomes. Hoping for an amazing rate of return to be the solution to all financial matters can lead to repeated disappointments.

Far too many people don't consider protection as a foundation of their financial plan. Yet, protection and a fund for emergencies is critical. The world is evolving and changing fast. Having a foundation in place is not only prudent, but it can also provide peace of mind that allows you to both navigate hardships and capitalize on opportunities.

The Financial Pyramid

The financial pyramid has long been a strong and solid approach to personal finance. The foundation is the first element of importance since anything could happen at any time. It's based on creating that first layer of financial protection by accumulating savings for emergency purposes as well as using personal insurance products to mitigate financial strains during times of illness, an accident, or even the loss of life of a family member.

Savings should be funds that are easily available and stored without any attached risk to value. The ideal cash safety net may vary from person to person, yet for most it is about six months' worth of bill totals.

The personal insurance needed can be quite subjective.

In general, if you're single, you're likely to have as your primary protection what's considered to be *living benefits* in case of a disability caused by illness or injury. This can take the shape of a wage replacement such as disability insurance or a tax-free lump-sum payment after the diagnosis of a covered condition like those often issued by a critical illness policy.

When you have a family and dependents, the protection should encompass the above living benefits as well as life insurance to address a premature death. This can help to assist with loss of household income as well as the loss of a primary person raising the family.

In either case, the need for a financial safety net is fundamental, and without it a financial catastrophe could emerge. For many widowed survivors and others suffering from a severe illness or accident, the financial burdens can become insurmountable. With this financial awareness, you can co-create a plan that encompasses a balanced and secure financial portfolio with both protective and growth aspects in place. A well-built financial structure will accompany you throughout the years like a great friend who has your back.

The common financial pyramid:

The focus on capital growth as well as increased risk is implemented after the base of the financial pyramid is stable. This stability comes from emergency funds and insurance coverage, which enables management of financial risks should something occur in the short term.

In contrast, and unfortunately for many, the priorities have not rested on a solid foundation. The lack of protection and lack of liquid emergency capital has many people experiencing heightened financial anxiety. As shown here, *Bank on Yourself* author Pamela Yellen easily illustrates the inherent challenge with this approach where the priorities are actually upside-down.

Pamela Yellen's Financial Instability Pyramid:

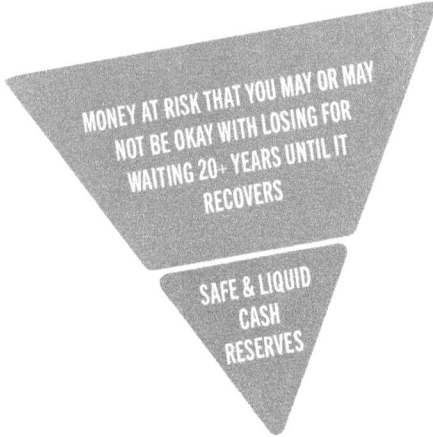

FINANCIAL INSTABILITY PYRAMID

MONEY AT RISK THAT YOU MAY OR MAY NOT BE OKAY WITH LOSING FOR WAITING 20+ YEARS UNTIL IT RECOVERS

SAFE & LIQUID CASH RESERVES

Financial Protection

The most important step and the foundation for putting your financial house in order is an insurance strategy. The blocks of a well-positioned protection strategy include life insurance (in case of an early or late death), long-term care (to assist with health care costs typically later in life), health insurance (regular health care costs including minor or major), disability insurance (income replacement in case of injury or illness), and critical illness insurance (lump-sum benefit for a critical illness that would need extra recovery time and usually has added costly treatments).

In most cases, these benefits are tax-free, and we have seen many people benefit from having such protective solutions in place. In fact, if they did not have such protection, the financial well-being of the family would have been devastated.

Another critical element of the foundation of the financial pyramid is the ability to have access to cash. Liquid capital for emergencies and even opportunities is a must. Where you keep this cash is another question and one that we will cover more as well. Yet, one should have anywhere from three to 12 months of capital available.

A protection portfolio is a type of portfolio that's gaining more recognition and appreciation in the industry and with clients in general. Having the right financial tools in place, including protection, can be argued to be a fundamental part of a financial portfolio and therefore be an asset. Often, we see people hesitate, as the new subject matter is *not fun*. And for some, there's a strong degree of embedded fear. This is human. Just remember that "talking about sex won't make you pregnant, and talking about death won't make you die."

So, besides having your regular health care needs covered, the following three protection building blocks are insurance products that most people should consider having.

Building Block 1: Disability Insurance

We call this insurance for your income, and it's also often described as wage replacement. Long-term disability insurance is considered a vital piece of your financial well-being. According to Statistics Canada, one in five Canadians have a disability,[58] and the 1985 Commissioners Individual Disability Table A tells us that one in three working-age Canadians will become disabled and unable to work before they turn age 65.[59] Similar statistics are also true in the U.S.

The World Health Organization estimates the most common forms of disability are mental disorders (31%), cancer (16%), cardiovascular diseases (12%), injuries (8%), musculoskeletal (5%), and other miscellaneous causes (28%).[60] From these statistics, we can discern that less than 10% of disabilities are caused by accidents.

You can obtain disability insurance coverage for illness and injury combined, or just one or the other. If budget is an issue, then the less costly accidental only can certainly provide a first step toward peace of mind.

Ideally you should either have disability coverage through an employer benefit program or with a private plan. The benefits of a private plan are numerous and may provide more coverage and

---

58   Stuart Morris, Gail Fawcett, Laurent Brisebois, and Jeffrey Hughes, "A Demographic, Employment and Income Profile of Canadians with Disabilities Aged 15 Years and Over, 2017," Statistics Canada, November 28, 2018, https://www150.statcan.gc.ca/n1/pub/89-654-x/89-654-x2018002-eng.htm.
59   "Individual Disability Valuation Standard Report of the Joint American Academy of Actuaries/Society of Actuaries Individual Disability Tables Work Group," American Academy of Actuaries, December 2015, https://www.actuary.org/sites/default/files/files/IDTWG_Table_Report_121915_0.pdf.
60   "Global Health Estimates: Life Expectancy and Leading Causes of Death and Disability," The Global Health Observatory, World Health Organization, accessed November 30, 2023, https://www.who.int/data/gho/data/themes/mortality-and-global-health-estimates.

other options with or without integration with an employer plan. The optional coverage provided by a private plan may be obtained beyond the standard two to five years and include coverage to 10 years and to age 65, 70, or even a lifetime. Payments under private plans can also begin after 0, 30, or 60 days as compared to most employer plans that mandate an elimination period of 90 days. Additional features private plans can include partial return of premiums every six or seven years or for predetermined ages. We always recommend a private plan either as a stand-alone, as a supplement to a group product, or to enhance an employer benefit program. Having a private plan can provide important long-term protection—especially if your employment situation changes. Most benefit programs only allow continued protection for a specified period of time after a participant leaves their employment.

On average, the amount insured under a disability program is limited to approximately two-thirds of your gross annual wage or earnings. This basically means that if you earn $60,000 per year, you can expect approximately $40,000 of net claim benefits. Yet if you earn $200,000 per year, the insurers will not go as high as $132,000. To increase their coverage, clients usually add debt-only disability coverage or bulk up on critical illness insurance.

Working with an advisor that understands each element and the strengths and weaknesses of each plan is key.

Many individuals and families have more peace of mind as a result of knowing they have disability insurance, whether it's offered through their employer or acquired personally. It's worth noting that some insurers offer disability coverage even without a medical exam. These plans have limitations but can be a strong solution for those less medically insurable.

Building Block 2: Critical Illness Insurance

As a complement to an protection portfolio, you should seriously consider critical illness insurance. We refer to this type of protection as insurance for savings. If you're beset with a critical illness, we want you to be able to have immediate access to the best health care anywhere in the world.

This form of insurance was suggested to insurance companies in South Africa in 1983 by Dr. Marius Barnard, brother of Dr. Christian Barnard, who performed the world's first human heart transplant. Dr. Marius Barnard observed that many of the people that he treated for cancer (and other critical illnesses) were subject to a significant amount of additional suffering due to financial stress. He was so passionate and determined to find a solution that he spoke to life insurance companies, explaining the urgency and stating that the life coverage alone does not benefit the family until the person passes away and that he was seeing very many clients recover from their critical illnesses only to find themselves in a difficult if not desperate financial situation because of their conditions. Eventually, Barnard helped South Africa's Crusader Life launch the world's first critical illness insurance policy.[61]

Soon after, other life insurance companies around the world

---

61   Andrew Rickard, "Critical Illness Insurance Pioneer Dr. Marius Barnard Dies at 87," Insurance Portal, December 3, 2014, https://insurance-portal.ca/article/critical-illness-insurance-pioneer-dr-marius-barnard-dies-at-87/.

accepted Dr. Barnard's challenge. They developed contracts to cover a claim (mostly tax-free) with a lump sum if the policyholder is diagnosed with a particular illness on a predetermined list, as specified in the insurance policy. Interestingly, North American policies are now some of the best in the world, as rates are locked in and do not change if there's an unusually high claim incidence with a particular disease.

Besides an individual analysis and assessment, the rule of thumb for the benefits of critical illness policies is one year's worth of income. This would theoretically cover you for a year of stress-free recovery from one of the big three (cancer, heart attack, and stroke) or any of the major illnesses indicated in the policy. Some policies can be obtained even without a medical exam, while others can be obtained even if you have cancer or some other covered conditions. The new coverage would simply not cover the pre-existing conditions. Other features can be a return of all premiums paid, limited pay periods on permanent coverage, and unique corporate solutions for executives, officers, and partners.

These lump-sum payments can insulate you from using your savings or draining your retirement nest egg and, in the case of a registered plan, suffering a potential tax hit.

The most common illnesses claimed on critical illness policies are:

- Cancer (69%)
- Heart attack (10%)
- Stroke (4%)

- Coronary surgery (2%)
- Other (15%)[62]

Furthermore, statistics show that 1 in 8 women experience breast cancer,[63] 1 in 4 people experience heart disease, 1 in 20 experience a stroke,[64] and, perhaps most surprising, many people survive these illnesses. Survival rates are 62% for cancer,[65] 90% for heart attack,[66] and 75% for the first stroke.[67]

Survival requires money. Critical illness insurance helps, and just about any advisor we have ever met has such a policy in their personal portfolio.

Many of our clients see this coverage as an asset—and a form of forced savings if the return of premium option is chosen. Again, peace of mind is increased knowing that you will be more financially secure if you experience a critical illness.

---

62 "Your Client Guide," Critical Illness Insurance, October 2022, https://iaa.secureweb. inalco.com/cw/-/media/documents-repository/individual-insurance-savings-and-retirement/individual-insurance/2022/10/transition-client-guide.pdf.

63 "Key Statistics for Breast Cancer," American Cancer Society, last updated January 12, 2023, https://www.cancer.org/cancer/types/breast-cancer/about/how-common-is-breast-cancer.html.

64 "Learn about Stroke," World Stroke Organization, accessed August 31, 2023, https://www.world-stroke.org/world-stroke-day-campaign/why-stroke-matters/learn-about-stroke.

65 "What's Driving the Improvement in U.S. Cancer Survival Rates?", City of Hope, January 26, 2023, https://www.cancercenter.com/community/blog/2023/01/cancer-survival-rates-are-improving.

66 Richard N. Fogoros, "How Many People Survive a Heart Attack?" Verywell Health, last updated May 11, 2023, https://www.verywellhealth.com/how-to-survive-a-heart-attack-1745323.

67 Lauren Hellicar, "How Many Strokes Can a Person Survive?" Medical News Today, January 31, 2023, https://www.medicalnewstoday.com/articles/how-many-strokes-can-a-person-have-and-survive.

Building Block 3: Life Insurance

None of us are getting out of here alive. Almost sounds like a line from a movie, doesn't it? Yet few truths could be more accurate. The unexpected death of a loved one can almost certainly cause emotional upheaval as well as financial hardship for the survivors. Having an estate plan, even a simplified one, can make a big difference to your finances as well as to your peace of mind.

Keeping the will, the health directive, and the power of attorney (POA) updated is critical for every family, whether or not you own a business. In general, according to Canada's financial consumer agency, approximately half of Canadians have a will, yet more than half of the wills and POAs need to be updated since the current versions no longer reflect their wishes.[68]

For many estates, capital may be needed for debts such as a mortgage, capital gains taxes, final expenses, charitable contributions, educational plans, and business succession and transition, as well as many more possible reasons.

So, how do most people deal with this need for capital at the end of a life? The usual options are basically:

1. Liquidating assets.
2. Borrowing funds using other assets as collateral.
3. Creating a cash reserve by systematically saving.
4. Using life insurance.

---

68   Tim Hewson, "Number of Canadians without Wills significantly under-reported," LegalWills Canada, June 6, 2016, https://www.legalwills.ca/blog/canadians-without-wills.

Let's look briefly at these options a little closer to see what would make the most financial and practical sense:

1. **Liquidation**: Despite being likely the most common method (and it will get the job done if needed), often it's not the most ideal. Issues such as business cycles or fluctuating real estate values can negatively affect the amounts received. Costs of a sale in commissions, accounting and legal expenses, and taxes may need to be paid on the gain.

2. **Borrowing calculation**: It might be more efficient to borrow against assets than to liquidate them. However, adding the element of uncertainty surrounding repayment due to assets possibly being tied up in probate can make it difficult to find a lender, which necessarily reduces the reliability of this option. Survivors may not have the income to support debt. And if they do, how much time will you have and how will you determine who carries which portion of debt? For example, let's assume there is no life insurance, and there is a need for $500,000 to cover a capital gain tax liability. The borrowing option at an interest rate of 5.5% with a 10-year repayment schedule would result in 10 payments of $66,333. totalling $663,338. This is a major liability and an expensive option (Appendix, A.1).

3. **Saving calculation**: Saving consistently for retirement is a challenge. This means saving for heirs is less realistic than one may think. Besides the behavioral aspect, the biggest challenge here is one never really knows when these funds would be needed as life (and death) is unpredictable. Let's

say we need $500,000 and have a savings account at a conservative rate of 4% and a tax rate of 49.8 %. One would have to save $44,748 over 10 years to achieve the goal of $500,000. This means that $447,480 of actual net capital will be required. The reality is that it is likely these funds will be used for many other possible reasons. It's also tax inefficient (Appendix, A.2).

4. **Life insurance**: This age-old proven product of our evolved society can remove the financial risks related to the death of an individual, whether premature or otherwise. Many of the qualities of life insurance include being tax-free to the beneficiaries (in most cases), available for relatively short-term needs (temporary insurance), and offering options to provide coverage for less cash flow, including Term 10, Term 20, Term 30, and even 40-year terms. In addition, life insurance policies are also available as a permanent means of insurance without expiry or change in cost. Some are with and some are without cash or investment values. Access to cash values can be tax-free (in most cases) and a death benefit payment to a beneficiary is often kept separate from estate processes such as probate. This saves additional taxes and, most importantly, time. As with savings, life insurance requires immediate action to implement. However, unlike the borrowing and liquidation methods, assets within the estate will not need to be sold or leveraged. For the sake of our comparison, let's say we choose a permanent policy with a maximum payment period of 20 years, growing cash values, and a guaranteed death benefit for life. Even if you live past

100, the required cash flow would remain unchanged. In the case of a 40-year-old male with a starting death benefit of around $150,000 and maximum deposit option payments into a 20 pay wealth accumulator PAR policy, the cash flow required would hypothetically be the annual amount of $8,801.73 times 20, equalling a total of $176,034.60, thereby making insurance often the least cash flow and the most efficient option. Interestingly, it should be noted that with this example, the death benefit actually grows to almost $1 million around the age of 80, with cash values in excess of $700,000 that could be used for retirement as well.

As can be seen, life insurance is often the best way to fund an estate and prepare for the unexpected passing of a loved one.

So which type of life insurance is best?

Cost, Value, and the Duration of Life Insurance

So many things financial are subjective, and we know that in most cases one gets what one pays for. Financial products are no different. It serves to look at the bigger picture and be open to the features and possibilities. This topic is so important that it deserves much attention. In many ways, participating life insurance could be referred to as Investment Grade Life Insurance (IGLI), and we like to think of PAR as the Swiss army knife of financial tools, as it allows us to do so much from a planning perspective.

Your immediate need for protection may be simple and short-term. Or it could be complex in order to protect you, your family, and your business. An intelligent approach would be to choose a solution that can continue to be optimized in the future. For example, a term life insurance policy that was originally taken out as mortgage protection may be converted later to a PAR policy, which is a tax-advantaged, simple yet sophisticated asset.

In our financial planning process, we utilize calculators that help us both determine our clients' human life value and the specific financial needs of their family and other beneficiaries of the coverage. To do this, we use several common financial inputs like earning potential, standard of living, mortgages, capital gains, and college expenses, along with other factors such as bereavement time.

When we look at the numbers, we usually see that the lowest cost protection today turns out to be the more expensive in the long term. It's also littered with more uncertainty. As we indicated above, term life insurance should be viewed as temporary insurance, and the mechanics of term life insurance are pretty straightforward. If you die within a specific time period, the insurance company will pay a death benefit in dollars to your beneficiaries. Of course, this means the only way to collect is if you die *within the specified period of time*. These term insurance contracts are seen as less expensive than permanent solutions since the financial outlay at the outset is lower. However, term insurance contracts are priced exactly the way they should be because the insurance company actuarially determines and applies the probability within their statistical models that you will outlive the chosen term period. The longer the term, the higher the likelihood of an adverse event and the more "costly" the coverage becomes. As you continue to read you will see the logical fallacy in the discussion around cost, especially as it relates to permanent insurance.

Term life insurance is often thought to be the least expensive form of protection since price dictates this decision most of the time. But the truth is that using term life insurance actually requires more cash flow than what might otherwise be required over the long-term. To explain this further, we came up with a metaphor related to car insurance, which most of us are familiar with.

Let's say you pay $100 a month for car insurance. That's $1,200 a year.

Now let's say you have to pay that every year until you're 89 years old. Then the insurance company says, "We don't want you on our roads. You're too old. That's it, no more car insurance coverage for you."

To which you reply, "But what about all that money I paid over the years?"

"It's the cost of doing business," the insurance company says.

But what if the insurance company had said to you, "Okay, Plan A will require $100 per month. But there's a Plan B. With Plan B, you pay $300 a month."

"Why would I consider that?" you say.

"Hear us out," the company says. "Yes, with Plan B you pay $300 a month. That's $3,600 a year. But you only pay the $300 per month for 20 years. Then you're insured for the rest of your life."

"I'm listening," you say.

"On top of that, what if that $3,600 a year over 20 years ($72,000) that you put in to Plan B continues to grow, and we pay you a dividend? At the end of 20 years, you've got that $72,000 in an account with compound growth. Oh, and you've got access to the cash in the policy for whatever purpose you might need, including retirement."

In this example, there were several obvious benefits to Plan B:

1. Insurance for life.

2. No increase in cost over the lifetime.

3. No expiry of the coverage and no need to ever get another medical exam to qualify for coverage.

4. Every dollar spent continues to grow with time.

5. The accumulated cash values within the policy can be utilized as emergency savings in the short term and they can become your own opportunity fund as well as your retirement nest egg.

Yes, all of this with more cash flow up front, yet less in total. So in this example can you really identify a cost? You get all the money you ever put in along with the growth, and you have access to your cash for opportunities along the way. This is not exactly how a PAR policy works, as it can take a number of years for the cash value to catch up to the deposits into the contract, and there are necessarily conditions around accessing the cash value that include an interest charge for borrowing. However, the general essence of the agreement is not far off what it looks like in real life, especially over the long term. Let's then look at a real example.

We have prepared a table that shows a comparison for a 40-year-old male between Term 10, Term 20, and Permanent Whole Life Insurance (with cash value).

To properly review the table, we recommend that you review and take note specifically of the following:

On Line 1, the initial death benefit. It starts the same: $100,000 for all the life policies.

Line 2: The yearly premium for the permanent policy is more than the term options.

Skip to Line 5: After 10 years, the permanent policy offers a net gain (its cash value worth versus what you've paid up to that point) of $1,969. Meanwhile, the two term policies offer a net cost of $1,652 and $1,956 for the then 10-year and 20-year term policies respectively.

Now look at Lines 8 and 9: For the permanent policy, you've paid a little over $80,000 but the value is worth $8,000 more than what you've paid. There are no cash values on term policies.

Skip ahead to Line 15: Thirty years in, the permanent policy shows a net gain of more than $71,000 while the term policies show net losses in the five figures.

Graphic		Term 10	Term 20	Permanent 20 year paid up Whole Life with Cash Values (Equity)
1	Initial Death Benefit	$100,000	$100,000	100,000
2	Cost Per Year	($165)	($196)	($4,023)
3	Year 10 Total Paid	$1,652	$1,956	$40,230
4	Total Cash Value at Year10	-	-	$42,199
5	Net Cost/Gain	($1,652)	($1,956)	$1,969
6	Death Benefit at age 50	$100,000	$100,000	$129,006
7	Cost/Yr – Year 11 (age 51)	($644)	($196)	($4,023)
8	Year 20 Total Paid	$8,089	$3,931	$80,460
9	Total Cash Value at Year 20	-	-	$88,786
10	Net Cost/Gain	($8,089)	($3,931)	$8,326
11	Death Benefit at age 60	$100,000	$100,000	$176,615
12	Cost/Yr – Year 21 (age 61)	($1,448)	($2,669)	-
13	Year 30 Total Paid	$22,572	$30,618	$80,460
14	Total Cash Value at Year 30	-	-	$152,305
15	Net Cost/Gain	($22,572)	($30,618)	$71,845
16	Death Benefit at age 70	100,000	100,000	235,429
17	Cost/Yr – Year 31 (age 71 to age 80)	($4,419)	($2,269)	-
18	Total Paid at age 80	$62,346	$54,636	$80,460
19	Total Cash Value at age 80	-	-	$239,241
20	Net Cost/Gain	($62,346)	($54,636)	$158,781
21	Death Benefit at age 85 (statistical mortality)	-	-	$376,198

This shows the net cost or the gain after this period of having the life insurance product. A negative number represents a cost, and a positive number represents a gain or a premium deposit against a policy with cash value.

Now, go to Lines 18 and 19. When you're almost 80 years old, will you want to have paid more than $50,000 for zero cash value? Or would you rather have paid $80,000 spread over 20 years to have a cash value that's a little less than a quarter of a million dollars?

That's how the cheapest option can wind up costing you more, especially when you consider the death benefit.

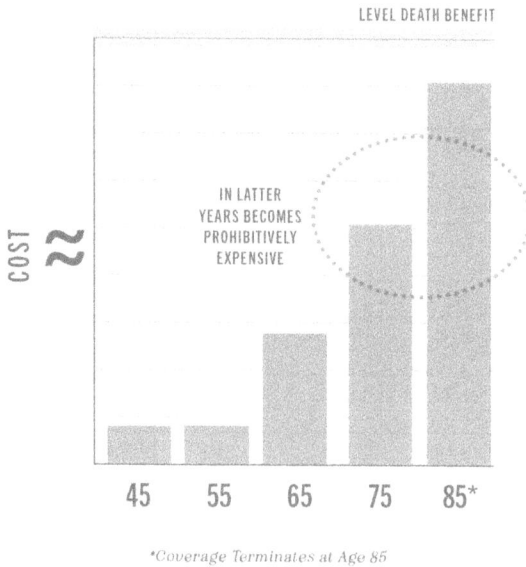

LEVEL DEATH BENEFIT

IN LATTER
YEARS BECOMES
PROHIBITIVELY
EXPENSIVE

COST

45   55   65   75   85*

*Coverage Terminates at Age 85

Making a choice on the initial price alone is seldom a good idea for any purchase. On the other hand, obtaining term life insurance is still an excellent first step in creating affordable protection for a family and business. We are of the view that term insurance should be viewed as an option to buy permanent insurance in the future. Term insurance essentially "locks in" your health for the period of the contract, which is very important since we all know that our health can change over time. We sometimes kid around and say that we are all "one banana peel" from being uninsurable.

Term insurance's affordability is both its strength and its curse. It's easily ignored and commonly brushed aside without reflecting on whether it's addressing the need in the best way possible, or if there are now additional factors which should now be considered.

It's perfectly logical to first implement a term policy to create risk management against financial headwinds with potential health or insurability variables. Once in place and risk has been addressed, then when more certain and financially capable, there could be a good reason to convert some or all of the term coverage to a permanent policy.

One example of dealing with a young family and their financial first steps is to design a hybrid policy that has permanent insurance from day one. Let's say this amount is $50,000, which can be paid for in full in 20 years. This policy will accumulate dividends and cash values from day one. In addition, the death benefit will continue to grow over time. Now we can add a term rider to this policy to ensure that the total coverage is equal to what we determined during our needs analysis, which could include additional coverage for a mortgage and other commitments.

For the sake of this example, this additional amount covered by a term rider may be $950,000 over 20 years. The term rider is an addition to the policy; however, it can be separated and can act separately from the policy as needed. As time goes on, more of the $950,000 covered by the term rider can be converted to permanent coverage. The end goal for a family may be to convert $300,000 of the term rider to permanent coverage and provide for more asset growth and death benefit coverage in the future. If planned properly, the family may choose not to renew the term portion of the policy as they have effectively replaced the term coverage with permanent protection. If there is now sufficient coverage, the family will benefit from not having to pay much higher prices on the renewal of the term rider.

We should add, *with emphasis,* that insurance is not like most products. You cannot just buy it when you're ready. You must qualify and be healthy enough to be considered an acceptable risk by an insurance company. And insurance underwriting is more than a medical check-up. Insurance companies need to be able to identify health risks and create an actuarial profile of a given applicant to properly price the coverage and protect the interests of the other policy holders with PAR contracts.

Many times, we have seen underwriting discover a negative health event that the regular physician had missed. This due diligence by the insurers is a good thing since they keep the insurance companies financially strong and healthy to be able to pay claims efficiently and reliably. This also helps to keep dividends flowing because the insurance company portfolio is strong and stable.

The fact is, less than 3% of all active policy claims do not get paid.[69] The main reasons for this are suicide within the first two years

---

69 Holly Bennett, "When Doesn't Life Insurance Pay Out?," NerdWallet UK, August 2, 2022, https://www.nerdwallet.com/uk/insurance/life-insurance/reasons-life-insurance-wont-pay-out/.

of a new life insurance policy (whereby the premiums are returned to the estate) and proven fraud. Both incidents are quite rare.

Permanent Life Insurance Basics

The first big difference between term and permanent life insurance is that permanent life insurance guarantees to pay a death benefit regardless of when the death occurs. The solution is permanent.

There are basically three types of permanent life insurance:

- Term100: Pure permanent insurance with no asset component. You pay the policy premium each year until the contract requirements are fulfilled.

- Universal Life Insurance (UL): There are several different types of universal life insurance policies. The main difference with UL polices is that they in essence separate the asset from the insurance. The owner of the policy can direct the funds inside the asset, which may be similar to an investment fund attached. The insurance works like a Term100 policy that is funded by the asset. The investing feature of UL policies shifts the risk for returns from the insurance company to the policy holder.

- Whole Life Insurance: These policies may be participating or non-participating. Non-participating policies do not pay dividends and instead pay performance bonuses or other similar types of returns. Whole life insurance combines the asset and the insurance into one contract, and there are also several different features and benefits available depending on the insurer. The insurance company manages the asset component for the benefit of policy holders in the case of whole life insurance.

Life insurance should be a staple in one's portfolio. It should be coverage without any significant degree of negative volatility. The policy should be there for you regardless of how well or poorly any markets or investments perform. We believe that whole life insurance should be part of a diversified portfolio. That's why we favor whole life policies for most situations.

Is It Ever Too Early to Get Insured?

Many well-known people have been able to use the benefits of the compounding growth of participating whole life insurance. Interestingly, John McCain, despite being generally quite wealthy, secured his initial campaign financing by using his $3 million in a life insurance policy as collateral.[70]

Other notable examples include Doris Christopher, who in 2002 sold her kitchen tool company the Pampered Chef to Warren Buffett for a reported $900 million. Yet, seven years earlier, she launched the company with a life insurance loan on her policy.[71]

---

70   "McCain Took Life Insurance Policy for Loan," UPI, February 1, 2008, https://www.upi.com/Top_News/2008/02/01/McCain-took-life-insurance-policy-for-loan/19831201873248/.

71   "What Famous Names Have Used Whole Life Insurance Cash Values to Stay in Business?," Cash Value Solutions, March 1, 2021, https://cashvaluesolutions.com/blog/what-famous-names-have-used-whole-life-insurance-cash-values-to-stay-in-business.

Even during the Great Depression, JC Penney used a loan against his then $3 million life insurance policy to resuscitate his retail stores after the 1929 crash.[72] In Canada, we also have firsthand testimonials from billionaire Jim Pattison on how he has enjoyed the living benefits of his long-held whole life insurance policy. He has admitted that it was also used as collateral for his first car lot acquisition.[73]

Investing in your own health, or that of your child or grand-child, can become an amazing financial tool for that person throughout their lives. This tool has been a favourite of the well-to-do, and now more than ever the average person is once again tapping into its benefits. To be able to use this financial Swiss Army knife as both a protection tool and an investment diversifier can serve one well over a lifetime.

Garrett B. Gunderson and Michael G. Isom wrote in their book *What Would the Rockefellers Do?* That it's possible to create a family fortune that lives on in perpetuity. Gunderson and Isom describe how, with large fortunes, both the Vanderbilts and the Rockefellers aimed to leave wealth behind to future generations.[74] (We'll go into specifics of how the Rockefellers did this—and the Vanderbilts' mistakes—in Spotlight B.)

As history has shown, the Rockefellers kept their fortune

---

72 "What Famous Names."

73 Don Anderson, "Jim Pattison Leveraged His Life Insurance Policy, Why?," Legato Wealth Management, November 30, 2023, https://www.legato.ca/pattison-kroc-disney.html.

74 Garrett B. Gunderson and Michael G. Isom, *What Would the Rockefellers Do?: How the Wealthy Get and Stay That Way ... And How You Can Too* (Salt Lake City: Garda Insurance, 2016).

while the Vanderbilts lost much of their great wealth. Intelligent financial planning and a game plan to keep the money together enabled the Rockefeller family to continue building wealth effectively using what they describe as the "Rockefeller Method."

This method is based on the utility of a participating whole life insurance policy as a bedrock financial tool for life. Control of capital, tax-advantaged growth, and compounding dividends, cash flow, liquidity, and eventual insurance that was paid for by pennies on the dollar has continuously enriched families all over the world. In their book *Entrusted: Building a Legacy that Lasts*, David York and Andrew Howell discuss the challenges of making family wealth survive more than a few generations.[75] Preserving and protecting financial wealth requires an understanding of, and a solid plan for, counteracting the three primary forces that erode wealth over multiple generations:

1. The division of assets among the generations
2. Transfer taxes and capital gains taxes
3. Business risks and third-party attacks

Our experience has shown us that as a result of these three forces, financial wealth doesn't last past the third generation in 90% of high-net worth families.[76]

As in America, Canadian insurers for the most part offer both

---

75   David R. York and Andrew L. Howell, *Entrusted: Building a Legacy that Lasts* (Salt Lake City: YH Publishing LLC, 2015).

76   Anne-Lyse Wealth, "Generational Wealth: What It Is & How to Build It," Empower, January 31, 2023, https://www.empower.com/the-currency/money/how-to-build-generational-wealth.

life and critical illness insurance for children. As an aside, many parents choose the critical illness plan as a forced savings vehicle, as one can get 100% of all paid premiums back after the 20th year.[77] This creates financial protection against a serious childhood illness and what can come with that in terms of expenses and/or time away from work for the parents. Yet, once the child is older, the option exists to keep the policy going or to cash it in and use the money toward any possible need.

However, and more on topic, whole life insurance for children makes a lot of sense for many since one can lock in a low cost of insurance due to youth and health. Naturally it's a financial tool for parents that need time to grieve a loss of a child. Yet, this purpose in of itself is a rare consideration. The main purpose is as a solid financial staple/bedrock item for the child's ongoing financial capabilities.

In addition, most design the policy to be paid up in full in 20 years. This allows the individual to benefit from the ongoing protection even for their future families—not to mention the compounding dividend growth and growing nest egg. The cash value can be utilized for education, a business start-up, the down payment for real estate, or anything else that may be needed.

Here's a simple example as profiled by Equitable Life—labelled as 'Forward thinking with Equimax Whole Life insurance for children' – and it is for your child – not on your child. It's a payment of $2,400 per year ($200/month) for 20 years for a boy with an age of 0. Most people don't know that you can insure a

---

77   "Critical Illness Insurance," Bankers Life, accessed August 31, 2023, https://www.bankerslife.com/supplemental-health-insurance/critical-illness-insurance/.

child as a newborn!

Using their Equimax Estate Builder participating whole life insurance, and based on the current dividend scale of 6.25%, the cash value is $59,799 at age 21, $114,693 at age 31, and $825,665 at age 65. The policy also provides a death benefit of $1,465,418 at the age of 65.

The plan will keep going past age 100, yet assuming mortality age to be 85, both these numbers simply keep compounding to $2,255,532 of cash value and a death benefit of $2,773,961. Critical Illness could also be added on this 20-year plan and could be designed to be maintained without cash outlay after policy year 20. It is easy to see the amount of flexibility one has with the set-up as well as the utility that can be enjoyed.

We hope that everyone now sees that the base of the financial pyramid must be rock solid. Protection needs to be implemented as soon as is feasible. Legacy and estate matters must be addressed while simultaneously addressing the need for living benefits. And, if possible, why not set up the entire family with the best possible financial building blocks from day one?

There's another factor that's often omitted when implementing financial protection measures: communication. Your family (and possibly your business partners) should understand what financial realities are ahead if a disability, critical illness, or death occurs.

Knowing this will create peace of mind for everyone.

FINANCIAL $POTLIGHT B
CAPITAL RISKS AND ASSET DIVERSIFICATION

Understanding risk and diversification goes beyond a balance of income, stock market shares, and real estate investing.

The act of investing is an ancient practice, and the modern landscape is the result of more than a thousand years of evolution. The first step on one's investment journey is to simply begin. The statement may be simple, but it's not easy. For this reason, it's important to start by first understanding risk and diversification. Once you're able to understand and invest with your risk profile in mind, you will be able to progress and optimize where it's needed.

As we evolve into the next level of our financial pyramid, we must delve into the spotlights of capital risks and the need for diversification.

Capital Risks

"What's the worst-case outcome?" is a great question. It's the first question the wealthy ask when considering a financial move. Rather than starting by asking "How much can I make?" they ask, "How much can I *not* lose?"

They approach any kind of financial risk by first looking at the downside rather than the upside. They put protecting what they already have ahead of making more, even decades before the conservative retirement years.

And when uncertainty rules, the wealthy know that more risk does not necessarily result in more reward. As a matter of fact, they're very good at finding opportunities to obtain rewards without risk. To quote someone who knows a bit about making and keeping money, Warren Buffett's first rule is "Don't lose." And rule number two is "Don't forget the first rule."[78]

You don't have to be wealthy to apply this line of thinking to your financial life. Always focus on the end result and don't be afraid to envision the worst-case scenario—it just might help you avoid it.

Obviously financial portfolios go up and down. Markets and individual industry sectors naturally have risks. Asset appreciation or depreciation can be temporary or long in duration. It helps to understand that when an asset depreciates, it

---

78 "Warren Buffett: 'Rule #1: Never lose money. Rule #2: Never forget rule #1.'," GrahamValue, September 6, 2018, video, 0:55, https://www.youtube.com/watch?v=vCpT-UmVf3g.

can feel like a very long time before it regains the value of the investor's original purchase price, and there's always a chance it may never again reach that value. Values could even go to zero, and anyone who has ever invested knows this reality. Changes can be sector and asset specific, or they can be very broad and structural.

Broader market risk, which may be referred to as **systematic risk**, cannot be simply reduced by diversification because the market as a whole is the risk. Examples include natural disasters, weather events, inflation, changes in interest rates, war, and even terrorism. However, and as we'll elaborate on later in this chapter, our approach to diversification actually helps mitigate systematic risks as well as unsystematic risks.

Unsystematic risk (non-market risk) is intrinsic to the investment itself and can be reduced by diversification.

The main unsystematic risks are:

- Stocks or equities have *equity risk,* which relates more to the performance of the company issuing the stock.

- *Currency risk* exists when the asset or shares are in a currency other than yours. The price of the foreign shares may remain the same, but changes as your own currency can impact exchange rates and, thus, the value of your investment.

- If your investment is a debt instrument—like a bond—then there's also *interest rate risk.* With bonds, there's an indirect relationship between the value of bonds and the interest rate. If the interest rate goes up, the market value of bonds drops.

- *Foreign investment risk* is present when investing in foreign countries through assets like emerging funds. The potential for your return on your investment may be high, yet this risk exists because countries (and/or their governments) may change policies that may work against the growth potential of your asset.

- *Liquidity risk* is the possibility of the inability to sell your investment. This can result from a lack of bids for the asset (i.e., interest by other buyers) or conditions or terms related to the specific investment.

- *Credit risk* concerns debt instruments, such as bonds. It's possible the entity issuing the bonds (governments or companies) may run into financial challenges that render the credit asset worthless.

- *Horizon risk* is specific to you. What's your investment timeline? Is it close, or decades away? If it's near, and the asset experiences a temporary drop in value, then the sale would be theoretically premature. Knowing the horizon is important but, unfortunately, life also presents surprises. For example, say you plan to hold a solid asset for a decade or more. Then life deals you a job loss. Now the horizon risk is closer because you may be forced to liquidate your investments prematurely, and possibly at the worst time.

- *Longevity risk* is also specific to you—it's the possibility of outliving your savings and investments. What if you retire at age 65 then live to age 95? Will your retirement nest egg last you 30 years?

- *Sequence of returns risk* is tied to the timing of your investment withdrawals. Will the investment performance of your portfolio go up or down when you begin retirement? The sequence of returns, either up or down, can dramatically impact your investment account balances when you're withdrawing income for your retirement. For example, if you begin withdrawing funds from your portfolio and the market experiences a significant downturn, as it did in 2008, down approximately 25% to 35%, the withdrawal would hurt your investment balance tremendously because you're taking funds from an account that has already experienced a significant decline in value. In the years leading up to retirement, the portfolio would have an opportunity to regain some of the decline in market value in subsequent years. The investment portfolio is in essence experiencing two forces (the withdrawal and the loss of value) that are reducing your balance. If the negative trend were to continue for a number of years, this could mean that your investments will not last as long as initially projected.

- *Tax risk* is the risk related to changes in taxation. This can be brutal and must be recognized as a potential signifi-cant factor that can impact your future. Understanding where a government may go with its policies will help you understand where best to place your hard-earned dollars.

Asset Diversification

Financial diversification is the idea and act of putting your capital in different financial products and assets to reduce your exposure to any one particular risk. It's a fancy way of saying, "Don't put all your eggs in one basket."

Most of us are familiar with the idea of diversification. While the specifics may vary, most of us know that any financial investment with the potential for us to make money or build wealth also comes with some degree of risk because we may lose money. The one sure thing when it comes to money is there's no such thing as a sure thing.

Intelligent diversification reduces risk and volatility.

Let's add some real-world perspective. Since 1982, an investor would have lived through six recessions (plus possibly another one in 2024, as many predict), five significant market crashes and, more specifically, twelve bear markets ranging from a 1-month duration (February 2020 to March 2020) to a 31-month duration (March 2000 to October 2002), of which two of the stock market crashes had a decline of 50% or more including Black Monday[79] in 1987. In addition, an investor over the same time period would have seen 12-plus wars involving the U.S. directly and indirectly, a dot-com bubble, a real estate bubble, impeached presidents, the 2008 financial crisis, 45-plus policy interest rate increases in Canada and the U.S., and a global pandemic. Specifically,

---

79   Matthew DiLallo, "The Biggest Stock Market Crashes in History," Motley Fool, May 18, 2023, https://www.fool.com/investing/stock-market/basics/crashes/.

on average, each market drop has seen a decline of 35% and the average duration has been 37 months.

An important question for you is, would you have been able to endure and maintain your financial game plan during these times?

Panic, ignorance, doubt, and poor counsel and decisions as well as tremendous emergencies influence our minds and behavior. Everyone has regrets when it comes to past investment choices and saving decisions, and the amount of information available on the internet has seemingly not changed the chances of success for most of us.

With proper asset diversification and planning, these decisions become easier, stress is reduced dramatically, results will be more stable, and retirement will be experienced with more confidence.

We think that the key to a resilient portfolio is to have it spread across distinctively different asset classes. This will usually result in higher long-term returns, greater liquidity, and easier access to capital in times of emergencies, which in turn reduces the chance of panic selling when instead opportunistic buying should occur. Believe it or not you can have this all simultaneously with lower risk.

So are you truly diversified?

In the last few decades, many companies grew through mergers and acquisitions. As a result, some equity portfolios may not be as diversified as you would think. Owning stock in company

A and in company B may not necessarily mean that your assets are divided between two different companies if company A has acquired company B.

Ray Dalio, who has served as the co-chief investment officer of the world's largest hedge fund, has shared his analysis on Investopedia of a diversification matrix that provides an effective bird's eye view on this subject.

In a nutshell, Dalio shows, and it is evident from reading his work, that the power of diversity *is reduced when pairing uncorrelated assets.*[80]

This concept is the "holy grail" according to Dalio and is crucial for the journey up the proverbial mountain as we accumulate assets to get to our financial summit. Yet just as important, on the way down the mountain as we distribute, spend, and enjoy our well-earned freedom, we should be able to live our life on our own terms.

Again, as we have already said in this book, the journey down a mountain can be very treacherous. When you reach the point in your life when work is optional, you should have some level of income security. For the person coming down the mountain, cash flow and capital maintenance are critical.

---

80   Hiranmayi Srinivasan, "Ray Dalio on the Latest Addition to His 'Principles' Series, and How to Invest Today," Investopedia, February 3, 2023, https://www.investopedia.com/ray-dalio-on-the-latest-addition-to-his-principles-series-and-how-to-invest-today-7105045.

Using Two Economic Powers for Real Diversification

Our first step into what we consider real diversification begins with a distinction that few realize. In a presentation at the American College Center for Retirement Income, Dr. Wade Pfau explained that there are distinctions of how growth occurs with various assets. Most assets function on the well-known economic power (as he puts it) of *appreciation and growth*. You try to buy low with the hope of selling high.

But Dr. Pfau points out there's a second economic power many people are unaware of—the economic power of *actuarial science*, which involves using mathematical and statistical methods to assess risk on human life spans. Utilizing the first (appreciation and growth) as well as the second economic power (actuarial science) makes diversification much more effective.

Before we step into the second power, let's review the common growth assets that many have relied on—sometimes to their dismay.

Capital's First Economic Power—Growth and Appreciation Dependent Assets

It seems that all these asset classes like equities (stocks), mutual funds, segregated funds, real estate (residential, commercial, public, and private REITs), cryptocurrencies and NFTs, and even fixed income mostly function on appreciation of value.

Yes, some have tremendous cash flow benefits too, such as dividends and bond yields, rent, and the sale of options. But for the most part, these assets are meant to appreciate (that is, be worth more later than when originally bought) due to more demand than supply.

This idea is the main driver of success when investing and planning for retirement. But your investing can and will experience volatility, which is the reason for diversification in the first place. Naturally, your investment advisor will ask you to complete the aforementioned investor profile and questionnaire. This in turn will assist the advisor in creating an investment mix of assets.

However, with economic changes, world events, or a crisis, all too often markets will swing lower. It may not always make sense, yet it does happen often. As of this writing, recent increases in interest rates have brought decreased stock market valuations in tandem with lower real estate values. Even the cryptocurrency sector, supposedly uncorrelated to the stock and real estate markets, had a meltdown in 2022.[81] As a result, diversification with respect to the first economic power has lacked effectiveness.

To recover from losses, you need both an increase in valuations and time to recover your losses. For example, a portfolio loss of 10% requires an 11.1% gain to restore the portfolio to whole (a 20% loss needs a 25% gain and a 35% loss requires a 54% gain to restore the portfolio to whole). If you're near retirement or already

81   David Gura, "2022 Was the Year Crypto Came Crashing Down to Earth," NPR, December 29, 2022, https://www.npr.org/2022/12/29/1145297807/crypto-crash-ftx-cryptocurrency-bitcoin.

retired and have a significant exposure to market volatility, a severe decline in the market is a major challenge. You are in effect still relying on one economic power.

However, if you are still in your income-producing years or are not relying on your portfolio to generate an income, negative volatility can work in your favor. You can continue to buy, presumably at lower prices, creating a lowered average price for your valuable assets. This, however, needs time to bear fruit and requires a willingness and commitment to stay the course. It's imperative to not interrupt a recovery by panic selling.

When touching on the value of staying the course, we must highlight here the incredible importance of the right behavior, which always outweighs any asset allocation. The following image of the Greed and Fear Index truly captures the effect emotions can have on your investments and their outcomes. No amount of diversification can survive a breakdown in the commitment to your strategy.

GREED/BUY
Highest level of
Financial Risk

" I'm very
pleased
with my
investment. "

" It's only a temporary
downturn. I'm in it
for the long term. "

EUPHORIA   ANXIETY

EXUBERANCE   DENIAL

ENTHUSIASM   FEAR   REPEAT UNTIL BROKE ...

OPTIMISM   DESPAIR   OPTIMISM

PANIC   RELIEF

CAPITULATION   HOPE

DISCOURAGEMENT   DISMAY

" The market is not
going in my favour. "

Best time for
investing
FEAR/SELL

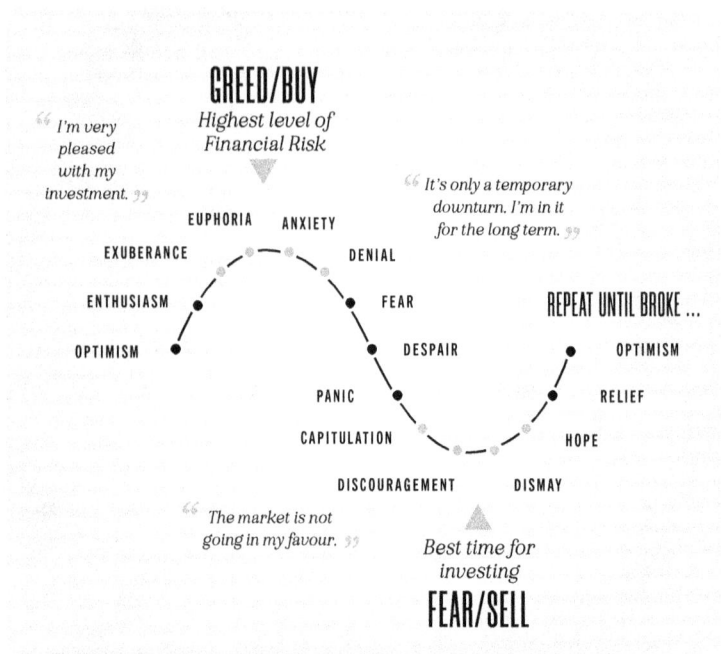

Good portfolio management can certainly assist with these issues, yet they're often reactive and not proactive, and therefore cannot be timed perfectly. This is why your strategy must be consistently updated and evaluated against your desired outcomes. For example, the shift from equity to bond portfolios should happen over an extended period of years and not in the middle of a business cycle.

Looking Sharpe

Professional money management utilizes many metrics, and we find the "Sharpe Ratio" very relevant to our discussion of asset diversification and risk.

The Sharpe Ratio (SR) is broadly respected and used as a comparative tool when evaluating a strategy, a fund, and portfolio performance. It was developed in 1966 by Nobel laureate William F. Sharpe and is used to understand the return of an investment compared to its risk.[82] There are several factors built into the ratio, but for our purposes all you need to know is that a high ratio is good when compared to similar portfolios. For example, a SR of 1.4 is more desirable than a SR of 0.85.

To be fair, there's a flaw in this metric—it assumes investment returns are normally distributed. But for our purposes, we will ignore this flaw because we know that normal distributions are not typical. After all, that's why we need diversification in the first place. For our purposes and as an interesting reference, we will briefly look at the Sharpe Ratio on the assets described in the categories of the first and second economic powers.

Equities, Indexes, and Segregated Funds

This category of investments is the "poster child" for the first economic power of growth and appreciation and is commonly referred to as a share in the ownership of a publicly listed and traded company—meaning you own that company's stock. A stock portfolio can exist based on simply owning a basket of these equity shares of different companies. An equity portfolio can also be diversified across several sectors such as technology, energy,

---

82   Rebecca Baldridge and Benjamin Curry, "Understanding the Sharpe Ratio," Forbes, last updated December 14, 2022, https://www.forbes.com/advisor/investing/sharpe-ratio/.

hospitality, etc.

Without getting into the various types of shares that are available, most people obtain equity shares as a stand-alone asset, or they opt to acquire stock indirectly through mutual funds, which consist of a basket of shares as chosen by a portfolio manager. Recent years have brought about the rise of *exchange-traded funds* (ETF). An ETF is a fund that trades on an exchange (as its name implies) and generally tracks a specific index. An ETF applies its own diversification model using a fixed pre-set basket of securities with a relatively small management fee. An example is the index on the *Standard and Poor's Top 500* companies. The index is traded as a stock, namely the "spiders" as traders so often refer to it (ticker symbol SPY). Indexes resemble many sectors and special baskets.

Segregated funds are like mutual funds, yet they are funds managed inside an insurance wrapper on the asset. In a nutshell, segregated funds are structured as deferred variable annuity contracts with life insurance benefits and other special features that vary. In brief, some of the features are guarantee of principal, automatic resets as fund values increase, lifelong income with accessible liquidity, and the ability to bypass the probate process if the owner of the investment passes away. The features contained in the contract can save money and a lot of time.

It goes without saying that equities have created a tremendous amount of wealth throughout history. However, nothing that performs that well is ever as easy as it looks. The growth is real, it's possible to succeed, and it is also possible to experience a significant decrease because of general market conditions and/

or specific stock challenges including ownership, management, market share, etc. Indexes can serve to buffer volatility and as such can assist in muting the up and down swings. Having said all of this, it is probably more obvious now that having all your eggs in equities, even an index, will not be diversified enough over the long term.

Looking at the Sharpe Ratio metric of the world's most popular index, the S&P 500 index (SPY), its ratio has a range—and this depends on which time period of comparative performance. The Sharpe Ratio on the SPY over the last five years was 0.41 with a standard deviation (volatility) of 18.71%. Decent performance with dramatic swings. The performance of the S&P 500 index over the last 5 years has been 8.996%. Further references show 0.62 as well, yet it is not over 1.0, as one may expect from this volatile growth-oriented investment asset.[83] As we look at the other assets that typically represent the first economic power, we will also consider their respective Sharpe ratios. This understanding may help explain why portfolios almost never perform as well as one would assume.

The Hedge: Precious Metals

Many people debate the role of gold and silver in a portfolio, and both have traditionally been a diversification tool to mitigate risks such as currency devaluation and inflation. Yet the hedge's volatility can also create losses.

---

83 "S&P 500," Backtest by Curvo, accessed November 29, 2023, https://curvo.eu/backtest/portfolio/gold--NoIg4g9gNgJiA0xQBECiAGTBBdBlAnGAELoICMAulUA.

It's worth mentioning that some investment advisors see gold and silver as an option to use as money in times of uncertainty or societal upheaval.

Still others feel that the value of gold is too high to ever be used as a currency tool. Its active purchasing power is timeless, and many people and cultures see it as a form of mobile security. In fact, it has been said that during Roman times one ounce of gold could buy you a fantastic robe, leather belt, and good quality sandals. Interestingly, today an ounce of gold can still buy you a quality suit, shirt, tie, and shoes.

Silver, on the other hand, could be a currency again if needed, and its practical use for industrial purposes has an embedded demand that will likely never cease. An example is its use in solar cells. It has been estimated that there is not enough silver on the planet to meet the demand for it in the use of solar panel manufacturing.

The less-utilized platinum is also worth considering for diversification. But it may be more volatile than gold, and not necessarily a hedge but an asset that rises and falls with the greater market direction.

Looking at the most popular precious metal, the Sharpe Ratio on gold is 0.35 with a standard deviation (volatility) of 17.65%. Decent performance with dramatic swings also—more than most would wish for a hedging purpose. Interestingly, the performance of gold on an annual compound growth rate is 5.57% from

December 1978 to April 2023.[84]

REITs

Real estate is an amazing asset historically.

Real estate with respect to owning your own home or a rental property is a great diversifying asset. History shows its undisputed strength and versatility. We will take a deeper approach to this asset class in the near the end of the book as it deserves a chapter on its own.

However, within the context of this chapter and with a focus on asset diversification (and especially non-physical asset diversification), real estate investment trusts—commonly known as REITs—are an excellent diversification tool.

There are two types—private REITs and publicly traded REITs. Private REITs are usually available directly from the issuer or via an *exempt market dealer*. Publicly traded REITS are bought and sold similar to mutual funds, stocks, or exchange-traded funds.

Be aware that publicly traded REITs have a blind spot. Often when the markets go down, a lot of REIT investors will sell the REIT—even though the whole asset class categorically does not need to be sold off.

For instance, back in the 2008–2009 financial crisis, real estate

---

84 "Gold," Backtest by Curvo, accessed August 31, 2023, https://curvo.eu/backtest/portfolio/gold--NoIg4g9gNgJiA0xQBECiAGTBBdBlAnGAELoICMAulUA.

was, in general, depreciating rapidly. Panic selling occurred and people lost their homes and walked away from mortgage obligations. Yet when people were losing their homes left, right, and center, where did those people end up living? They rented apartments.

The result was those REITs that included rental properties that so many investors exited were actually still solid investments during that period. The apartment buildings were full and not losing a dime of revenue. REITs are a great way to diversify, but we suggest you explore going into well-managed private REITs as an additional option so there's less chance of it being affected by panic selling.

REIT Sharpe Ratios should be specified according to the exact REIT category, yet for this brief overview we can reference www.reit.com and see that the Sharpe Ratio range is between a low of -0.009 (self-storage) and a high of 2.13 (health care facilities). General quotes of standard deviation (volatility) hover around 9.0%. In general, performance has a range for 3.1% to 4.3% for public REITs, and often 10% plus for private REITs.

Crypto and NFTs

No doubt, there's a ton of diversity in this sector. As technology and society evolve, there are going to be new opportunities to invest that we can't even imagine yet.

The key is to understand what you're investing in, and we can't stress enough that you should truly know what you're dealing with. During the second half of 2022, the "strong" cryptocurrency market began to decline as a result of steady selling. Some of the crypto exchanges ended up going bankrupt, and this spurred on further declines in this sector. Early 2024, on the other hand, shows much strength in the crypto currency sector. Again, its critical to know what you are doing here and beware of online promises.

We have heard of people mortgaging their homes to buy Bitcoin and Ethereum.[85] For some, that bet may have worked; yet for many the timing may have resulted in significant losses and hardship.

If your advisor can't help you with this and you choose to take a self-study approach, we would advise you to be extremely careful. We will abstain from providing the Sharpe Ratio on these assets, as the range and options are simply too vast at this time for this discussion. Much needs to be confirmed in this sector with respect to the regulatory environment and the nature of the crypto details at hand.

Using Capital's Second Economic Power to Diversify

It's been said the rich are just different from the rest of us. But have you ever stopped to consider that the rich may not be so different after all?

In their book, *What Would the Rockefellers Do?* Garrett B.

---

85   Michelle Fox, "People Are Taking Out Mortgages to Buy Bitcoin, Says Securities Regulator," CNBC, last updated December 11, 2017, https://www.cnbc.com/2017/12/11/people-are-taking-out-mortgages-to-buy-bitcoin-says-joseph-borg.html.

Gunderson and Michael G. Isom discuss the difference between the Vanderbilt and Rockefeller fortunes. During the 1800s, both families amassed fortunes that are incredible even by modern standards.[86]

The Vanderbilt fortune was approximately $100 million, roughly $200 billion in today's dollars. The family lived modestly and donated significant amounts to create Vanderbilt University, several churches, and numerous other philanthropic causes.[87]

Even with such largess, the patriarch of the family, Cornelius Vanderbilt, passed roughly 95% of his wealth on to his son, William. To his credit, William did well, too. He doubled the fortune despite living for only nine years after taking control of his father's wealth.[88] But things start to go awry with the generation following William Henry Vanderbilt. They were a spending generation—so much so that a mere 48 years after Cornelius's death, one of his direct descendants managed to die broke.[89]

In contrast, there's oil magnate John D. Rockefeller. In 1937, he was the richest man in America. In today's dollars, his wealth would be approximately $250 to $350 billion.[90] But rather than pass his wealth along to his children, he taught them to keep the money together. Their primary financial tools for keeping the

---

86   Garrett B. Gunderson and Michael G. Isom, *What Would the Rockefellers Do?: How the Wealthy Get and Stay That Way ... And How You Can Too* (Salt Lake City: Garda Insurance, 2016).

87   Gunderson and Isom, What Would the Rockefellers Do?, 2-3.

88   Gunderson and Isom, What Would the Rockefellers Do?.

89   Gunderson and Isom, What Would the Rockefellers Do?.

90   Gunderson and Isom, What Would the Rockefellers Do?, 4.

money together were trusts and life insurance contracts. The second generation's wealth came in the form of income generated from the wealth John D. created.

Today, there are more than 150 Rockefeller family members, all of whom continue to receive income in enviable amounts.[91] So, what was the difference between the way the two families managed their generational wealth?

The first difference between the two families was their behavior and mindset. Each generation of Rockefellers focused on leaving a legacy of financial empowerment for the following generation. The Rockefellers realized the value of their human capital and what their contributions could mean over time. Second, to accomplish their mission, they realized the importance of having two economic powers rather than just one.

As we have discussed at length in this chapter, the first power is the *growth power* (which is sometimes also referred to as *accumulation power*). The second power, as Dr. Pfau told us above, is based on actuarial science, which, to remind you, involves using mathematical and statistical methods to assess risk on human life spans.

Long-performing life insurance companies have mortality data that is decades, sometimes even centuries, old. Using mathematical and statistical methods, actuarial science applies probability and statistics to define, analyze, and solve the financial implications of uncertain future events. Life insurance and pension plans are the two main applications where actuarial science is

---

91   Gunderson and Isom, What Would the Rockefellers Do?.

used to determine costs and values.

Because it's rooted in actuarial science, the performance of the second power is unrelated to that of the growth power.

Also, because the second power is tied to your longevity, you can benefit from what we might call a "longevity dividend." And frankly, if it turns out you are *not* blessed with longevity, then the benefit for your family is more significant with a much higher internal rate of return on a tax-free death benefit.

What's Old Is New Again

In the past, long before 401(k)s and registered retirement savings plans, many people saved using the distribution power of whole life insurance as a long-term savings method—not just for the protection for their loved ones, but also for retirement, emergencies, or additional investment opportunities.

In the 1950s people conventionally saved with their savings account, life insurance policy, and home ownership. Guarantees and conventional real estate appreciation held fast for most Americans as the investment landscape showed growth with low volatility.

Today, in combination with real estate and intelligent hard assets, you would certainly want to combine the power of life insurance and/or annuities with the first power (growth) of retirement accounts to optimize your retirement assets and reduce volatility risk over the long term.

Permanent Participating Whole Life Insurance

This unique financial tool (some call it investment grade life insurance) participates in the profitability of life insurance companies. As a policyholder you're treated like a shareholder. Actuarial science and hundreds of years of data help the insurer meet claims lawfully and efficiently while at the same time producing a profit for shareholders and/or policyholders.

Insurers that are listed on the stock exchanges are labelled *stock* companies. They also offer strong dividends for policyholders. However, mutual insurers (those that are basically owned by the participating whole life policyholders) often perform the best in terms of dividend returns.

What's unique and makes these companies incredibly stable is the fact that they are well run, profitable, and greatly benefit from the methods that they use to assess and diversify risk. Even though the insurers have a diversified and very conservative investment portfolio by design and regulation, what keeps profitability incredibly stable throughout history, regardless of recessions, wars, pandemics, stock market bubbles, and retracements is the fact that insurance companies have excellent cash flow (in the form of yearly premiums) coupled with long-term liabilities that are well understood and are only realized when claimed. What is also not well known is that the insurance companies make significant profits with term policies—most of which expire or are canceled.

Why? Because most of the coverage is taken out by individuals or businesses on people who are under the age of 65 when the risk of a claim on a properly underwritten life insurance policy is very low. What generally happens to term policies when people reach the age of 65? They renew at higher prices for a new term that may be much shorter than the original term.

Most customers either renew or stop renewing because the new price can be an increase of 300% to 400% on average.[92] Eventually either the situation becomes cost prohibitive or the insurer will only convert the policy to a permanent policy that will necessarily require higher premiums for the coverage. So, in essence, it's either a lack of planning, a lack of understanding, or both, which leaves many people unaware that their options will become very limited after decades of paying premiums on term policies. It is indeed unfortunate and sad to think that no coverage is available in the end since they could not or did not maintain the policy into their later years.

Because of the immediate estate enhancement, the opportunity for long-term tax-advantaged growth, and great comparative performance coupled with low volatility (lower than that of a GIC or CD), many will find that participating whole life insurance as an asset serves short-, mid-, and long-term goals alike—all for a lower cost and less risk than many other asset classes.

It's important to state here that with our financial pyramid and the analogy of having our financial house in order, whole life has the required features and characteristics to continue pushing

---

92   "How Age Affects Life Insurance Rates," Investopedia, last updated June 7, 2022, https://www.investopedia.com/articles/personal-finance/022615/how-age-affects-life-insurance-rates.asp.

upward through the various layers of our pyramid almost simultaneously. In a sense, with its protection benefits, its investment performance, and its ever-ready liquidity, it's like rebar that solidifies our financial house through all the vertical layers and floors.

Sharpe Ratios are not often considered when one speaks about life insurance. Yet, over the years some have run the numbers and have concluded that for an average 40-year-old male, non-smoker, the SR with equitable life wealth achiever is 0.84. Volatility since 1992 is between 1.44% and 1.65%. This is more stable than the government of Canada's five- to 10-year bonds.

Get In Early

The second economic power hinges on your health and longevity and actuarial data that you don't have. Life insurance companies do have this data. They are the only parties able to essentially write a bond on your life.

Ideally, if you're buying an insurance policy, buy it as early in life as possible while you're healthy. This makes the cost low and allows you to build cash values with uninterrupted compounding over years and decades in the policy that can help you in your retirement.

In 2022, we found that many clients regretted not diversifying the assets more into participating whole life policies. In addition to insuring themselves and their spouse, many parents and grandparents now diversify their capital into policies on their children and grandchildren.

What If I'm Too Late?

If for whatever reason time is not on your side, don't worry. One option for you might entail buying an annuity.

An annuity is a financial asset with an insurance company where you make a payment or series of payments and then receive regular money back in return. An annuity is like life insurance, only the payments are reversed. In the case of life insurance, one trades a series of payments (premium) for a lump-sum payment at the end (death benefit). With an annuity, you make a lump-sum payment or a series of payments for a specified time period in order to receive a series of payments that can last for the rest of your life. It guarantees you a certain amount of money for life and can help shield you from any volatility in your stock portfolio. An annuity is a late-in-life financial tool to take risks off the table. It's an excellent diversification tool in this phase of your life. You can obtain a guarantee that at least your bills will be paid.

Two Powers, One Strategy

We have to be upfront and say that combining both the first and second economic powers (growth/appreciation and actuarial/distribution) can be a challenge when working with financial advisors today. This is because the two powers are rooted in very different financial tools and most advisors tend to be more fluent in one than the other, depending on their background.

By and large financial advisors are well-meaning people.

However, as in any profession, advisors are prone to only promote strategies they know well and recommend financial assets they are comfortable with. And why wouldn't they? After all, you're asking them to protect and grow your money. You certainly don't want them trying out something new and untested with your money! That's why sometimes it seems as if money managers want to keep all your money under their management. And, yes, it seems as if insurance guys only want to sell you insurance.

The implementation of a two power type of diversification utilizes the first economic power to grow the assets that will be used when you start to take an income from your assets (i.e., it is usual to draw down registered and non-registered plans in the beginning of retirement). This allows the second economic power, as is implemented in cash-value life insurance contracts and annuities, to continue compounding late into life to ensure that you never run out of money.

The second economic power can also become a volatility buffer. If markets are down one year, the retiree would withdraw from cash values and thereby not make negative portfolio returns worse by withdrawing. Then, when markets are more positive, the funds can be returned and withdrawals could resume using assets benefiting from the first power. The option of being able to switch between the two powers buffers the eventual drawdown of assets against any headwinds suffered by market conditions, taxes, and even emotions.

In the end, you get to choose who you work with. You can find advisors who are open to working collaboratively with advisors outside their area of expertise. This will provide you a means of developing a cohesive retirement strategy that harnesses both growth power (money's first economic power) and distribution power (money's second economic power).

Lastly, an Aspect of Diversification—Making Versus Taking and Keeping

Your greatest liability throughout life is taxes. With that in mind, remember that it's what you keep that matters, regardless of the investment path you take.

This means any well-designed diversification strategy should include tax optimization. Or to put it another way, minimize the amount the taxman takes from you. If you're making good returns on an investment but it's tax-inefficient, a significant portion (i.e., taxes) is not going back into your wealth. The net result is your returns aren't as good as they might be, and compounding growth could be negatively affected.

While tax planning is relevant to diversification and government-sponsored plans are great solutions, it's important to recognize that when the government gives you certain tax benefits, it can just as easily change them or even take them away. So, you want to be diversified outside of government plans as well.

Interestingly, the second economic power is also more tax-advantaged for most than the first. So, its implementation into your retirement strategy is very important in the short term for risk management and the long term for income.

FINANCIAL SPOTLIGHT C
RRSPS, TFSAS, & 401(K)s —THE HOLY GRAILS OF FINANCIAL PLANNING?

RRSPs and TFSAs can help you build capital and cash flow in the future—but you should also understand the limitation with each.

You've probably never heard of Ted Benna. However, unless you're lucky enough to have a rich relative who left you a fortune, Benna's probably had more of an impact on your retirement than any other person in the last 40 years.

Benna is widely regarded as the father of the 401(k). He did not write the tax code that paved the way for the creation of the plan in the U.S. That happened in 1978 when, without a lot of fanfare, changes were made to the Revenue Act in the United States.[93]

But once the changes came into law in 1980, Benna is credited with putting together a few financial pieces that were not specifically contemplated in the Revenue Act. In other words, the Act did not say that he couldn't do what he did.[94] Without getting bogged down in arcane tax specifics, Benna recognized changes in the Act that allowed him to redesign a pension plan for a client. This plan was effectively the first 401(k) ever created.

Over time, Benna's redesigned plan has grown into an apocryphal death knell marking the end of company pension plans in favor of individual RRSPs and 401(k)s in Canada and the U.S., respectively.

In a 2018 article in *Barron's* magazine, Benna denied killing company pension plans or even saying that he wanted to see the plans replaced, as has been long rumored. He maintained pension plans were already on the way out thanks to the changes in the Revenue Act and regardless of the plan he created.[95]

Like Dr. Frankenstein, failing to see the long-term ramifications of unleashing his creation on the villagers, Benna admits that as forward-thinking as he was, even he couldn't foresee the trillions

93 Kathleen Elkins, "A Brief History of the 401(k), Which Changed How Americans Retire," CNBC, last updated January 5, 2017, https://www.cnbc.com/2017/01/04/a-brief-history-of-the-401k-which-changed-how-americans-retire.html.

94 Financial Administration Act, R.S.C., 1985, c. F-11, https://laws-lois.justice.gc.ca/eng/acts/f-11/fulltext.html?wbdisable=true.

95 Sarah Max, "The Inventor of the 401(k) Thinks It Has Gone Awry," Barron's, November 16, 2018, https://www.barrons.com/articles/the-inventor-of-the-401-k-thinks-it-has-gone-awry-1542413142.

of dollars that would be poured into these individual retirement plans in the decades that followed.

In the article, Benna also clarified he does not like the investment structure of modern plans. Nor is he pleased with how complicated these plans have become. Benna points out that when the 401(k)s and RRSPs first started, employers paid all the fees. But the financial services industry saw opportunities to create additional features for more compensation. This created complexity in the plans. In turn, this complexity drove up the cost of fees to maintain these plans. The led employers to dump the fees on employees. Benna describes this as "a tragedy." When even the guy who created the plans is frustrated by aspects of his creation, it pays for you to understand those limitations as well.

It's likely that every person who's reached the age of majority in Canada has probably heard of a registered retirement savings plan (RRSP) and a tax-free savings account (TFSA). Unlike its southern cousin the 401(k), the RRSP was created in 1957. The popularity of the RRSP in Canada seems to have followed the rise of the 401(k) that occurred when the financial services industry in the U.S. saw what a boon it could be for advisors.[96] The advertisements for these plans abound, especially during RRSP season, that 60-day window after December 31st each year when individuals can contribute to their plans and get a tax deduction for the preceding year.

According to Statistics Canada, the country's official source for national statistics, in 2020 over 6.2 million Canadians put

---

96 Julia Kagan, "Registered Retirement Savings Plan (RRSP): Definition and Types," Investopedia, last updated December 19, 2022, https://www.investopedia.com/terms/r/rrsp.asp.

aside a total of $50.1 billion for their retirement by making contributions to their registered retirement savings plan (RRSP). Compared with a year earlier, contributions increased 13.1% in 2020, while the number of contributors increased 4.9%.[97]

The report goes on to say that this broke a 12-year trend of reductions in contribution rates that started in 2008. Interesting that 2008 was also the last major market correction before COVID, and in fact the report noted that COVID assistance may have contributed to the increases in 2020.

In 2008 we also entered a period in which interest rates and government spending eased, and that has radically changed the economic outlook for many Canadians.

Why are these accounts so popular? Well, an easy answer is that they have been a boon for the financial services industry. And, we might add, just because a financial tool is profitable for the service providers does *not* make it a bad tool.

Tax Free, So What?

We can keep the conversation about tax-free savings accounts short. From a purely technical perspective, putting funds into a TFSA is a no brainer. Anytime a financial tool can shelter funds from tax, it's worth looking into. That's why insurance tools are so

---

97   "Registered Retirement Savings Plan Contributions, 2020," Statistics Canada, last updated April 1, 2022, https://www150.statcan.gc.ca/n1/daily-quotidien/220401/dq220401a-eng.htm.

powerful. When no tax is imposed on an account's earnings, the math is clear.

However, what's the impact long-term and what other considerations are there?

In 2009, when TFSAs were started, the annual dollar limit a person could contribute was $5,000. In 2013, the limit was increased to $5,500. In a radical move in 2015, the conservative government increased the limit to $10,000. Then in 2016, a new liberal government reduced the limit a person could contribute back to $5,500, only to then increase the dollar limit to $6,000 in 2019. The annual dollar limit is set to be indexed to inflation with raises rounded to the nearest $500.[98]

As an interesting exercise, we have done a calculation based on the current limits adjusted for inflation for a period of 47 years from age 18 to age 65. Using an earnings rate of 3%, the amount that would be accumulated over that period would be around $780,000. The amount of tax-free income would be approximately $400,000. (Appendix, C.1).

All in all, that seems like a pretty good deal. However, there are a few considerations that need to be addressed. The first issue is the impact of inflation. At first glance you might say that the account is "inflation-protected" by increasing the contribution room. However, that may not be the case. To be conservative, in

---

98   "Tax-Free Savings Account (TFSA), Guide for Individuals," Government of Canada, last updated January 6, 2023, https://www.canada.ca/en/revenue-agency/services/forms-publications/publications/rc4466/tax-free-savings-account-tfsa-guide-individuals.html.

our example we used a low 2% inflation rate for the increase in the contribution room, and this assumption held in terms of the increase to TFSA contribution limits until the end of 2023. The Consumer Price Index (CPI) rose 3.9% in 2023 and, accordingly, the TFSA contribution limits are set to increase to $7,000 in 2024, which marks the first time that these limits have gone up two years in a row. The question is whether the CPI is a good measure of inflation. Michael Saylor, who was the former CEO of MicroStrategy, made a splash in 2020 by using the company's cash to purchase $250 million worth of Bitcoin. Saylor is quoted as saying that inflation is a vector and that everyone should define a market basket of products, services, and assets that you desire, weight them subjectively, and you will have your own index. Anyone that has seen the increases in food or fuel prices in the last few years can appreciate Saylor's perspective. So, increasing the contribution room by the CPI most likely will not protect you from inflation.

The next issue to address is access to the capital of the account. You can access the capital in your TFSA at any time. However, you can only contribute up to your contribution room and your with-drawals are added back to the contribution room in the calendar year after the withdrawal. That means that if you had $100,000 in your TFSA at the start of 2022 and you made your contribution of $6,000 for that year but withdraw $40,000 in June, you cannot put those funds back into the TFSA until January 2023.

We think that this mechanism was put in place for simplicity and for monitoring activity in these accounts by the government, which is fine. But it makes accessing and using your TFSA as a financial tool a bit cumbersome.

Given the rules surrounding withdrawals, your TFSA is not as effective as an emergency/opportunity fund. Therefore, we find ourselves likely using the TFSA as a buy and hold asset with low contribution limits. Because of this, we find ourselves right back where we started in the arena of investments, mutual funds, and the like, which are the domains of the large financial institutions.

What's Right with RRSPs?

There's a lot of confusion regarding RRSPs, and we need to deal with that first. The first issue is the tax deduction. A lot of people put money in their RRSPs to get a tax refund. We argue that's not the right way to look at it.

Using a simple example, let's say a person earns $100,000 per year. They're in the 30% tax bracket. Now let's say they contribute $10,000 to an RRSP. In order to determine their cash flow, the math is as follows:

- $100,000 salary – $10,000 contribution = $90,000
- $90,000 x .30 (the tax rate for their tax bracket) = $27,000
- $90,000 – $27,000 = $63,000

Now let's look at the cash flow to an individual who does not make a contribution:

- $100,000 salary – $30,000 (taxes calculated at 30% of salary) = $70,000

So, the individual who contributed to the RRSP has cash flow of $63,000 and the person who did not has cash flow of $70,000. Where is the tax refund? The answer is that the tax refund is *inside the RRSP* rather than in your pocket. The refund reduces your investment into the plan, and it does not increase your cash flow. We repeat the tax refund does not increase your cash flow because it does not consider the cash outlay or investment in the RRSP. The math is as follows:

- 100,000 x .30 = $30,000 (which would be withheld from your paycheques)

- $70,000 – $10,000 RRSP contribution = $60,000

- $60,000 + $3,000 sent back by the government after you file your tax return (which is the government contribution toward your plan)

Your investment is $7,000 in the $10,000 RRSP.

What confuses most people in the scenario above is that they have contributed the $30,000 in withholdings during the year, and when they file their taxes they get $3,000 back to get to the proper amount of tax of $27,000. However, the math is still the same. For your contribution, $7,000 comes from your pocket and the other $3,000 is the government's money. What does that mean? Let us show you.

If we take the total of $10,000 and split that balance into $7,000 being your money and $3,000 being the government's money, we could track those two buckets separately. Let's say we use a 6% earning rate over 40 years (Appendix, C.2 and C.3).

We see that we have about $72,000 in your bucket and we have almost $31,000 in the government bucket. Once you retire, if you decide to take $10,000 a year for 10 years in retirement and you're still at a tax rate of 30%, you would essentially get 10 payments of $7,000 and the government would get 10 payments of $3,000.

And if the tax rate went down to 20%, the government would get $2,000 each year. Or if the rate went up to 40%, the government would get $4,000 each year. This all assumes of course that there is no additional growth in the account during the 10 years of withdrawals, but you get the point that the government contribution is not your money.

An interesting point here that's seldom mentioned is that the government's money has also benefited by *the growth of the investments held inside the plan*. You probably didn't realize the government is a very real partner in your investment strategy, whether you like it or not.

Looking at the above scenario, you could say you end up winning if you're in a lower tax bracket in the future. But that might also mean you have less income in the future. Who wants to have less income in retirement?

Another issue related to RRSPs is that we lose the tax advantages of certain types of income. This includes dividend income and income from capital gains. In Canada, currently only 50% of income from capital gains is subject to tax. But inside an RRSP, all income, including dividends, and capital gains are taxed at the higher rate of ordinary income—meaning that money inside an RRSP loses the tax advantage that would be there if it were held outside the RRSP. The trade-off, of course, is that you pay the lesser capital gains tax now while getting to defer the higher tax you pay on capital gains inside the RRSP.[99]

Also, dividends represent a distribution from a corporation that has already been subject to corporate tax. To compensate the individual taxpayer, the rates on eligible and ineligible dividends are lower than other income *unless that income is earned inside an RRSP.*

If that dividend income is earned inside an RRSP, it's subject to higher rates. Only interest income is subject to the same rate inside an RRSP as it would if earned in a non-registered account. Accordingly, from a tax efficiency perspective, it is better to hold interest bearing instruments inside an RRSP.

What About the Holy Grail of Financial Planning?

One theme that is consistent throughout this book is that there's no such thing as a perfect tool for your finances. Maybe RRSPs and TFSAs are not the Holy Grail of financial planning. But they do serve a purpose, and if these tools work inside your financial strategy, then that's great. Just be sure your expectations are informed by understanding the strengths and weakness of these tools.

---

99   "A Closer Look at Capital Gains Tax," TD Bank, accessed August 31, 2023, https://www.td.com/ca/en/investing/direct-investing/articles/capital-gains-tax.

TFSAs are limited in their impact due to the amount of the contributions that individuals can make into these plans. RRSPs are limited due to excessive fees, the loss of tax attributes on certain types of income earned in the plan, and the inherent uncertainty with the impact of taxation in the future. One question that we like to ask our clients is, "Do you think tax rates are going to be higher or lower in the future?" Also, the repayment of tax on withdrawal makes RRSPs cumbersome to use as an opportunity fund.

Now we will look at how the RRSP actually works and show you the complexity of this structure and what could go wrong.

Let's start with an individual who is 30 years old and has $100,000 in his plan and is contributing $20,000 per year. If those funds are invested at a rate of 8% over a period of 36 years to age 65, that individual will have $ 5,638,224 (Appendix, C.4). At this point many of us would stop—why would anyone need to do anything else? Just for fun, let's continue.

Now let's say that this individual has an employer match of contributions. However, the match is limited to your first $3,000 of contributions (Appendix, C.5). Your account value is now up to $6,244,435, which is incredible. You might ask why the rate of return has only gone from 8% to 8.38% given that we're being matched. Shouldn't the rate of return double?

Actually, no, because the match is limited to $3,000. Many people fail to recognize the limits of the employer match that are marketed to employees to encourage excitement and participation in the plan.

Now let's look at the benefit of the tax deferral. Let's say this person lives in Alberta and makes $150,000 per year. You will notice that the account value did not change (Appendix, C.6). However, the net contributions changed from $820,000 to $518,480 because the government has returned a part of your contributions on your tax return. Remember, the government is your partner in this plan! But hey, the rate of return is just over 10%—can life be any better?

Now it's time to look at some other aspects of the plan that are often overlooked. The first area is management fees. There are lots of reports on management fees being over 3%, and for our purposes let's just use a rate of 2%.

Now that had an impact (Appendix, C.7). We lost all the benefit of the tax deferral and our gross account value dropped from $6,244,435 to $3,571,084. What's shocking is that we lost $2,673,351 of account value because of a 2% management fee with a dollar value of $977,579. Remember that we can't pay the fees at the end and that each payment reduces the opportunity for the funds used to pay the fee to grow.

It's realistic that we get 8% return year over year without any down years for a period of 36 years. It's possible as the S&P 500 with dividends has averaged over 11% since inception.

However, with both the Dow Jones Industrial Average and the S&P 500, no dividends have averaged around 7.59% since inception. The TSX, on the other hand, has averaged 7.94% over the last 43 years. In addition, as we know, most portfolio managers add fixed income and similar instruments to reduce volatility.

When we reduce the return to 6% in our example, the account value is now down to $2,202,155. (Appendix, C.8).

Now let's see what it looks like coming down the mountain. In Canada you must start withdrawing your RRSP when you are 71. In this scenario we assumed that you live to age 90 and you take steady withdrawals beginning at age 66. We have also assumed that you would have an additional $30,000 from CPP and other sources at retirement. Your rate of return has reduced further to just over 4% (Figure C.9).

Your withdrawals would be just over $133,000 per year and you would net around $90,000 (Appendix C.10 and C.10a). Is that enough? Maybe or maybe not. However, what could go wrong?

- You may not get a 6% rate of return, as generally portfolio managers try to reduce volatility even further later in life.

- Tax rates may change to be higher in the future.

- If you pass away, unless you have a surviving spouse or other individual that you can transfer the plan to, the entire amount will be taxable.

As you can see these plans have a lot of complexity and they're considered "sticky" funds for financial institutions. They're also a source of a lot of fees. These funds are not available as an emergency and opportunity fund unless you're willing to pay the tax. They operate as designed—as a pension fund. If you want to participate in these plans, you should be prepared to treat them as they are designed.

FIGURE C.9

REGISTERED RETIRED SAVINGS PLAN REFLECTING WITHDRAWAL PHASE

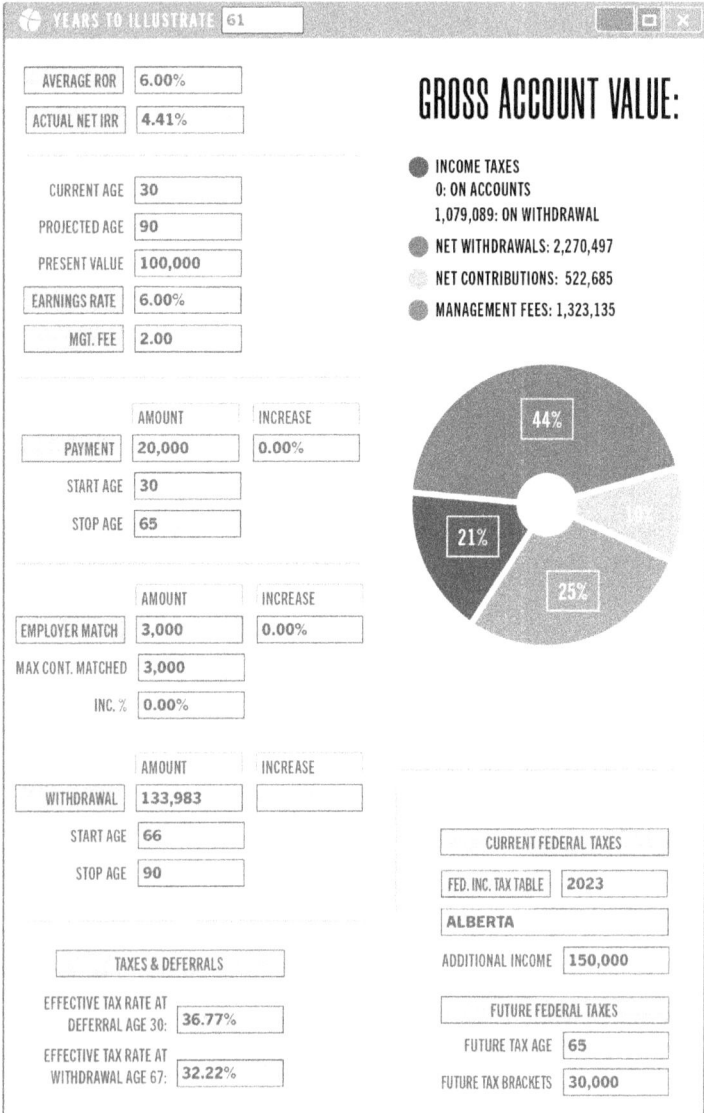

YEARS TO ILLUSTRATE	61

| AVERAGE ROR | 6.00% |
| ACTUAL NET IRR | 4.41% |

GROSS ACCOUNT VALUE:

- INCOME TAXES
  0: ON ACCOUNTS
  1,079,089: ON WITHDRAWAL
- NET WITHDRAWALS: 2,270,497
- NET CONTRIBUTIONS: 522,685
- MANAGEMENT FEES: 1,323,135

CURRENT AGE	30
PROJECTED AGE	90
PRESENT VALUE	100,000
EARNINGS RATE	6.00%
MGT. FEE	2.00

	AMOUNT	INCREASE
PAYMENT	20,000	0.00%
START AGE	30	
STOP AGE	65	

	AMOUNT	INCREASE
EMPLOYER MATCH	3,000	0.00%
MAX CONT. MATCHED	3,000	
INC. %	0.00%	

	AMOUNT	INCREASE
WITHDRAWAL	133,983	
START AGE	66	
STOP AGE	90	

44%

21%

25%

CURRENT FEDERAL TAXES	
FED. INC. TAX TABLE	2023
ALBERTA	
ADDITIONAL INCOME	150,000

TAXES & DEFERRALS	
EFFECTIVE TAX RATE AT DEFERRAL AGE 30:	36.77%
EFFECTIVE TAX RATE AT WITHDRAWAL AGE 67:	32.22%

FUTURE FEDERAL TAXES	
FUTURE TAX AGE	65
FUTURE TAX BRACKETS	30,000

FINANCIAL $POTLIGHT D
BUY TERM AND "SPEND" THE DIFFERENCE

Strategies are great ... as long as you stick with them.

In the 1970s, a man named Arthur Williams started his company Primerica with this simple philosophy: *buy term and invest the difference.*

This catchy slogan was so successful for the company that Williams was able to buy the NHL's Tampa Bay Lightning franchise. Today the phrase "buy term and invest the difference" is still used and associated with popular financial-entertainment personalities Dave Ramsey and Suze Orman.[100]

However, as with many of the other financial concepts

---

100 "Buy Term and Invest the Difference: Common Sense or Nonsense?" Internet Insurance Guru, April 2, 2018, https://medium.com/@internetinsuranceguru/buy-term-and-invest-the-difference-common-sense-or-nonsense-1bb77ed9f1ef.

discussed in this book, we have a bit of a different take and often refer to the strategy as "buy term and *spend* the difference." In our experience, this is exactly what most people do. Rather than investing the money, they save from buying "cheaper" term insurance—they spend it (see logical fallacy regarding pricing of term insurance in "Financial $potlight A: Financial Protection and Safety for You and Your Family").

To illuminate the facts around buying term insurance and investing the difference, we're going to use a tale of two men. Let's call them John and Bill. (Full disclosure: This example was published by the Equitable Life insurance company in their flyer "Building a Stronger Investment Portfolio with Equimax Whole Life 1782 and the Supplemental 1782B.")

The facts in the case study prepared by Equitable Life are as follows:

1. John and Bill are both 45 years old, insurable, and non-smokers.

2. They have maximized their registered savings, which would generally include RRSPs and TFSAs.

3. They both have $750,000 in non-registered savings.

4. They can afford to spend $30,000 annually for the next 20 years to help them achieve their financial goals.

5. They live in Ontario and are subject to the highest rate of tax.

This may seem like an extreme example and lots of questions may come to mind:

- Do they have a family?
- What do they do for work given they have maximized their RRSPs and they have $750,000 in the bank?
- Do these guys have a life?

However, leaving these questions aside for a moment, let's continue.

John and Bill both want to leave a legacy. John buys a $1 million *term* insurance policy for 20 years while Bill purchases a $750,000 *whole life* policy with a term 20 rider for $250,000. (A term rider is simply a term insurance policy added to a whole life insurance contract.) The 20-year term policies will not be renewed after they expire.

In this example John, holder of the term policy, will have $28,280 a year added to his non-registered account (which is the $30,000 annually less the premium for the term insurance of $1,720) (Appendix D.1).

Meanwhile, Bill will have $6,183 annually to add to his non-registered account after making the required deposits to the whole life insurance and the cost of the term rider—which are $23,817 per year for 20 years (Appendix, D.2).

After 20 years, using a 5% rate and a 53% tax rate (Ontario personal tax rates), John (term) will have $1,921,805 and Bill (whole life) will have $1,352,724 in their non-registered accounts respectively.

At this point both John and Bill want to use their money to fund their lifestyle. Now both John and Bill have a choice to make. Do they take interest only or do they wind down the entire amount in their non-registered savings?

Their choice will depend on several factors, including what other assets exist to fund the withdrawal phase. In this specific situation, in addition to the $1,352,724 in his non-registered savings, Bill also has the whole life insurance contract that has a cash value of $659,763 (Appendix, D.3).

There are several options that Bill has with the cash value of the policy, which include taking a policy loan, taking the annual dividend in cash, and surrendering the policy for cash value.

The dividend on the policy at year 20 is $25,596, which can be withdrawn in *cash*. There are tax considerations that need to be examined when you're looking at which strategy may be right for your situation.

Now what might happen when John and Bill reach the age of 66? Let's look at a situation where John takes interest only from his account while Bill winds down his non-registered account completely. Using the same earnings rate and the same tax rate, John will have net withdrawals of $903,248 versus $1,737,277 for Bill. And the taxes paid by John over that 20-year period are just over $1 million whereas Bill has paid $433,645 over the same time period (Appendix, D.4).

At the end of the 20-year period, John still has the $1,921,805 and Bill has a cash value of just over $2 million in the life insurance contract. In addition, Bill has a death benefit of $2,424,100 (Appendix, D.5).

It's important to note at this point that John and Bill do not have the same assets when they're 85 years old. The most significant difference is that the insurance contract that Bill owns has an adjusted cost basis of $0 when he is 85, which means that any withdrawals from the policy will be 100% taxable.

Another significant difference is that if both John and Bill passed away when they're 85, Bill will leave $2.4 million to his estate tax-free versus the $1.9 million that John will leave to his estate.

Now let's take a closer look at that difference related to distributions from the insurance contract now that Bill is 85 years old, and any cash distributions would be 100% taxable. If the earnings rate stays the same, John will continue to get just over $45,000 net spendable taking interest only.

If we take cash surrenders of the same amount from the insurance contract for Bill, based on the illustration, the amount of cash value gradually decreases to $1,992,789 at year 100 (Appendix, D.6). They're essentially in the same position if John continues to take interest only. However, because John has his funds in a non-registered account, he has the option to use his capital, obtain more cash flow, and pay less in taxes than Bill if he chose to do the same.

However, do you think that John is going to significantly change how he spends his money suddenly when he turns 85?

When considering the use of the non-registered funds, which of the two brothers had more flexibility, control, and security over their cash flows from age 65 to age 100? We would argue that would be Bill. Having his funds in the insurance contract gives Bill more flexibility over his cash flow and allows him to spend down on the entire amount in his non-registered account. John would have to pay more taxes over time by maintaining his capital potentially over concern about running out of money. We have left out the impact of the registered accounts for the purpose of other examples, as we don't have any information on those accounts from the Equitable flyer.

Impact of Earnings and Tax Rate Changes

We have looked at the above scenario using different earning rates and tax rates for the accumulation stage and the distribution stage. The impact is that if the earning rate increases or the tax rate decreases, it would increase the assets available to both John and Bill. Accordingly, if those situations happened, John might end up leaving more assets to his heirs.

But there's more to the story.

Remember, to achieve this result John was subject to taking only the earnings on his account, whereas Bill was able to draw down the entire amount in his non-registered account. This resulted in a significant reduction in taxes and a significant amount of additional cash flow for Bill during the 20 years leading up to his 85th birthday. As one can see in the example, Bill was able to enjoy over $800,000 of additional cash flow.

When talking about rates of return, another question comes up: Is a 5% earnings rate net of fees a respectable rate of return?

We addressed this same issue in the "Qualified Plan" chapter. And our conclusion was that there are a lot of headwinds associated with obtaining rates of return above 4% to 5% consistently over long periods of time—not to mention the benefits of having flexibility, access, and control of your money without interrupting the compounded growth of such funds.

There are two key issues that we believe make the argument toward having whole life insurance as a key part of your wealth strategy. The first issue that has been explained in depth throughout this book is volatility. Most of us are not wired to deal with volatility and generally how the industry deals with this issue is to add fixed income instruments to the portfolio, which historically have underperformed—especially when taking management fees into consideration.

The second issue is sequence of returns risk. Although the hope is that we don't have to deal with volatility in our assets during the accumulation stage, we're better able to deal with it because we're still working and adding capital and have time to make up losses. It's when we stop adding capital to our assets and start to withdraw funds that significant market downturns can hamper the ability of our assets to cover our needs for our lifetime.

In fact, a series of market downturns in the first five years in the drawdown phase can be catastrophic.

To illustrate this point, let's take the ending portfolio balance for John at the age of 65 in our first example in this chapter, which was $1,921,805. For this example, we will assume that John has no other assets and needs this portfolio to last 30 years without running out of money with an assumed inflation rate of 3%.

We looked to find a period in history using the S&P 500 with dividends (the best of the best) where there were a series of losses at the beginning. That period started in the year 2000. We ran a simulation with the starting portfolio of $1,921,805 and steady withdrawals of $100,000 per year along with other attributes including Ontario tax rates, additional income (CPP, etc.) of $30,000, and 2% management fees. The result was that we ran out of money in year 14 (Appendix, D.7).

We reversed that exact scenario, and the result was that we still had just over $450,000 in year 20. (Appendix, D.8). With the challenges in the market and changes in technology, volatility may increase in the future. We must be prepared for it or risk running out of money during what should be the best years of our lives.

In this Spotlight, we hope we've made it clear that participating, dividend-paying whole life insurance is an amazing asset that can be used in many situations to provide protection and safe and reliable cash flow later in life.

FINANCIAL $POTLIGHT E
INFINITE BANKING

Main Idea: Be your own bank (for the most part).

This is a topic close to both our hearts. Separately, we were both introduced to the financial services industry through advisors that practiced infinite banking or a derivative of it called *bank on yourself.*

The founder of the infinite banking concept was a man by the name of R. Nelson Nash. Nelson, who passed away in 2019, was a God-fearing man and a walking encyclopedia. He lit up the room everywhere he went and was committed to sharing his knowledge with everyone he encountered.

Nelson was originally a forester after receiving a degree from the University of Georgia in 1952. Being a forester meant that Nelson was trained to think long range and many generations into the future.[101]

---

101 "R. Nelson Nash's Obituary," Nelson Nash Institute, March 29, 2019, https://infinitebanking.org/banknotes/the-following-is-r-nelson-nashs-obituary/.

Nelson conceived the infinite banking concept in the 1980s when he was caught in a real estate deal with partners and the debt associated with the deal was structured so that each partner was responsible for the whole debt if the other partners could not pay. Unfortunately, Nelson was left holding the bag.[102]

At that time, interest rates were high. Nelson was looking at 23% interest on $500,000, which is the equivalent of over $1.6 million in today's dollars. Nelson prayed to find a solution for his predicament. He soon discovered he had funds inside a whole life insurance policy that was purchased many years before. He could access the cash to pay down the debt, which would allow him to take back control of his situation.

After this experience Nelson vowed to rid himself of the "snakes and dragons" in his life. For him, these were the banks. Nelson was a life insurance agent for over 30 years with two mutual life insurance companies. From his work experience and his close call with the banks, Nelson formed his infinite banking concept.

The Concept

The concept is centered around using a dividend-paying, participating whole life insurance contract (preferably from a mutual company) to control the finance function in your life. Let's break down that statement. We've discussed participating

---

102 "Nelson Nash's Becoming Your Own Banker – Part I, Lesson 2: How the Infinite Banking Concept Got Started," Nelson Nash Institute, accessed August 31, 2023, https://infinitebanking.org/banknotes/nelson-nashs-becoming-your-own-banker-part-i-lesson-2-how-the-infinite-banking-concept-got-started/.

whole life insurance in other areas of this book. Participating life insurance (or PAR life insurance as it is commonly referred to) is a type of insurance contract in which the owner of the contract "participates" in the financial performance of a block of similar policies.

A block may be better described as a group of policies that have been underwritten by an insurance company. Underwriting is a process used by insurance companies to examine the risk related to the person being covered by the contract.

Think of the multiple health and lifestyle questions (as well as the medical tests) that are usually undertaken in connection with being approved for life insurance. When the risk is assessed by the insurance company, they make an offer to the individual or entity that's applying for the insurance. The offer requests a certain payment of money—both now and in the future—in exchange for a specified amount of coverage. The coverage, also known as a the "death benefit," remains in place as long as the owner continues to make payments or until the contract ends on the passing of the person covered under the policy.

PAR life insurance is special in that the policy pays a dividend that can be taken in cash or used to purchase more insurance. The dividend that's paid on the policy is generally not taxable if it's used to purchase more insurance. As a result, the death benefit and cash value continue to increase. (The cash value, simply stated, is the value that the insurance company is willing to pay at any point in time to complete and cancel the contract.)

Insurance in any form works due to the law of large numbers. This essentially means the risk of claims in any one year is reduced by the number of policies in the pool and the continued payments that are being made by the remaining participants. In other words, the risk is spread around among the policies. The more policies, the less risk to be absorbed by the insurance company.

The reference to a mutual company is a company that's willing to provide all the services and administration for the particular PAR life insurance block for a fee such that all the residual income from the block is left for the owners of the contracts in the block. A stock company may also provide PAR life insurance. However, there's an additional element of profit that is taken for the shareholders of the stock company, thus potentially reducing the return to the owners of the contract. This point has been debated by many professionals and is not worth going into any further for our purposes here.

The process of infinite banking may be broken down as follows:

- Deposit funds into a policy.
- Continue to make deposits over time.
- Borrow against the policy cash value.
- Pay the loans back to the insurance company with interest, releasing the collateral and thus increasing the cash value.
- Rinse and repeat.

Later in this chapter we will provide examples. Before that, though, we need to discuss something else first.

The Pitch

A presentation on infinite banking can be a unique experience. Some of the larger organizations in Canada and the U.S. that openly promote the strategy put on sessions that are well done and entertaining. We have thought long and hard about the information provided in these presentations—specifically the effectiveness, relevance, and usefulness of the material provided. After careful consideration, we believe much of the material obscures and confuses the person considering the strategy. However, we will let you be the judge.

One of the first places to start in explaining the pitch is the grocery store example. Nelson came up with a wonderful analogy that most people will identify with.

The presenter asks what it would be like if you started a business by opening up a grocery store. To open a grocery store you would have to find a location and construct a building. You would also need to fill that building with attractive displays and showcases and purchase equipment and inventory. The setup of the grocery store would cost a lot of money.

The process of constructing the grocery store is meant to symbolize the setup of your insurance contract and putting capital inside that contract.

Step 1: Deposit Funds into a Policy

Now that your grocery store is established, it's time to open the doors to your customers. The staff needs to be trained, the inventory needs to be stocked, and the prices must be right—the customers demand it. This requires more money!

Step 2: Continue to Deposit Funds into the Policy

If the prices are right at the grocery store, you'll sell your inventory and earn $0.60 for a can of peas whilst it cost you $0.57. We feel that this passage, which is more fully explained in the book, is illustrating that the deposits are growing over time, and if you take policy loans and pay them back with interest, you're observing the spirit of the infinite banking process.

Steps 3 and 4: Take Policy Loans and Pay Those Loans Back Over Time with Interest

Continuing with the grocery business, if you turn your inventory over 15 times you break even; if you turn it over 17 times you make a profit; if you turn the inventory over 20 times you retire early. This excerpt relates to a concept known as the velocity of money, and that money must move to create wealth. We have studied the infinite banking concept for years, and the process of continuing to make deposits, taking loans, and paying them back is in essence self-correcting. If the individual was only taking loans for lifestyle, then the process of paying back the loan would have a more significant impact on cash flow over time, and thus correct the behavior. The process in theory would encourage loans and behavior toward more productive uses, increasing cash flow over time and redirecting funds to activities that enhance wealth accumulation.

Step 5: Rinse and Repeat.

After this point, depending on who is making the presentation, the conversation might then move toward the following:

- The problems with Registered Retirement Savings Plans (RRSP)
- Potential issues with deferred taxes related to RRSPs
- The volatility of stock markets
- The use of average versus actual returns by investment professionals
- Spending patterns by a typical household
- An airplane flying into a headwind versus a tailwind
- The amount of interest paid on a 25-year mortgage
- How banks work
- How you can borrow at 6% and save at 4% and make money
- How you can borrow at 20% and save at 10% and make money
- Whether you either pay up or give up interest
- Money needs to be in motion
- The miracle of compound interest
- Fractional reserve lending
- How people buy cars
- Starting ahead versus finishing ahead

- Human factors such as Parkinson's Law
- The money pool

And then finally after you have sat in a chair or in front of a screen for hours, you can talk about the tool: dividend-paying, participating whole life insurance, or PAR life insurance.

The above points are interesting, that's for sure. But we believe that most of the discussion invites comparisons which are not complete, reducing the usefulness of the exercise. The concept of opportunity cost is relevant, but it can be taken too far. People are going to consume some of their income. There's no such thing as recaptured interest. And how banks work is not really relevant because you and I *cannot become our own banker.*

We cannot borrow against collateral without having sufficient deposits to match the loan like a bank can. We must capitalize and make deposits to the insurance contracts. We cannot lend money that we don't have. Instead, when you're using the lending provisions inside a PAR life insurance contract to access cash value as part of a financial strategy, you're using leverage. Most of us understand the process of borrowing money.

The Real Story

This part is very important so please sit up and really dig in. After reading the above you might think that PAR life insurance is not a great financial tool, and that would be a big MISTAKE.

PAR life insurance is an incredible financial tool. As we pointed out in the beginning of this book, our human brains have the tendency to throw the baby out with the bathwater when we hear information that's either contrary to our opinion or reinforcing a previously held negative opinion. Even if the pitch might be somewhat misleading, please do not discount this financial tool.

Is it possible to use the policy loans toward a home renovation, a dream vacation, or to fund a year at college for one of your children? The answer is YES, YES, and YES.

Can you use your cash value (via a policy loan) to pay for an emergency surgery or to take part in an attractive real estate deal? Again, the answer is YES and YES.

Getting to the Heart of the Matter

You may be getting a sense of a few of the issues with the infinite banking concept.

For instance, would someone finance their home with a policy loan if they had sufficient cash value? From a pure economics point of view, a person probably wouldn't finance their home with a policy loan since it's likely that you will always be able to get a better rate outside the policy from a bank.

However, if someone wanted to reduce their exposure to banks then they might consider doing so. And some argue that the infinite banking concept is not about rates. The more ardent supporters of infinite banking rest on their belief in the process and method used by the strategy.

We agree that the process is very important. Individuals and businesses that learn to use the policy loan provisions to obtain capital for their business or to progress their family wealth do change their habits. They start to understand where their money is coming from and what "leaks" may exist in their finances that have stopped or slowed their financial progress.

Where we diverge in our thinking from infinite banking theory is that we believe interest rates matter—especially when considering using the policy later in retirement as a source of cash flow or income. If you take a policy loan later in life in order to avoid paying taxes, the compounding is now in essence working against the equity that you have in the policy. The interest is now compounding and increasing the loan. Although policy returns move with interest rates, the rate on the loan is probably going to be higher than the rate earned inside the policy. When it comes right down to it, everything matters, and when we hear statements like "it's not about rates," we see a possible red flag that we should pay attention to.

Another issue that someone may have with infinite banking is the question around whether someone really gets ahead by using their policies to buy cars, vacations, and to pay for renovations. The short answer is YES. The reason for this answer is that whether you have a PAR life insurance contract or not, an individual is most likely purchasing those items anyway.

However, the reason you're getting ahead is that you're adding more capital to the plan. The process of repaying policy loans is taking funds from future consumption for the repayment of borrowing. Most people don't see that in the first 6 to 10 years, you can only borrow the capital that you have contributed to the policy. After that you'll start to see some real growth.

If you're going to use your PAR life insurance for financing consumption, then you should really look at ways to increase your savings rate inside the policy. After you pay each loan off according to your amortization schedule, you'll have adjusted your finances to accommodate that payment. If you convert some of your term life insurance or apply for a new policy, you will have increased your savings rate and your future legacy—both of which are good ideas.

Using your PAR life insurance for an emergency/opportunity fund is a no brainer for us. If you have good opportunities to create additional cash flow by redeploying the funds inside your PAR life insurance, you should definitely do that!

Also, if you want to maintain the leverage on a particular asset that has a reducing schedule for loan repayments, you can use a policy to maintain the leverage. Over time, a PAR insurance contract can act as an excellent flow through mechanism to maintain the gearing of a deal if that makes sense to do so. For example, a typical issue with real estate investors is that their assets are depreciated for tax purposes and the amount of the deduction decreases over time, which causes them to keep buying properties. And they must continue to make debt repayments on their properties when they would like to keep the financing in place and use their funds elsewhere. To maintain a set level of financing, a real estate investor could deposit the funds for the debt repayment into a PAR contract and use a policy loan to repay the financing. By doing so, you could maintain a set amount of financing in place (as the borrowing against the policy is an unstructured loan and you can pay interest only) and have another stable asset to provide for legacy and/or further distributions in the future. There is more complexity to implement the above strategy, as the cash value available in the policy will not match the amount used in the debt repayment, which will require some additional cash flow in the short term. However, this point illustrates that there are many ways to use the incredible financial tool called PAR insurance.

———◈———

Building capital inside PAR life insurance is a wonderful pay yourself first strategy—not to mention a great place to store cash. This financial tool is excellent to use as a volatility buffer and to protect from sequence of return risks as mentioned in other Spotlights.

We once heard another advisor say that "the world is designed to take our money away from us." After years of listening to client stories and assembling financial strategies, we think that the statement is true; there are lots of ways financial institutions and shopping platforms get us to part with our money. A practice of consistently depositing capital into a financial tool is a good thing.

Infinite Banking Can Be Taxing

We would be remiss if we did not talk about some of the negative tax consequences of taking policy loans.

The infinite banking concept was conceived in the U.S. There are different tax rules in the U.S. than those in Canada. In Canada, a policy loan reduces the adjusted cost basis of a life insurance contract. The adjusted cost basis is simply the amount of money that you put into the contract less the net cost of pure insurance less policy loans. If the adjusted cost basis of an insurance contract is negative due to a policy loan, there's an income inclusion, and the income is subject to the tax rate for other income (which is the same as interest income). However, there's an offsetting deduction for a repayment of a policy loan as well. Accordingly, there are ways to deal with adverse impacts. However, if your income varies or the inclusion pushes you into a higher tax bracket, there could be a real cost.

What this also means is that if a person intends to use a leveraged strategy as part of their retirement, you will need to get a third-party bank involved. In our practice, we suggest that clients do a pay down strategy, which leaves the life insurance as the last asset. This practice will ensure that the life insurance contract has had the most time to compound. Then we'll look first to use cash dividends and the surrender of death benefit before we will look to take a loan to fund retirement. The reason for our stance in this area is that due to changes in interest rates and interest rate differentials, the interest charge on a policy loan could severely reduce the value of your assets and impair or compromise your standard of living.

The abundant tax benefits of having whole life insurance have been discussed quite thoroughly in the other chapters of this book.

A Word on Universal Life and Indexed Universal Life

We recommend that these types of policies are not used for infinite banking. And to be honest, universal life and its variants are, in our view, very special financial tools that should only be used in conjunction with a specialist when designing and using these products.

Further Exploring Infinite Banking

While we believe there's a lot to like about the infinite banking strategy, as we said before, there are areas of the strategy where we differ. We don't believe in any one financial tool or strategy as a silver bullet or the one golden solution for everyone.

Still, there's so much we do like about infinite banking—from both a financial and a self-empowerment perspective. If you're inclined to explore it for yourself, we highly encourage you to do so. Be sure to work with a financial planner or insurance agent who thoroughly understands infinite banking concepts and, ideally, has a track record of helping clients implement infinite banking strategies.

Most importantly, be sure the person you're working with has completed training to understand the nature of participating whole life and how policy loans work. Finally, we recommend that this specific strategy is implemented inside a holistic planning framework. What we mean by this is that saving inside a whole life insurance contract is great; however, it is only one step in a journey of many steps up the mountain toward your goals.

FINDING THE REAL VALUE IN REAL ESTATE

Investing in real estate can get complicated, but it can be simple to decide if an opportunity is worth pursuing.

We have personal friends who started their journey into real estate by purchasing a four-plex for around $250,000. A four-plex has four units that can be rented, meaning there was the potential for more cash flow than a single residence. Because of this and because our friends had good jobs, the bank allowed them to take a personal line of credit for the down payment on the four-plex.

In the 20 years since they purchased it, that four-plex has grown to a value of over $600,000. The rate of return can't be calculated. Why? Because our friends have no money in the deal. They achieved what's called an *infinite return*.

What's more, this one purchase was the impetus for building

(not buying, building) another four-plex a few years later. Then they purchased a couple of duplexes. Over time, they have built a multi-million-dollar real estate portfolio and cash flow for the rest of their lives all through this powerful asset class called real estate—and with virtually *no personal money up front.*

It seems we're all fascinated by investing in real estate. After all, it's the one asset we either own or rent in order to put a roof over our heads. In recent years, the interest in real estate has only grown, as evidenced by the many television shows on renovating, staging, selling, and flipping real estate. And stores like Home Depot, Lowes, and Rona are just the most well-known of the many home and building stores that have become a major part of our economy over the last few decades.

But owning or renting a home for our personal use is one thing. Investing in real estate is another matter. Direct investment in real estate may come with significant outlays of capital, increases in personal leverage (i.e., debt), and exposure to significant loss either through damage or nonpayment by tenants.

What's more, the rules and regulations regarding residential rentals tend to favor the tenants in disputes. For those less inclined to invest directly, it's possible to include real estate investing in their financial portfolio without purchasing a rental unit, condo, or apartment building thanks to alternative real estate investment opportunities like real estate investment trusts (REITS) and other indirect ownership financial tools.

It's not our intention to outline all the ways you can own and participate in real estate as an asset. There's a lot of information about that on the internet and in other books. But we do want to understand and evaluate real estate so that you can choose to take control of and increase your wealth using this powerful asset class.

As we see with many of the financial tools we have already examined, there's a lot of information relating to investing in real estate that can confuse us. Terms like *cash on cash return*, *cap rate*, *internal rate of return*, and *hard money loan* can be daunting.

Our advice is this: Don't worry about all that.

Instead, use some basic information to assess an investment into real estate. Think of what follows as a quick, "back-of-a-napkin" calculation when first considering a real estate investment deal. It will also show you how powerful of a wealth-building tool real estate investing can be.

Let's say you're looking at investing in a warehouse situated on a sizable lot in an industrial section of town. For this example, we're going to use the real estate analysis calculator that's available at Truth Concepts to show you exactly how to perform an analysis. The basis inputs for the calculator are as follows:

- Value of the property: $465,000 (land and building)
- Price of the property: $465,000

For this example, we're keeping it simple and making the value and price the same. But often you may purchase a property that's undervalued based on an assessment made by you or another knowledgeable party (i.e., bank, realtor, etc.). If the property was undervalued, then you would enter your valuation and the price you paid separately. Thus, we need two numbers to begin our calculation, which could be the same.

- Closing costs: $5,000 (legal fees, property assessments etc.—many times, closing costs are overlooked and can have an impact on the analysis.)

- Land value: $100,000

- Building value: $365,000 (This is important because the building can be depreciated for tax purposes whereas land can't. Don't worry, your tax person/accountant will handle the depreciation part. You just need to know what each part of your investment is roughly worth.)

- Loan amount: $302,250 (This is the amount of financing that can be secured on the deal. In this case it's 65% of the price of the property.)

Monthly Expenses

- Mortgage payment: This will be determined based on the interest rate and the loan term.

- Property taxes: These are generally based on an assessment. The property tax assessments may be available through the local municipality, or you can ask a realtor for this information.

- Insurance: This is based on a quote from an insurer or information from the current owner.

- Other expenses: These might include a capital reserve of 4%, property management fees of say 4%, and maybe a 5% vacancy rate.

A capital reserve is an estimate of additional funds that you would like to keep on hand for unexpected expenses. Property management is the percentage of the rent a third party would charge to manage your unit. The vacancy rate is an estimate of what portion of time during the year that your unit may not be rented or the time in between renters.

Expenses need to be carefully examined and could include other costs like utilities.

Gross Rental Income

Should be established through existing tenants, prior history, or relevant market rates. Again, the real estate agent should be very helpful with respect to these amounts.

Basic Tax Information

This should be based on the location of the property; in this case we are using Alberta rates.

Now the fun part, the analysis!

The first item to note is the holding period which in our case is five years or 60 months. The holding period should be the amount of time that you are prepared to own the asset. At the beginning we do not include an appreciation rate on the property. By appreciation rate we mean a rate that we expect the value of the property to increase in the future. In general, real estate follows inflation and is said to be a good inflation hedge. Another factor that impacts real estate values is the interest rate. When interest rates go down the value of real estate goes up, and when interest rates go up the value of real estate tends to go down.

The preliminary results are as follows:

Your down payment is $167,750.

We arrive at that amount by starting with the price of the property ($465,000), adding the closing costs ($5,000), and then subtracting the amount of the loan we took out to buy the warehouse ($302,250).

- $465,000 + $5,000 = $470,000
- $470,000 - $302,250 = $167,750

Your net average monthly cash flow is $923. We get that amount by taking the monthly revenue ($4,296) and subtracting your expenses ($537 property taxes + $250 insurance + $172 property management + 172 capital reserve + $215 for vacancy), your monthly loan payment ($1,767 based on the terms of the loan, which we used 5% over a 25 year amortization period), and taxes of $261 based on the highest Alberta personal rates and some rounding inside the program.

The net cash out after five years is $162,226. This is calculated as the selling price of the property ($465,000 as we have not factored appreciation) less the remaining loan ($267,734) less taxes ($35,040). The rate of return is 6.08%, which may seem odd given the net cash out is less than the $167,750 down payment. However, you also must consider the positive cash flow of $924 per month for 60 months, which equates to another $55,440 (Figure F.1).

Before we get to the analysis of the analysis, let's look at some other indicators of value that were presented by the realtor in the actual deal documents for this example. They were as follows:

1. Cap rate of 8%: This was calculated as total revenue of $51,552 less total expenses of $16,152 for a net amount of $35,400. If you take the net amount of $35,400 and divide it by 8%, you will get an amount of $442,500. However, the property is being offered at $465,000. So why is the cap rate of 8% being presented? In this case you could calculate the actual cap rate by taking the net amount of $35,400 and divide it by $465,000, which will give you 7.6%.

2. Gross rent multiplier 9.49: This is calculated as the property value of $465,000 divided by the gross rent of $51,552, which gives us a figure of 9. Again, you might ask why a deal document would disclose a number that would imply a value of $489,228?

3. Rate of return to capital invested 8.8%: This is calculated

FIGURE F.1

REAL ESTATE ANALYSIS #1

PROPERTY INFORMATION

PROPERTY VALUE:	**465,000**
PRICE OF PROPERTY:	465,000
CLOSING COSTS:	5,000
REALTOR FEES:	0
TOTAL PURCHASE PRICE:	**470,000**
LAND VALUE:	**100,000**
VALUE OF STRUCTURES:	**365,000**
BASIS FOR DEPRECIATION:	**470,000**

MONTHLY EXPENSES

TOTAL MORTG. PAYMENT:	(1,767)
PROPERTY TAXXES:	(537)
INSURANCE:	(250)
MAINTENANCE:	0
HOA FEES:	
PROPERTY MANAGEMENT:	(172)
CAPITAL RESERVE:	(172)
VACANCY:	(215)

1ST MORTGAGE INFO.

LOAN AMOUNT:	302,250
EXTRA POINTS:	**0.00%**
NET LOAN AMOUNT:	(302,250)
ANNUAL LOAN INT. RATE:	**5.00%**
LOAN TERM (MONTHS)	**300**
MONTHLY LOAN PAYMENT:	(1,767)

GROSS MONTHLY INCOME

GROSS RENTAL INCOME:	**4,296**
OTHER 1:	
OTHER 2:	
OTHER 3:	0

2ND MORTGAGE INFO.

LOAN AMOUNT:	0
EXTRA POINTS:	
NET LOAN AMOUNT:	0
ANNUAL LOAN INT. RATE:	
LOAN TERM (MONTHS)	
MONTHLY LOAN PAYMENT:	0

INVESTMENT ANALYSIS

MONTHS FOR ANALYSIS:	60	MNTH. TAX. INCOME:	542
MONTH TO SELL/RET. INV:		MNTH. INC. TAXES:	(260)
PROP. APPREC. RATE:	0.00%	NET. AVG. MONTHLY CASH FLOW:	923
DOWN PAYMENT:	(167,750)	FUT. PROP. VALUE:	**465,000**
NET MNTH. INC. AFTER EXP.:	**1,183**	FUTURE LOAN BAL.:	(267,734)
AVG. INTEREST PYMT.:	(1,192)	SALES FEES/ CLOSING COSTS:	0.00%
MNTH. INTEREST DED.:	1,192	DEPREC. RECAP. TAX:	(35,040)
YEARS FOR DEPREC.:	25	CAPITAL GAINS TAX:	0
MNTH. DEPREC. DED.:	1,217	NET CASH OUT:	**162,226**

BASIC TAX INFORMATION

INCOME TAX BRACKET:	**48.00%**
CAP. GAINS TAX BRACKET:	**24.00%**
DEP. RECAP TAX BRACK.:	**48.00%**

ROR: 6.08%

as the net amount of $35,400 less the total debt payments for the year, which is $21,204 ($1,762 multiplied for 12 months), totaling $14,196. Then you take $14,196 and divide that by the down payment of $167,750, which equates to 8.46%. Despite another discrepancy between 8.8% and 8.46%, what is this number telling us?

4. Overall rate of return with no expenses and no debt service 11.1%: This is calculated by taking the gross rental revenue of $51,552 divided by the value of the property of $465,000, which gives us an amount of 11.08%. Finally, a figure that works! This might be applicable to an investment of 100% of the capital and a triple net lease. Triple net means that the lessee pays all the expenses.

5. Rate of return to capital invested with first year principal pay down 12.65%: This is calculated as adding the annual principal paid on the debt of $6,289 to the $14,196 calculated in item 3 above divided by the down payment, which equates to 12.21%

The result? Utter confusion!

We have figures of 8%, 8.8%, 11.1%, and 12.65%, which is nowhere close to the rate of return over years of just over 6%. Why? The reasons include the period under analysis. The period in the calculations above is 12 months, or one year.

Another issue is that tax has not been factored into the analysis. We think that income taxes are relevant! Another issue is the expenses being included in the analysis. Expenses must always be examined very closely as part of your due diligence.

Returning to the analysis using Truth Concepts, there are some additional insights to glean. Let's add an appreciation rate of 3%. Real estate generally moves with inflation, and the increases over time can be even more significant. This factor moves the rate of return for our analysis to 11.29% from 6.09%. That's almost double what it was above before we factored in appreciation. Now this deal is starting to get our attention (Figure F.2).

Now, what if you could access more capital? For instance, let's consider funds in a whole life insurance contract. What would happen if you accessed, say, another $100,000 at a rate of 7% over the same period of 300 months?

Now the rate of return is 19.30% and there's still positive cash flow of $476 per month (Figure F.3). Are you starting to see how powerful of a wealth-building tool real estate investing can be? The rationale for the figures used is that generally the rate of a loan taken on a whole life insurance contract will be up to 200 basis points or 2% higher than a market rate loan on a first mortgage. However, depending on your specific situation it may not be much higher.

The other factor in favor of using the funds inside a PAR policy is control over the payments.

You could choose to pay only interest on a collateral loan taken on an insurance contract. In fact, if you have enough value

FIGURE F.2

REAL ESTATE ANALYSIS #2

PROPERTY INFORMATION

PROPERTY VALUE:	465,000
PRICE OF PROPERTY:	465,000
CLOSING COSTS:	5,000
REALTOR FEES:	0
TOTAL PURCHASE PRICE:	470,000
LAND VALUE:	100,000
VALUE OF STRUCTURES:	365,000
BASIS FOR DEPRECIATION:	365,000

MONTHLY EXPENSES

TOTAL MORTG. PAYMENT:	(1,767)
PROPERTY TAXXES:	(537)
INSURANCE:	(250)
MAINTENANCE:	0
HOA FEES:	
PROPERTY MANAGEMENT:	(172)
CAPITAL RESERVE:	(172)
VACANCY:	(215)

1ST MORTGAGE INFO.

LOAN AMOUNT:	302,250
EXTRA POINTS:	0.00%
NET LOAN AMOUNT:	(302,250)
ANNUAL LOAN INT. RATE:	5.00%
LOAN TERM (MONTHS)	300
MONTHLY LOAN PAYMENT:	(1,767)

GROSS MONTHLY INCOME

GROSS RENTAL INCOME:	4,296
OTHER 1:	
OTHER 2:	
OTHER 3:	0

2ND MORTGAGE INFO.

LOAN AMOUNT:	0
EXTRA POINTS:	
NET LOAN AMOUNT:	0
ANNUAL LOAN INT. RATE:	
LOAN TERM (MONTHS)	
MONTHLY LOAN PAYMENT:	0

INVESTMENT ANALYSIS

MONTHS FOR ANALYSIS:	60	MNTH. TAX. INCOME:	542
MONTH TO SELL/RET. INV:		MNTH. INC. TAXES:	(260)
PROP. APPREC. RATE:	3.00%	NET. AVG. MONTHLY CASH FLOW:	923
DOWN PAYMENT:	(167,750)	FUT. PROP. VALUE:	540,152
NET MNTH. INC. AFTER EXP.:	1,183	FUTURE LOAN BAL.:	(267,734)
AVG. INTEREST PYMT.:	(1,192)	SALES FEES/ CLOSING COSTS:	0.00%
MNTH. INTEREST DED.:	1,192	DEPREC. RECAP. TAX:	(35,040)
YEARS FOR DEPREC.:	25	CAPITAL GAINS TAX:	(18,036)
MNTH. DEPREC. DED.:	1,217	NET CASH OUT:	219,342

BASIC TAX INFORMATION

INCOME TAX BRACKET:	48.00%
CAP. GAINS TAX BRACKET:	24.00%
DEP. RECAP TAX BRACK.:	48.00%

ROR: 11.29%

FIGURE F.3

REAL ESTATE ANALYSIS #3

PROPERTY INFORMATION

PROPERTY VALUE:	465,000
PRICE OF PROPERTY:	465,000
CLOSING COSTS:	5,000
REALTOR FEES:	0
TOTAL PURCHASE PRICE:	470,000
LAND VALUE:	100,000
VALUE OF STRUCTURES:	365,000
BASIS FOR DEPRECIATION:	365,000

MONTHLY EXPENSES

TOTAL MORTG. PAYMENT:	(2,474)
PROPERTY TAXXES:	(537)
INSURANCE:	(250)
MAINTENANCE:	0
HOA FEES:	0
PROPERTY MANAGEMENT:	(172)
CAPITAL RESERVE:	(172)
VACANCY:	(215)

1ST MORTGAGE INFO.

LOAN AMOUNT:	302,250
EXTRA POINTS:	0.00%
NET LOAN AMOUNT:	(302,250)
ANNUAL LOAN INT. RATE:	5.00%
LOAN TERM (MONTHS)	300
MONTHLY LOAN PAYMENT:	(1,767)

GROSS MONTHLY INCOME

GROSS RENTAL INCOME:	4,296
OTHER 1:	
OTHER 2:	
OTHER 3:	0

2ND MORTGAGE INFO.

LOAN AMOUNT:	100,000
EXTRA POINTS:	0.00%
NET LOAN AMOUNT:	(100,000)
ANNUAL LOAN INT. RATE:	7.00%
LOAN TERM (MONTHS)	300
MONTHLY LOAN PAYMENT:	(707)

INVESTMENT ANALYSIS

MONTHS FOR ANALYSIS:	60	MNTH. TAX. INCOME:	0
MONTH TO SELL/RET. INV:	0	MNTH. INC. TAXES:	0
PROP. APPREC. RATE:	3.00%	NET. AVG. MONTHLY CASH FLOW:	476
DOWN PAYMENT:	(67,750)	FUT. PROP. VALUE:	540,152
NET MNTH. INC. AFTER EXP.:	476	FUTURE LOAN BAL.:	(358,896)
AVG. INTEREST PYMT.:	(1,751)	SALES FEES/ CLOSING COSTS:	0.00%
MNTH. INTEREST DED.:	1,751	DEPREC. RECAP. TAX:	(34,527)
YEARS FOR DEPREC.:	25	CAPITAL GAINS TAX:	(18,036)
MNTH. DEPREC. DED.:	1,199	NET CASH OUT:	128,692

BASIC TAX INFORMATION

INCOME TAX BRACKET:	48.00%
CAP. GAINS TAX BRACKET:	24.00%
DEP. RECAP TAX BRACK.:	48.00%

ROR: 19.30%

inside the policy, no payment may be required. We would not recommend forgoing making interest payments on your collateral loan though, as discussed earlier in this book.

Of course, there's still much work to do. We alluded to due diligence, which is perhaps the most important step in the process (you'll find a helpful due diligence checklist on the Motley Fool website).

Despite the increased complexity of real estate, it's a very important asset and a significant difference maker in wealth accumulation. Hopefully the "back-of-a-napkin" analysis from Truth Concepts above will give you an early sense of whether a real estate investment opportunity is worth pursuing further.

FINANCIAL $POTLIGHT G
PENSIONS AND THE POWER OF ANNUITIES

In the end we all want a secure retirement and reliable pension funds that continue to pay regardless of market performance or economic cycles.

Joe and Lisa came to Eric for financial advice. At the time they were in their late 30s and making more money than ever before. Joe is a realtor with a professional corporation and makes more than $250,000 a year, while Lisa is a tech company executive making more than $150,000 a year. Despite their ample income, they wanted to make sure they didn't wind up outliving their retirement savings tomorrow.

For Lisa, her employer was matching her contributions to her RRSP (registered retirement savings plan). As discussed elsewhere in this book, RRSPs have their pros and cons, but in general, when your employer is matching your contributions, it makes sense to take advantage of what is essentially free money for you. Lisa opted to maximize the allowable RRSP contributions this way and will keep doing so as long as the company continues to match her deposits.

Joe's dynamics were different. His income sits in his corporation, and unused capital turns into retained earnings. For Joe to follow the RRSP path, he'd have to move money out of his company and use that money to maximize his RRSP ($30,780, the maximum contribution for 2023). But moving money out of his company would incur taxes no matter whether he took the money as a dividend or as a salary.

Oh, and when Joe retires, he will be taxed once more on the "harvest" at the regular income tax rate when he retires or is forced to take funds from the plan under the current rules.

None of this was ideal for Joe.

Instead, once we explored Joe's need for insurance and his desire to have short- and long-term savings, we saw that his corporate capital could be used more efficiently. We decided to use what's known as a Corporate Insured Retirement Plan (CIRP).

Essentially, it's a whole-life plan designed for immediate growth, strong immediate cash values, and insurance. We were able to guarantee returns, have dividend benefits, obtain insurance today if the worst happened, and secure a solid retirement plan. And the long-term tax advantages could be significant.

Joe and Lisa are doing many things right and are maximizing everything they can to rest easy about whether they're putting away enough for retirement. But for many people, the possibility of outliving their savings and retirement funds is a real concern.

Sadly, we believe the age of retirement *insecurity* is upon us.

Number One Concern

The possibility of outliving our savings and investment funds is a real concern for many. In fact, according to the LIMRA Secure Retirement Institute, 6 in 10 pre-retirees want guaranteed income for life.[103] That's their number one desired feature in a financial product.

Yet according to the article, one in four pre-retirees do not believe they will have a financially comfortable retirement.

Demographics in Canada are shifting with the ratio of older people (over 65) to younger people (15 to 64) projected to increase by more than 20% in the next two decades.[104] More and more hard-working folks from both Canada and the U.S. are looking for secure sources of retirement.[105] Longevity, inflation, and market risks add further pressure on retirement accounts that people hope will last their entire lifetime.

103 "Ready, Set, Retire? Not So Fast! Revisited: A Canadian Consumer Retirement Study," LIMRA, November 4, 2014, https://www.limra.com/siteassets/research/research-abstracts/2014/ready-set-retire-not-so-fast--revisited-a-canadian-consumer-retirement-study-2014/full-report.

104 Steven Globerman, "Canada's Demographic Crisis Threatens Incomes and Living Standards," Fraser Institute, October 25, 2022, https://www.fraserinstitute.org/article/canadas-demographic-crisis-threatens-incomes-and-living-standards.

105 Elena Holodny, "We're About to See a Mind-Blowing Demographic Shift Unprecedented in Human History," Business Insider, May 16, 2016, https://www.businessinsider.com/demographics-shift-first-time-in-human-history-2016-5.

But the longer you live, the longer your money needs to stretch. Interestingly, the probability of having a long retirement, according to the Society of Actuaries and American Academy of Actuaries looks like this:

- A 65-year-old man has a 50% chance of living to age 84, and a 25% chance of living to age 91.

- A 65-year-old woman has a 50% chance of living to age 87, and a 25% chance of living to age 93.

- A 65-year-old couple has a 50% chance of living to age 91, and a 25% chance of living to age 96.[106]

An increasingly female aging population is also becoming more common. Women now make up a larger share of seniors and widowers.[107] We assist many women in creating long-lasting retirement plans that have both pension and annuity qualities, all while enabling positive market participation.

Corporate and government-sponsored pension plans have always been sought after. However, according to Statistics Canada, guaranteed defined benefits from registered pension plans for men have declined from 52% to 37% between 1977 and 2012.[108] These workers' compensation packages had been one of the pillars of retirement income for many Canadians and Americans.

106 "Actuarial Life Table," Social Security, accessed November 30, 2023, https://www.ssa.gov/oact/STATS/table4c6.html.

107 "2020 Profile of Older Americans," Administration for Community Living, May 2021, https://acl.gov/sites/default/files/aging%20and%20Disability%20In%20America/2020Profileolderamericans.final_.pdf.

108 Marie Drolet and René Morissette, "New Facts on Pension Coverage in Canada," Statistics Canada, accessed August 30, 2023, https://www150.statcan.gc.ca/n1/pub/75-006-x/2014001/article/14120-eng.htm.

Many corporations cannot afford these defined benefit programs. They may offer defined contribution plans for which they will hopefully provide contribution matching. With a defined contribution plan you know your contributions, yet you do not know how much you will get when you retire as the benefits are not specified.

The defined benefit pension plan, where you know what you will receive when you retire, has seen an uptick within the public sector but a downtick in the private sector.

If you have a corporate or government pension, you're in a sweet minority. You either enjoy a defined and indexed benefit/retirement income that will last you for your entire life, or you have a defined contribution plan that culminates in a nest egg at retirement. If are like so many Canadians that do not have a company pension, you will have some decisions to make as to how to allocate your income and savings into retirement and how to optimize them for lifelong retirement funding.

Solutions to Longevity in Retirement

For many of our clients, the ride of the markets becomes more and more tiring as retirement comes closer. After years of working, saving, and sacrificing, the last thing you want to do is worry about market and retirement fund performance. Additionally, you want to know that your funds are tax-optimized and, should retirement be shorter than imagined, that remaining funds can be passed on efficiently and quickly to your heirs.

Thankfully there are some fabulous tools available for you to be able to create your own pension, even if you were not blessed by having a pension through your employment.

There are three financial vehicles that can help you accomplish the feat of creating a secure retirement. They are annuities, guaranteed minimum withdrawal benefit funds (GMWBs), and as already discussed above in this chapter, insured retirement plans (IRPs) using accumulated cash values of participating whole life insurance policies.

In many cases, clients choose to allocate enough of the retirement fund to one of these guaranteed income streams to at least cover the main bills for housing, food, utilities, and transportation. Knowing the basics are covered in and of itself creates peace of mind. The balance of your retirement income may come from a mix of conservative investments, fixed income, dividend-paying stock portfolios, or even real estate.

Let's have a closer look at creating our own pension using either an *annuity* or a *guaranteed lifetime income benefit* (GMWB) fund. Both choices require that you have successfully amassed a retirement fund that might be in a non-registered account or, more likely, is allocated in an RRSP, a TFSA, a RRIF or, if in the U.S., a 401(k), Roth IRA, etc.

Annuities

Annuities come in many different variations.

A simple way to think about an annuity is to consider it the opposite of life insurance. With life insurance you make periodic payments to get a lump-sum benefit at the end. With an annuity you make a lump-sum payment to obtain periodic payments for the rest of your life.

Annuities have evolved from a simple guaranteed lifetime product where you essentially bet to live a long time and a life insurance company by default takes the other side of the bet. A lifetime annuity promises to pay its owner income on a regular basis for the rest of their life in return for a lump-sum deposit or a series of deposits. The benefit is that you do not have to worry about running out of money in old age.

However, many do not like the idea that if they died much earlier than expected, the insurance company would be able to keep the rest of the unpaid funds. To address these concerns, many insurers began to add additional features to these contracts. Some include a minimum payment period, after which funds would then be transferred to the beneficiary of the annuity.

Other features include indexing for increases over time, multiple lives, term-certain, deferred, or immediate payouts, and a mix between fixed predetermined annuity payments and variable annuities. Choosing the right one will be a decision with your advisor based on the needed features, the amount available, your age, and estate considerations.

But how do they perform?

Getting a lifetime immediate annuity too early in life is not usually the best in terms of the yield on the amount paid.

For example, if you are a male, age 57, and you deposit a $250,000 registered lump sum into a lifetime guaranteed annuity with a 30-year guarantee (maximum), a 2% indexed feature to combat some inflation, the monthly income becomes $901 (early 2023) per month and growing.

This is $10,812 per year plus and $438,675.72 guaranteed in total for 30 years. This represents a gross yield of approximately 4.3% per year.

Later in life is when annuities hit their stride. Here are the same annuity features implemented at age 75. For example, if you are a male, age 75, and you deposit a $250,000 registered lump sum into a lifetime guaranteed annuity with a 15-year guarantee (maximum), a 2% indexed feature to combat some inflation, the monthly income becomes $1,431.17 (early 2023) per month and growing.

This is $14,311.70 per year plus and $296,997.72 guaranteed in total for 15 years. This represents a gross yield of approximately 6.86% per year. And as interest rates remain higher, these yields will look more and more favourable. These are definitely worth considering if you are over 70 years of age.

Many seniors consider annuities seriously, as they should. These vehicles can out-perform registered retirement income funds (RRIFs) that are allocated with as much as 50% in equities.

The appeal of RRIFs is control over investments, control over withdrawals, and having money for surprise needs as well. Yet will the RRIF last until age 92? Getting 6% or more net of fees will be a challenge for many with RRSPs, 401(k)s, RRIFs, etc. Annuities can provide reliable revenues that are higher than GICs and T-bills. Doing so without risk is even more difficult as bonds have been generally underperforming, and for many equity portfolios you literally need a seat belt.

In addition, annuities have better taxation—especially with non-registered funds. They do vary throughout the years, so the choice to purchase an annuity should be made in real-time with an advisor who can provide objectivity and options. Pushback usually revolves around access to funds. Yet, you don't have to annuitize the entire retirement portfolio. As mentioned, a portion that could ideally handle all the regular bills and provide some measure of certainty in an uncertain world.

Wishing to have a long life when you own an annuity is a given. And, interestingly enough, Canadian pensioner mortality tables indicate that Canadians who are members of pension plans are living longer than previously predicted.[109] If one dies prior to the short-term rate protection period or the guarantee period, then the beneficiary listed on the contract will receive the payments to the end/total of the guarantee period. There are also other options that can be considered such as a joint annuity. In many instances, an annuity can be a better and less stressful path to take versus GICs or balanced funds.

---

109 "The Retirement Dilemma," Guardian Capital, August 2022, https://www.guardiancapital.com/investmentsolutions/wp-content/uploads/gp/The-Retirement-Dilemma.pdf.

Another common question is about leaving a legacy.

How can I buy an annuity with my lump-sum retirement funds and still leave behind a financial legacy and inheritance? I want it all—a solid maximized retirement using the funds I worked for and saved and invested and the ability to leave behind a legacy?

You have worked hard and deserve to enjoy the maximum potential of your retirement assets. To achieve guaranteed income for life, minimize taxes, and preserve the value of your estate, many implement a strategy called the *insured annuity strategy*. It's worthwhile mentioning that many business owners also use the corporate insured annuity with corporate funds.

Our clients who have shifted from wealth accumulation to a focus on wealth preservation want their portfolio to include GICs, bonds, and fixed income investments. Added is the need to leave a legacy for their families. The adjusted portfolios may leave the principal intact for some, yet this stability is less than ideal when considering the need for guaranteed income and the impact of taxation. The insured annuity strategy offers a way to maximize after-tax retirement income and provide funds for the estate.

The strategy uses a combination of a life annuity coupled with a permanent life insurance policy. The key to implementing this strategy is to first obtain the life insurance policy before purchasing the annuity. Once approved for a life insurance policy (or perhaps solid early planning has resulted in having an insurance policy already in place), the annuity can be acquired. The annuity will make lifelong payments of capital plus interest, whereby the annuitant pays tax only on the prescribed interest amount. This prescribed rate feature actually provides the annuitant with higher after-tax income than would be received from a guaranteed investment certificate (GIC).

Since the capital used to buy the annuity is no longer available for the heirs, some of the cash flow is utilized to pay for the life insurance policy. When that time comes, the death benefit of the life insurance policy will be paid free of tax to the beneficiaries thereby replacing all or a portion of the capital that was used to purchase the annuity.

This strategy will produce lifelong income, preferential tax treatment of income, control over preserved estate via life insurance policy, peace of mind, and the elimination of probate costs and time.

The Guaranteed Minimum Lifetime Income Withdrawal Benefit, or GMWB

This option is somewhat of a hybrid solution for the need of lifetime income when using a registered or non-registered retirement asset. With this solution, the retiree would like to achieve predictable guaranteed income—indexed income that increases over time, like many annuities—yet wishes to maintain the ability to have access to funds in case of an emergency. Additional features include market participation as well as bypass of probate that saves additional time and money.

The solutions have income that never decreases and only increases, even if the markets are performing poorly. Many of our clients enjoy these features as both retirees and pre-retirees. Some of the offering insurers of these plans offer an aggressive net 4% annual performance bonus on funds even if the markets are less or negative. This, in effect, guarantees no losses leading up to retirement age and beyond as well as continued growth and compounding.

Calibrating your income needs with tax-efficient, reliable solutions makes a retirement experience more tranquil and joyous. In the end, money is about being able to live as fully as possible. Making sure your money will last and can be a part of your legacy is what we all want to do.

If, like many retirees, you're concerned about outliving your retirement nest egg, appreciate immediate liquidity, and would also like performance and even increases of payments as you grow older, then perhaps a properly allocated *guaranteed retirement income for life fund* is a great consideration for you.

As is the case with many recommendations we provide, there's usually more than one answer. It all begins with intention and taking stock of where you're at and matching your actions with where you wish to be. This approach will allow you and your advisor to create a pathway that enables you to meet your short- to long-term goals with peace of mind.

ONE BIG BRIGHT $POT
MAIN IDEA: YOU.

Hopefully, you can now see many financial blind spots that many people never do. You may also be able to identify with certain financial tactics we put in the Spotlights for you. But before we wrap up this book, we want to point out one final big bright spot in all of this: You have the power to apply everything in this book along the way on your financial journey.

Yes, you'll need an advisor or two (or more) to help you make the journey successful. But the compass for your journey—the thinking about your thinking—is already in hand. The only thing left now is for you to start your journey.

Where Are You Right Now?

If, as the saying goes, every journey begins with the first step, then we think it's just as important to know where you're starting from. This means taking an honest, clear-eyed look at your current finances, your old and new notions about money, your lifestyle habits and patterns, and your financial goals. Only then can you begin to chart a path toward where you want to go.

Look at Your Debt, Then Come Up with a Plan

You can't climb out of a hole at the same time you're digging it deeper. Maybe, at some point down the road in certain situations, it might make sense to take on debt to grow your wealth. However, in our experience, that's seldom the case, especially at the beginning of your financial journey. The first thing you should do is to stop your money from flowing away from you. You have to learn how to hang onto it before you can accumulate it.

Look at Your Revenue Creation

Where does your money come from? Once you understand where you get your money, you can then make decisions about how you might increase the flow of money coming to you. Maybe it's a better-paying job or a side hustle. Maybe it's investing in a rental property or getting a participating whole life insurance policy. There are a myriad of methods for making money. It's up to you (and your team of financial advisors) to determine which ways give you the most efficient path toward your financial goals.

Understand Your Spending

Live your life. Have fun. Just be sure to understand where your money goes and why you're spending it as you keep your long-term goals in view.

Ask

Ask questions of your advisors. Ask for clarification. Ask for examples.

Ask yourself questions about your actions. Ask yourself what you truly value. Ask yourself about your choices. Ask yourself about your goals. Ask yourself how you spend your time and why. Ask yourself about your thinking.

Ask who stands to profit from any given opportunity. Ask *How much do I stand to lose?* Ask *How much could I gain?* Ask if a decision you're facing brings you closer to or farther from your goals.

And never, ever be afraid to *ask* for help. For more advice, you can reach out to us any time at info@financialblindspotsbook.com.

LET'S KEEP THE CONVERSATION
GOING

Join the email list to receive exclusive content. Visit **www.financialblindspotsbook.com** to sign up.

For **special discounts** or bulk purchases, contact **info@financialblindspotsbook.com**

For speaking events, contact **info@financialblindspotsbook.com**

Seeking financial guidance? Contact us at **info@financialbindspotsbook.com**. We provide direct consultations with our team in Canada, and for US residents, we'll connect you with our trusted partners to address your financial needs.

THANK YOU FOR READING!

If you enjoyed *Financial Blindpot*,
please leave a review on Goodreads or on the retailer site where you purchased this book to help reach more readers like you.

ERIC B. WATCHORN

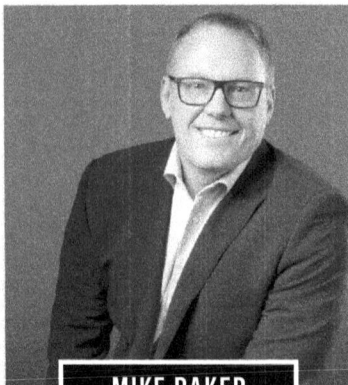

MIKE BAKER

APPENDIX

Table and Graphics (By Chapter)

Financial Blind$pot #5: Your Maximum Potential
FIGURE 5.2

YEARS TO ILLUSTRATE: 30		— □ ✕

CURRENT AGE:	30	**INCOME INCREASE:** 4.00%
CURRENT ASSETS:	0	
ANNUAL INCOME:	150,000	

	TOTAL INCOME
FIRST YEAR:	150,000
AVERAGE:	280,425
LAST YEAR:	467,798
CUMULATIVE:	8,412,741
COMPOUND:	8,412,741

	100.0% INCOME TO SAVINGS
FIRST YEAR:	150,000
AVERAGE:	280,425
LAST YEAR:	467,798
CUMULATIVE:	8,412,741
COMPOUND:	8,412,741

MAXIMUM POTENTIAL

100% SAVINGS @ 0.0%

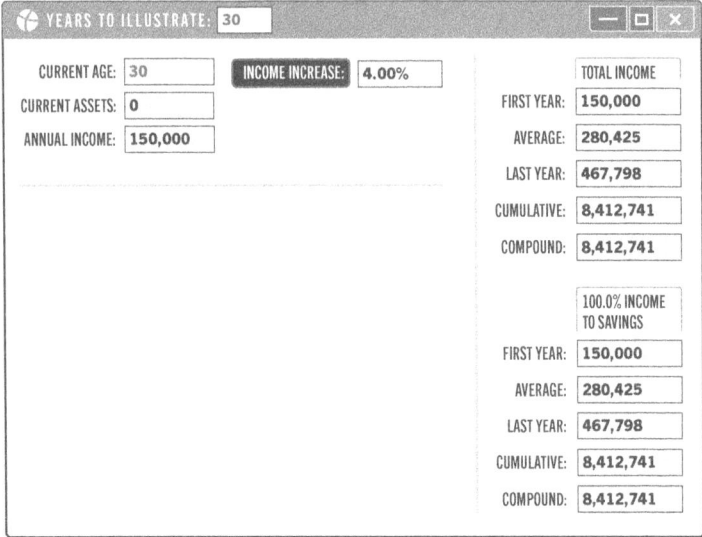

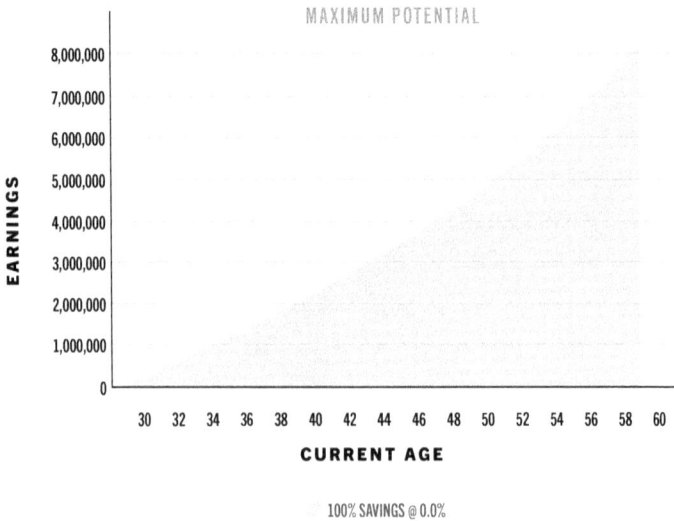

Continuing above scenario, add inflation or a pay increase of 4%

FIGURE 5.5

YEARS TO ILLUSTRATE: 30		

CURRENT AGE:	30	**INCOME INCREASE:**	4.00%		TOTAL INCOME	
CURRENT ASSETS:	0	**NET EARNING RATE:**	5.00%	FIRST YEAR:	150,000
ANNUAL INCOME:	150,000			AVERAGE:	280,425

LAST YEAR: 467,798

CUMULATIVE: 8,412,741

	TOTAL TAXES	DEBT PAYMENTS
% OF INCOME:	40.00%	34.50%
	ANNUAL COST INCREASE:	4.00%

COMPOUND: 16,987,082

25.5% INCOME TO SAVINGS

| TOTAL COSTS: | (3,365,096) | (2,902,396) |
| ACTUAL LOSS: | **(6,794,833)** | **(5,860,543)** |

FIRST YEAR: 38,250

AVERAGE: 71,508

LAST YEAR: 119,288

CUMULATIVE: 2,145,249

COMPOUND: 4,331,706

MAXIMUM POTENTIAL

EARNINGS

3,732,5058
1,732,508
(267,792)
(2,267,492)
(4,267,492)
(6,267,492)

30 32 34 36 38 40 42 44 46 48 50 52 54 56 58 60

CURRENT AGE

26% SAVINGS @ 5.0%   35% TO DEBT SERVICE   40% TO TOTAL TAXES

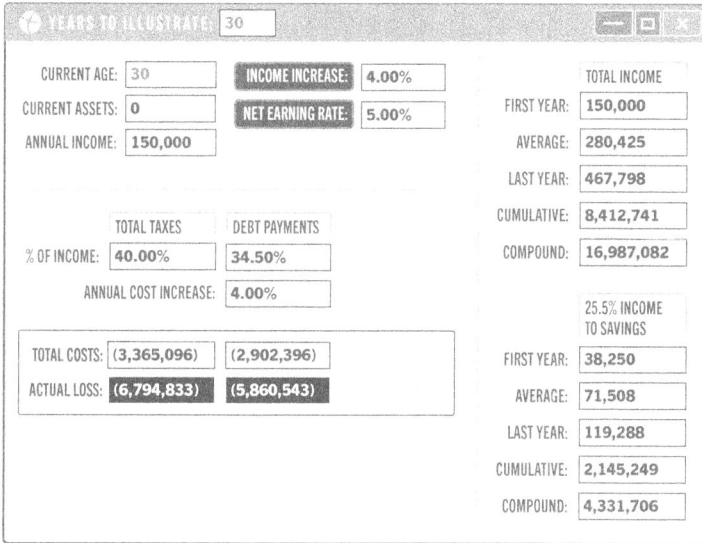

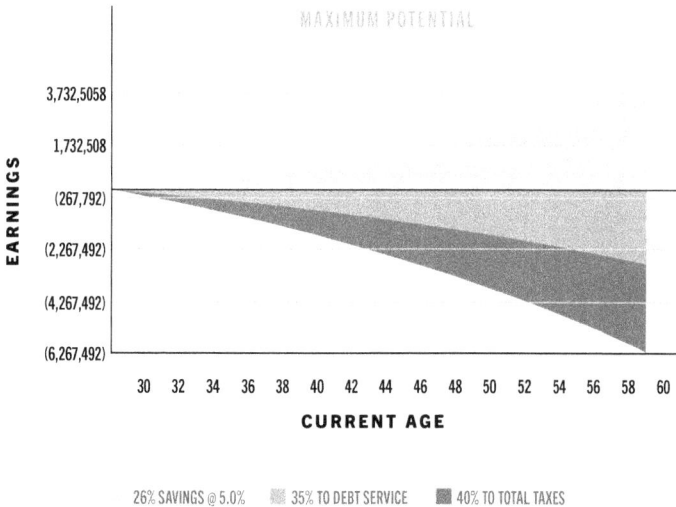

Continuing above scenario,
adding in 34% financing/debt and interest

FIGURE 5.7

| YEARS TO ILLUSTRATE: | 30 | | | | | | — □ × |

CURRENT AGE:	30	INCOME INCREASE:	4.00%		TOTAL INCOME
CURRENT ASSETS:	0	NET EARNING RATE:	10.00%	FIRST YEAR:	150,000
ANNUAL INCOME:	150,000			AVERAGE:	280,425
				LAST YEAR:	467,798
				CUMULATIVE:	8,412,741

	TOTAL TAXES	DEBT PAYMENTS	LIFESTYLE	COMPOUND:	39,066,513
% OF INCOME:	40.00%	34.50%	23.50%		
ANNUAL COST INCREASE:	4.00%	4.00%		2.0% INCOME TO SAVINGS
TOTAL COSTS:	(3,365,096)	(2,902,396)	(1,976,994)	FIRST YEAR:	3,000
ACTUAL LOSS:	(15,626,605)	(13,477,947)	(9,180,631)	AVERAGE:	5,608
				LAST YEAR:	9,356
				CUMULATIVE:	168,255
				COMPOUND:	781,330

MAXIMUM POTENTIAL

| EARNINGS | |
| 755,514 |
| (244,486) |
| (1,244,486) |
| (2,244,486) |
| (3,244,486) |
| (4,244,486) |
| (5,244,486) |
| (6,244,486) |
| (7,244,486) |
| (8,244,486) |

CURRENT AGE: 30 32 34 36 38 40 42 44 46 48 50 52 54 56 58 60

2% SAVINGS @ 10.0%   24% TO LIFESTYLE   35% TO DEBT SERVICE   40% TO TOTAL TAXES

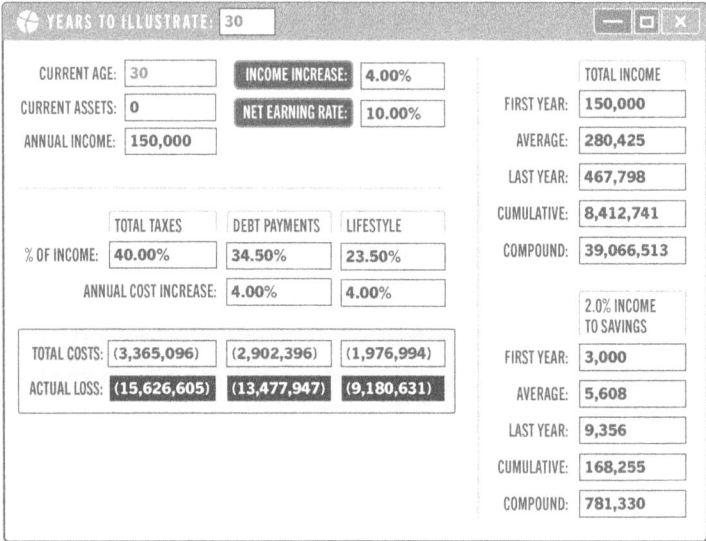

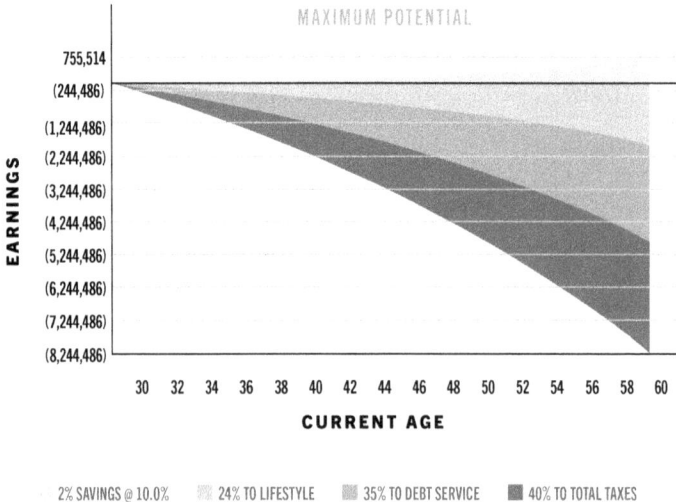

Continuing above scenario, increase earnings to 10%

FIGURE 5.8

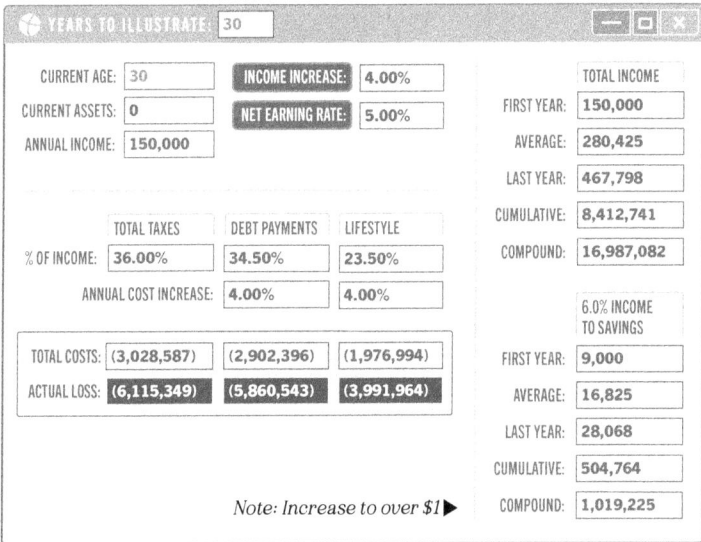

	YEARS TO ILLUSTRATE: 30		— □ ✕

				TOTAL INCOME	
CURRENT AGE:	30	INCOME INCREASE: 4.00%	FIRST YEAR:	150,000
CURRENT ASSETS:	0	NET EARNING RATE: 5.00%	AVERAGE:	280,425
ANNUAL INCOME:	150,000		LAST YEAR:	467,798

				CUMULATIVE:	8,412,741
	TOTAL TAXES	DEBT PAYMENTS	LIFESTYLE	COMPOUND:	16,987,082
% OF INCOME:	36.00%	34.50%	23.50%		
	ANNUAL COST INCREASE:	4.00%	4.00%	6.0% INCOME TO SAVINGS	

TOTAL COSTS:	(3,028,587)	(2,902,396)	(1,976,994)	FIRST YEAR:	9,000
ACTUAL LOSS:	(6,115,349)	(5,860,543)	(3,991,964)	AVERAGE:	16,825
				LAST YEAR:	28,068
				CUMULATIVE:	504,764
		Note: Increase to over $1 ▶		COMPOUND:	1,019,225

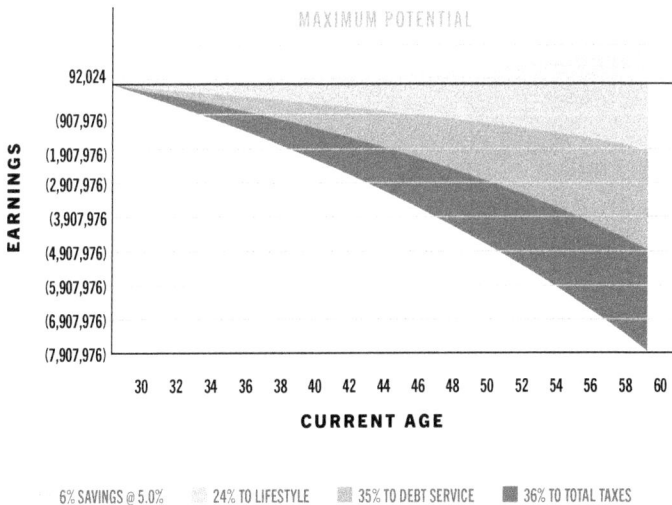

MAXIMUM POTENTIAL

EARNINGS

92,024
(907,976)
(1,907,976)
(2,907,976)
(3,907,976)
(4,907,976)
(5,907,976)
(6,907,976)
(7,907,976)

30 32 34 36 38 40 42 44 46 48 50 52 54 56 58 60

CURRENT AGE

6% SAVINGS @ 5.0%   24% TO LIFESTYLE   35% TO DEBT SERVICE   36% TO TOTAL TAXES

Continuing above scenario, lower taxes to 36%

FIGURE 5.9

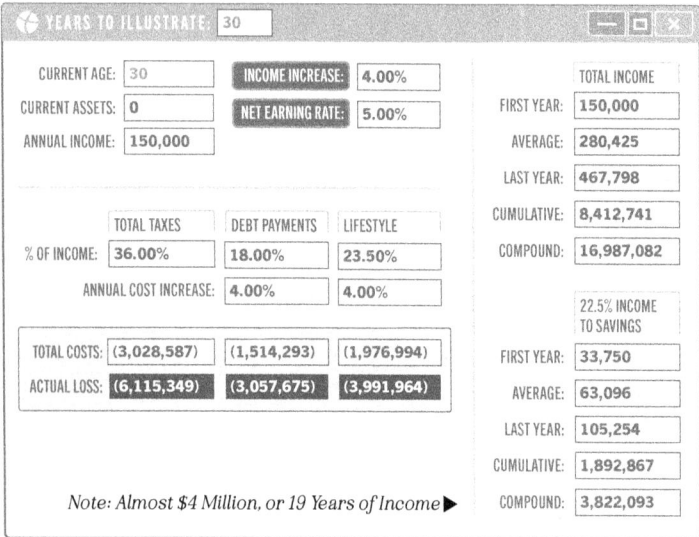

⚙ YEARS TO ILLUSTRATE:	30					▭ ▢ ✕

CURRENT AGE:	30	**INCOME INCREASE:**	4.00%			TOTAL INCOME	
CURRENT ASSETS:	0	**NET EARNING RATE:**	5.00%		FIRST YEAR:	150,000	
ANNUAL INCOME:	150,000				AVERAGE:	280,425	
					LAST YEAR:	467,798	

	TOTAL TAXES	DEBT PAYMENTS	LIFESTYLE	CUMULATIVE:	8,412,741
% OF INCOME:	36.00%	18.00%	23.50%	COMPOUND:	16,987,082
ANNUAL COST INCREASE:		4.00%	4.00%		

				22.5% INCOME TO SAVINGS	
TOTAL COSTS:	(3,028,587)	(1,514,293)	(1,976,994)	FIRST YEAR:	33,750
ACTUAL LOSS:	**(6,115,349)**	**(3,057,675)**	**(3,991,964)**	AVERAGE:	63,096
				LAST YEAR:	105,254
				CUMULATIVE:	1,892,867

Note: Almost $4 Million, or 19 Years of Income ▶   COMPOUND: 3,822,093

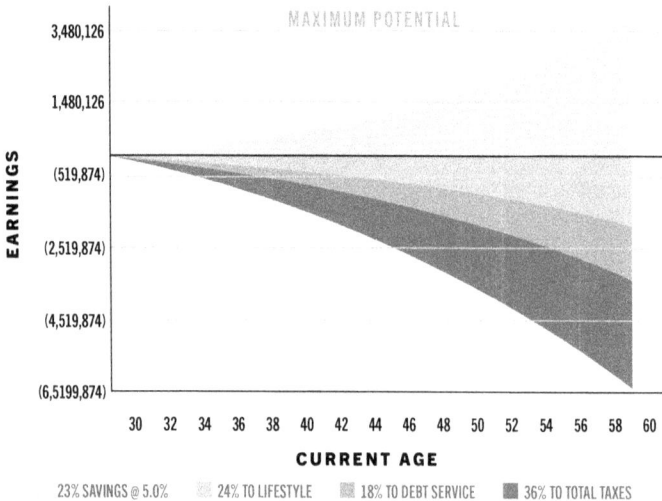

Continuing above scenario, lower debt payments by half

Financial Blind$pot #7: Understanding Financing & Opportunity Costs

FIGURE 7.1

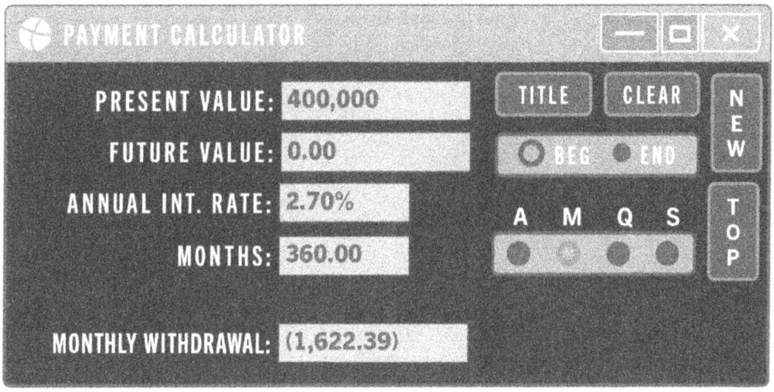

PAYMENT CALCULATOR

PRESENT VALUE: 400,000

FUTURE VALUE: 0.00

ANNUAL INT. RATE: 2.70%

MONTHS: 360.00

TITLE   CLEAR

BEG   END

A   M   Q   S

N E W

T O P

MONTHLY WITHDRAWAL: (1,622.39)

FIGURE 7.2

PAYMENT CALCULATOR

PRESENT VALUE: 400,000

FUTURE VALUE: 0.00

ANNUAL INT. RATE: 6.70%

MONTHS: 360.00

TITLE   CLEAR

BEG   END

A   M   Q   S

N E W

T O P

MONTHLY WITHDRAWAL: (2,581.11)

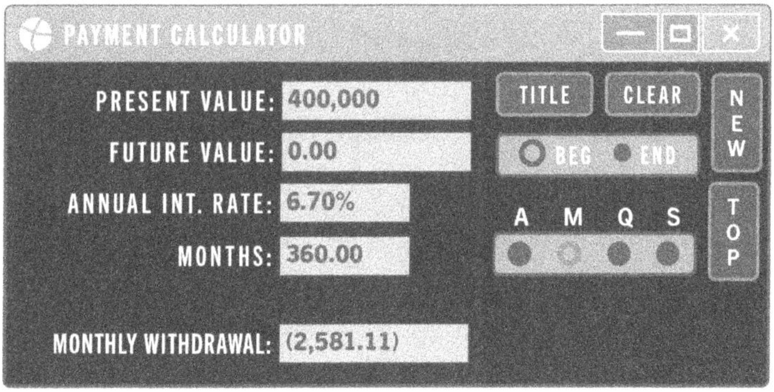

FIGURE 7.6

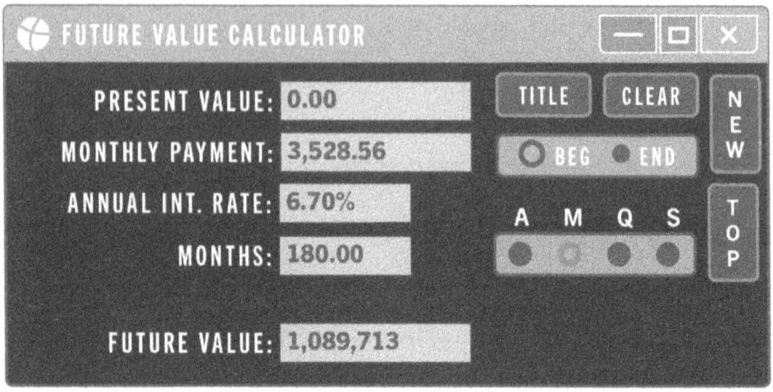

FIGURE 7.7

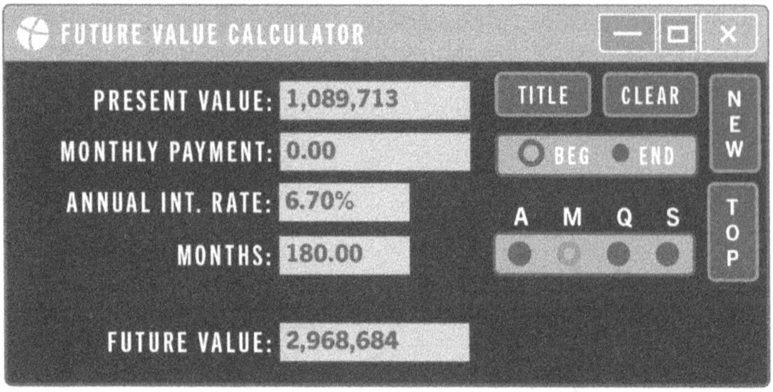

FIGURE 7.8

$947.45 DIFFERENCE FOR 180 MONTHS

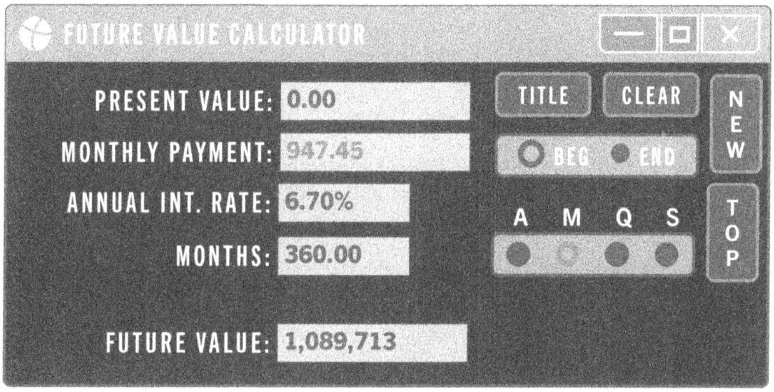

FUTURE VALUE CALCULATOR

PRESENT VALUE: 0.00
MONTHLY PAYMENT: 947.45
ANNUAL INT. RATE: 6.70%
MONTHS: 360.00

FUTURE VALUE: 1,089,713

TITLE   CLEAR
BEG   END
A   M   Q   S

NEW
TOP

FIGURE 7.9

PAYMENT CALCULATOR

LOAN BALANCE: (35,000.00)
FUTURE VALUE: 0.00
ANNUAL INT. RATE: 0.00%
MONTHS: 48.00

MONTHLY PAYMENT: 729.17

TITLE   CLEAR
BEG   END
A   M   Q   S

NEW
TOP

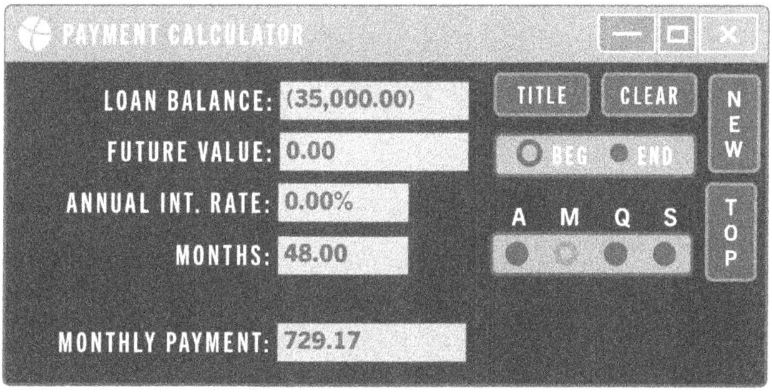

FIGURE 7.10

CALCULATING INTEREST BASED ON CAR PRICE LESS REBATE

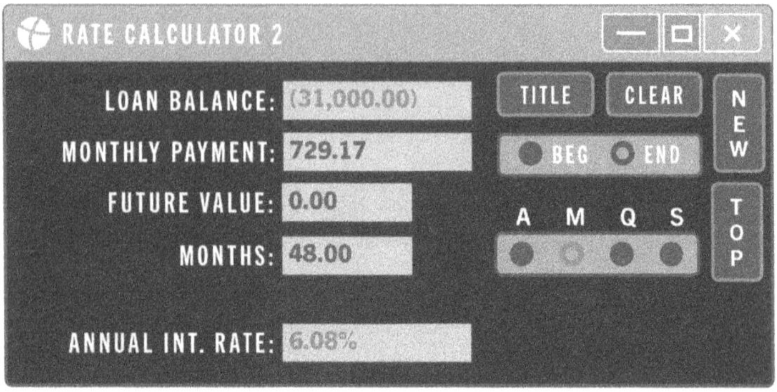

RATE CALCULATOR 2	— □ ✕
LOAN BALANCE:	(31,000.00)
MONTHLY PAYMENT:	729.17
FUTURE VALUE:	0.00
MONTHS:	48.00
ANNUAL INT. RATE:	6.08%

TITLE CLEAR NEW

BEG END

A M Q S TOP

FIGURE 7.11

AUTO EXAMPLE SET UP

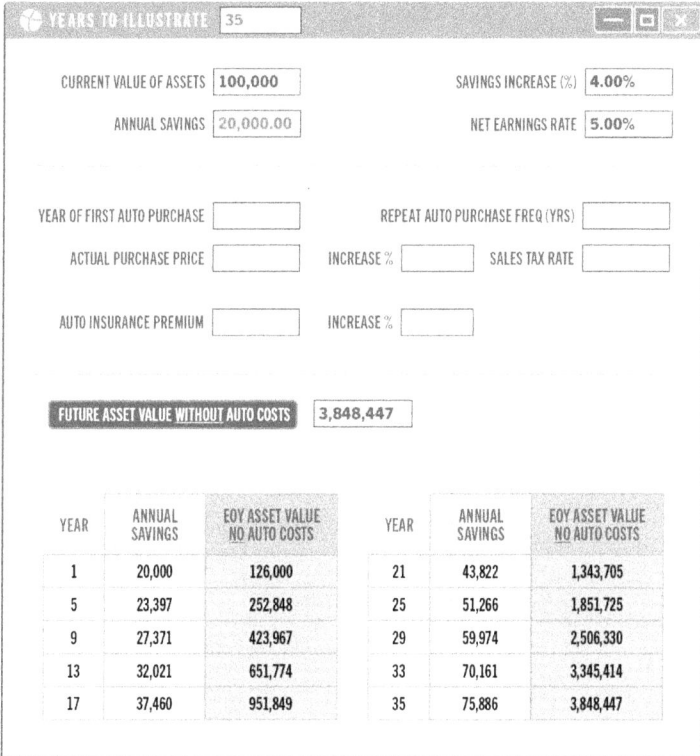

YEARS TO ILLUSTRATE	35		— ☐ ✕

CURRENT VALUE OF ASSETS	100,000	SAVINGS INCREASE (%)	4.00%
ANNUAL SAVINGS	20,000.00	NET EARNINGS RATE	5.00%

YEAR OF FIRST AUTO PURCHASE		REPEAT AUTO PURCHASE FREQ (YRS)	
ACTUAL PURCHASE PRICE		INCREASE %	SALES TAX RATE
AUTO INSURANCE PREMIUM		INCREASE %	

FUTURE ASSET VALUE WITHOUT AUTO COSTS | 3,848,447

YEAR	ANNUAL SAVINGS	EOY ASSET VALUE NO AUTO COSTS	YEAR	ANNUAL SAVINGS	EOY ASSET VALUE NO AUTO COSTS
1	20,000	126,000	21	43,822	1,343,705
5	23,397	252,848	25	51,266	1,851,725
9	27,371	423,967	29	59,974	2,506,330
13	32,021	651,774	33	70,161	3,345,414
17	37,460	951,849	35	75,886	3,848,447

FIGURE 7.12

CLIENT EXAMPLE: BUY CAR $35K EVERY 4 YEARS

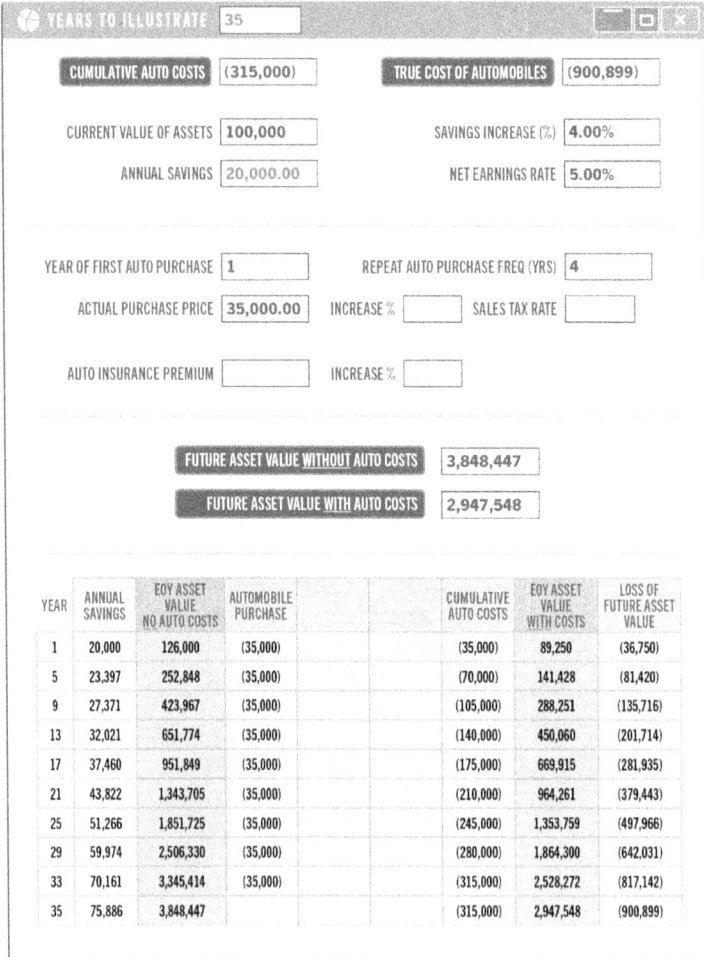

YEARS TO ILLUSTRATE 35

| CUMULATIVE AUTO COSTS | (315,000) | | TRUE COST OF AUTOMOBILES | (900,899) |

CURRENT VALUE OF ASSETS 100,000   SAVINGS INCREASE (%) 4.00%

ANNUAL SAVINGS 20,000.00   NET EARNINGS RATE 5.00%

YEAR OF FIRST AUTO PURCHASE 1   REPEAT AUTO PURCHASE FREQ (YRS) 4

ACTUAL PURCHASE PRICE 35,000.00   INCREASE %   SALES TAX RATE

AUTO INSURANCE PREMIUM   INCREASE %

FUTURE ASSET VALUE WITHOUT AUTO COSTS 3,848,447

FUTURE ASSET VALUE WITH AUTO COSTS 2,947,548

YEAR	ANNUAL SAVINGS	EOY ASSET VALUE NO AUTO COSTS	AUTOMOBILE PURCHASE		CUMULATIVE AUTO COSTS	EOY ASSET VALUE WITH COSTS	LOSS OF FUTURE ASSET VALUE
1	20,000	126,000	(35,000)		(35,000)	89,250	(36,750)
5	23,397	252,848	(35,000)		(70,000)	141,428	(81,420)
9	27,371	423,967	(35,000)		(105,000)	288,251	(135,716)
13	32,021	651,774	(35,000)		(140,000)	450,060	(201,714)
17	37,460	951,849	(35,000)		(175,000)	669,915	(281,935)
21	43,822	1,343,705	(35,000)		(210,000)	964,261	(379,443)
25	51,266	1,851,725	(35,000)		(245,000)	1,353,759	(497,966)
29	59,974	2,506,330	(35,000)		(280,000)	1,864,300	(642,031)
33	70,161	3,345,414	(35,000)		(315,000)	2,528,272	(817,142)
35	75,886	3,848,447			(315,000)	2,947,548	(900,899)

FIGURE 7.13

CLIENT EXAMPLE: BUY CAR $35K EVERY 4 YEARS, INCLUDING INFLATION, SALES TAX, AND INSURANCE

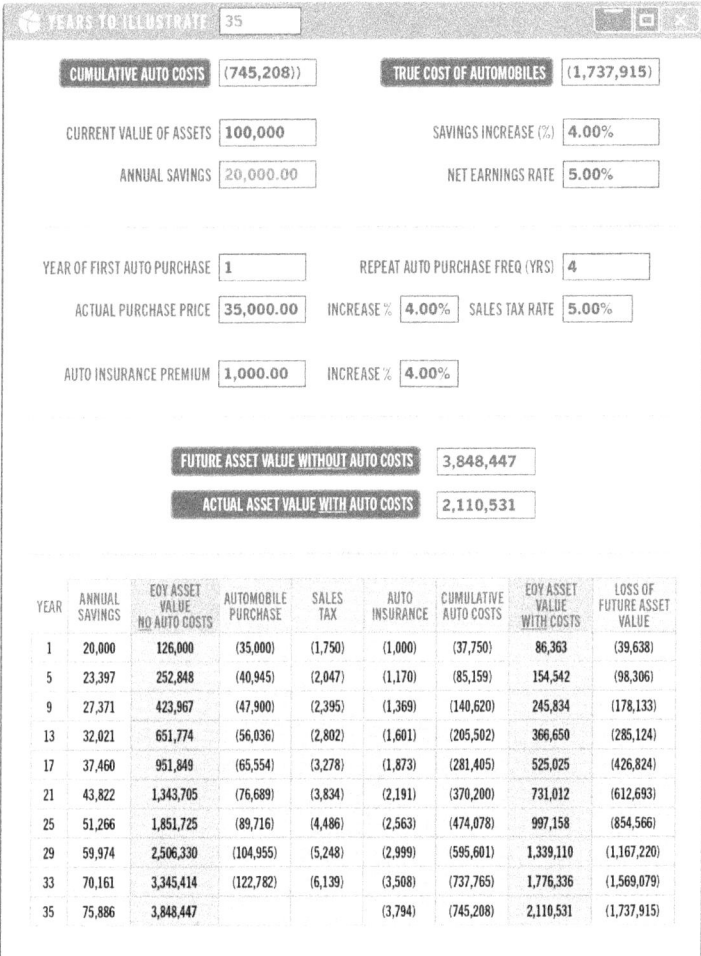

YEARS TO ILLUSTRATE	35				

CUMULATIVE AUTO COSTS	(745,208))		TRUE COST OF AUTOMOBILES	(1,737,915)

CURRENT VALUE OF ASSETS	100,000		SAVINGS INCREASE (%)	4.00%
ANNUAL SAVINGS	20,000.00		NET EARNINGS RATE	5.00%

YEAR OF FIRST AUTO PURCHASE	1		REPEAT AUTO PURCHASE FREQ (YRS)	4
ACTUAL PURCHASE PRICE	35,000.00	INCREASE %	4.00%	SALES TAX RATE	5.00%

AUTO INSURANCE PREMIUM	1,000.00	INCREASE %	4.00%

FUTURE ASSET VALUE WITHOUT AUTO COSTS	3,848,447
ACTUAL ASSET VALUE WITH AUTO COSTS	2,110,531

YEAR	ANNUAL SAVINGS	EOY ASSET VALUE NO AUTO COSTS	AUTOMOBILE PURCHASE	SALES TAX	AUTO INSURANCE	CUMULATIVE AUTO COSTS	EOY ASSET VALUE WITH COSTS	LOSS OF FUTURE ASSET VALUE
1	20,000	126,000	(35,000)	(1,750)	(1,000)	(37,750)	86,363	(39,638)
5	23,397	252,848	(40,945)	(2,047)	(1,170)	(85,159)	154,542	(98,306)
9	27,371	423,967	(47,900)	(2,395)	(1,369)	(140,620)	245,834	(178,133)
13	32,021	651,774	(56,036)	(2,802)	(1,601)	(205,502)	366,650	(285,124)
17	37,460	951,849	(65,554)	(3,278)	(1,873)	(281,405)	525,025	(426,824)
21	43,822	1,343,705	(76,689)	(3,834)	(2,191)	(370,200)	731,012	(612,693)
25	51,266	1,851,725	(89,716)	(4,486)	(2,563)	(474,078)	997,158	(854,566)
29	59,974	2,506,330	(104,955)	(5,248)	(2,999)	(595,601)	1,339,110	(1,167,220)
33	70,161	3,345,414	(122,782)	(6,139)	(3,508)	(737,765)	1,776,336	(1,569,079)
35	75,886	3,848,447			(3,794)	(745,208)	2,110,531	(1,737,915)

Financial Spotlight A: Financial Protection and Safety for You and Your Family

FIGURE A.1

PAYMENT CALCULATOR		− □ ×
LOAN BALANCE:	(500,000.00)	TITLE CLEAR N E W
FUTURE VALUE:	0.00	○ BEG ● END
ANNUAL INT. RATE:	5.50%	A M Q S T O P
YEARS:	10.00	● ○ ● ●
ANNUAL PAYMENT:	66,333.88	

FIGURE A.2

CASH FLOW		− □ ×
YEARS TO ILLUSTRATE:	10	CASH FLOW 1 44,748
CURRENT AGE:	0	INCRASE 0.00%
PRESENT VALUE:	0	
FIXED EARN RATE	4.00%	TAX BRACKET 49.8%

YEAR	BEG. OF YEAR ACCOUNT VALUE	ANNUAL BOY CASH FLOW 1	EARNINGS RATE	INTEREST EARNINGS	TAX PAYMENT	END OF YEAR ACCOUNT VALUE
1		44,748	4.00%	1,790	(891)	45,647
2	45,647	44,748	4.00%	3,616	(1,801)	92,210
3	92,210	44,748	4.00%	5,478	(2,728)	139,708
4	139,708	44,748	4.00%	7,378	(3,674)	188,160
5	188,160	44,748	4.00%	9,316	(4,640)	237,584
6	237,584	44,748	4.00%	11,293	(5,624)	288,002
7	288,002	44,748	4.00%	13,310	(6,628)	339,431
8	339,431	44,748	4.00%	15,367	(7,653)	391,894
9	391,894	44,748	4.00%	17,466	(8,698)	445,409
10	445,409	44,748	4.00%	19,606	(9,764)	500,000

Financial Spotlight C: RRSPs, TFSAs, and 401(k)s—Holy Grails of Financial Planning?

FIGURE C.1

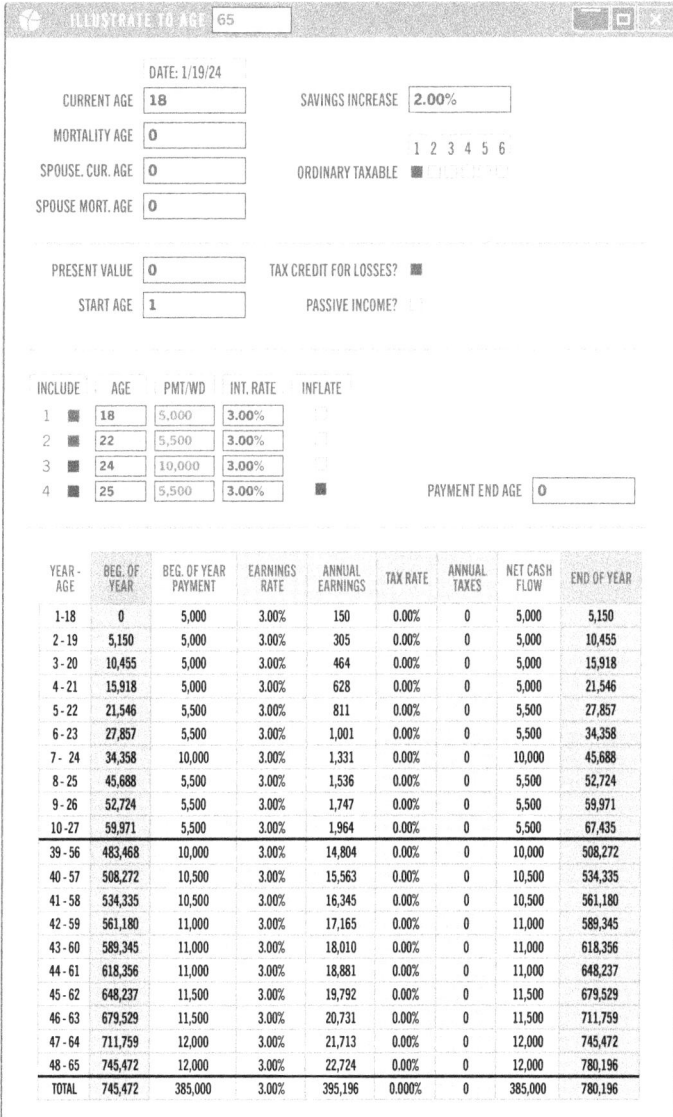

		DATE: 1/19/24					
CURRENT AGE	18		SAVINGS INCREASE	2.00%			
MORTALITY AGE	0			1 2 3 4 5 6			
SPOUSE. CUR. AGE	0		ORDINARY TAXABLE				
SPOUSE MORT. AGE	0						
PRESENT VALUE	0		TAX CREDIT FOR LOSSES?				
START AGE	1		PASSIVE INCOME?				

INCLUDE	AGE	PMT/WD	INT. RATE	INFLATE			
1	18	5,000	3.00%				
2	22	5,500	3.00%				
3	24	10,000	3.00%				
4	25	5,500	3.00%		PAYMENT END AGE	0	

YEAR - AGE	BEG. OF YEAR	BEG. OF YEAR PAYMENT	EARNINGS RATE	ANNUAL EARNINGS	TAX RATE	ANNUAL TAXES	NET CASH FLOW	END OF YEAR
1-18	0	5,000	3.00%	150	0.00%	0	5,000	5,150
2 - 19	5,150	5,000	3.00%	305	0.00%	0	5,000	10,455
3 - 20	10,455	5,000	3.00%	464	0.00%	0	5,000	15,918
4 - 21	15,918	5,000	3.00%	628	0.00%	0	5,000	21,546
5 - 22	21,546	5,500	3.00%	811	0.00%	0	5,500	27,857
6 - 23	27,857	5,500	3.00%	1,001	0.00%	0	5,500	34,358
7 - 24	34,358	10,000	3.00%	1,331	0.00%	0	10,000	45,688
8 - 25	45,688	5,500	3.00%	1,536	0.00%	0	5,500	52,724
9 - 26	52,724	5,500	3.00%	1,747	0.00%	0	5,500	59,971
10 - 27	59,971	5,500	3.00%	1,964	0.00%	0	5,500	67,435
39 - 56	483,468	10,000	3.00%	14,804	0.00%	0	10,000	508,272
40 - 57	508,272	10,500	3.00%	15,563	0.00%	0	10,500	534,335
41 - 58	534,335	10,500	3.00%	16,345	0.00%	0	10,500	561,180
42 - 59	561,180	11,000	3.00%	17,165	0.00%	0	11,000	589,345
43 - 60	589,345	11,000	3.00%	18,010	0.00%	0	11,000	618,356
44 - 61	618,356	11,000	3.00%	18,881	0.00%	0	11,000	648,237
45 - 62	648,237	11,500	3.00%	19,792	0.00%	0	11,500	679,529
46 - 63	679,529	11,500	3.00%	20,731	0.00%	0	11,500	711,759
47 - 64	711,759	12,000	3.00%	21,713	0.00%	0	12,000	745,472
48 - 65	745,472	12,000	3.00%	22,724	0.00%	0	12,000	780,196
TOTAL	745,472	385,000	3.00%	395,196	0.000%	0	385,000	780,196

ILLUSTRATE TO AGE 65

FIGURE C.2

RRSP BUCKETS 3K

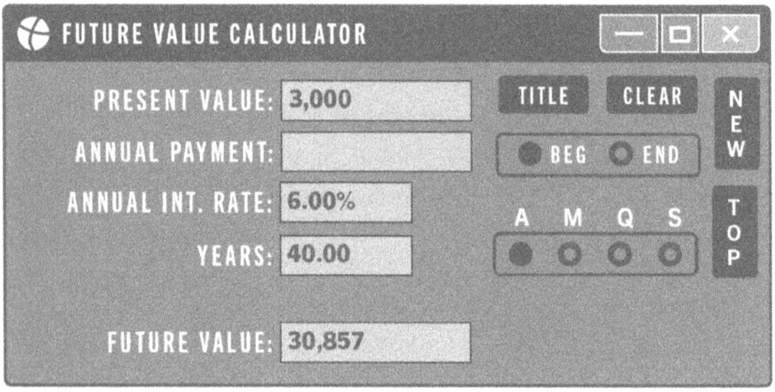

FUTURE VALUE CALCULATOR

PRESENT VALUE: 3,000
ANNUAL PAYMENT:
ANNUAL INT. RATE: 6.00%
YEARS: 40.00

FUTURE VALUE: 30,857

TITLE   CLEAR   NEW
BEG END
A M Q S   TOP

FIGURE C.3

RRSP BUCKETS 7K

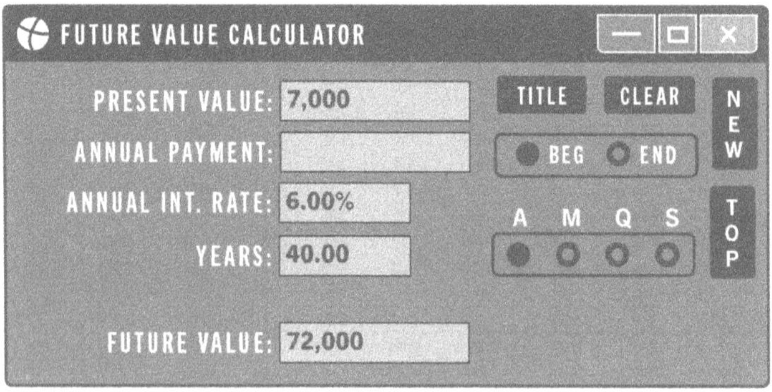

FUTURE VALUE CALCULATOR

PRESENT VALUE: 7,000
ANNUAL PAYMENT:
ANNUAL INT. RATE: 6.00%
YEARS: 40.00

FUTURE VALUE: 72,000

TITLE   CLEAR   NEW
BEG END
A M Q S   TOP

FIGURE C.4

QUALIFIED PLAN

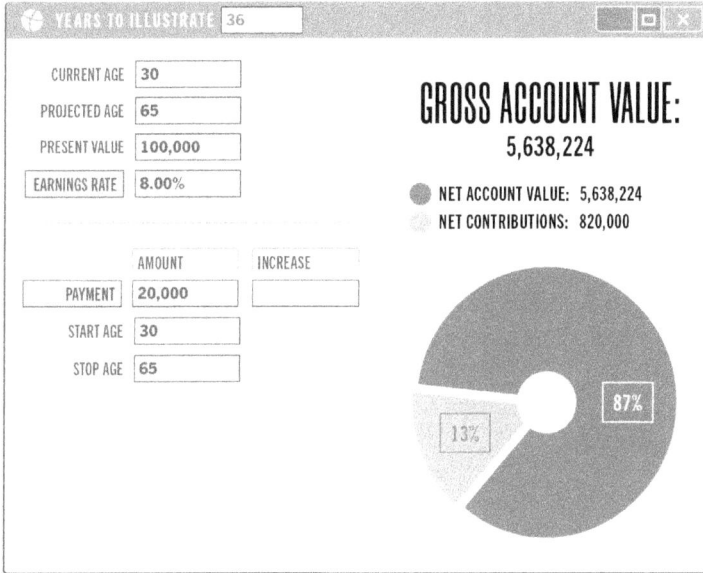

| | YEARS TO ILLUSTRATE | 36 | | | □ ■ × |

CURRENT AGE	30
PROJECTED AGE	65
PRESENT VALUE	100,000
EARNINGS RATE	8.00%

GROSS ACCOUNT VALUE:
5,638,224

● NET ACCOUNT VALUE: 5,638,224
◐ NET CONTRIBUTIONS: 820,000

	AMOUNT	INCREASE
PAYMENT	20,000	
START AGE	30	
STOP AGE	65	

87%

13%

FIGURE C.5

QUALIFIED PLAN

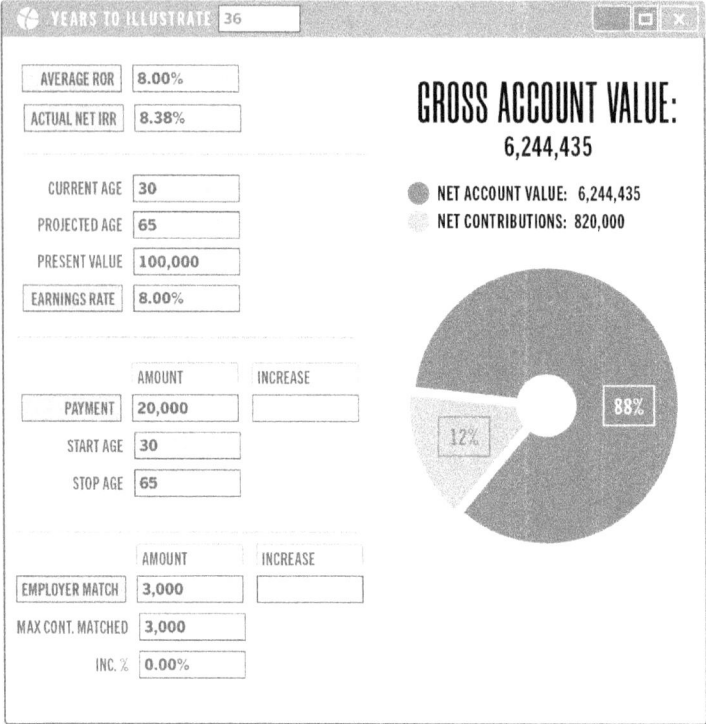

YEARS TO ILLUSTRATE 36

AVERAGE ROR 8.00%
ACTUAL NET IRR 8.38%

CURRENT AGE 30
PROJECTED AGE 65
PRESENT VALUE 100,000
EARNINGS RATE 8.00%

GROSS ACCOUNT VALUE:
6,244,435

NET ACCOUNT VALUE: 6,244,435
NET CONTRIBUTIONS: 820,000

	AMOUNT	INCREASE
PAYMENT	20,000	
START AGE	30	
STOP AGE	65	

	AMOUNT	INCREASE
EMPLOYER MATCH	3,000	
MAX CONT. MATCHED	3,000	
INC. %	0.00%	

88% 12%

FIGURE C.6

REGISTERED RETIRED SAVINGS PLAN REFLECTING THE IMPACT OF THE TAX DEFERRAL

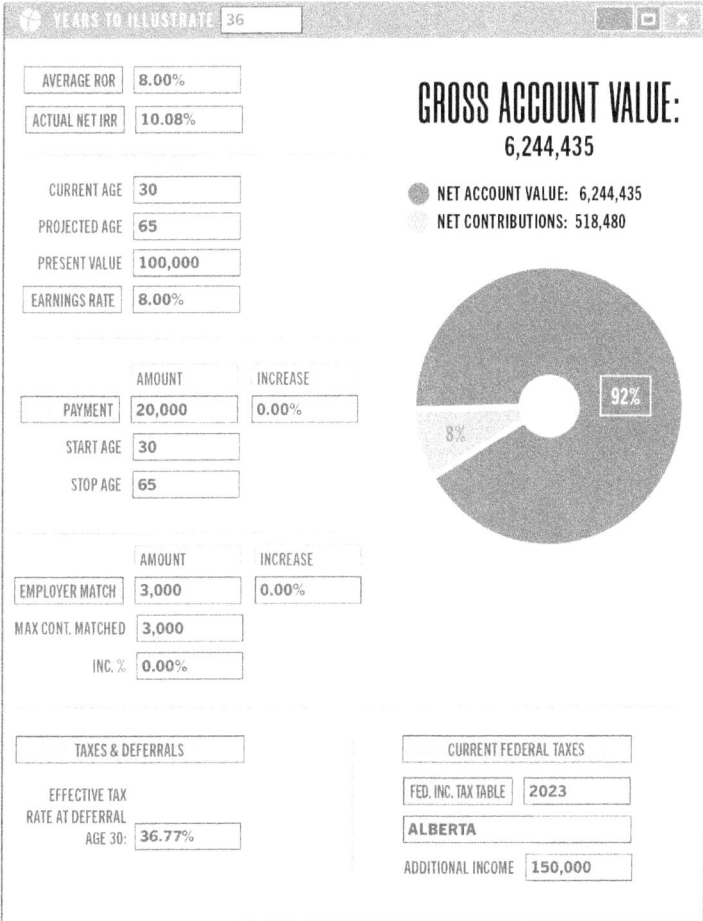

YEARS TO ILLUSTRATE 36

| AVERAGE ROR | 8.00% |
| ACTUAL NET IRR | 10.08% |

CURRENT AGE	30
PROJECTED AGE	65
PRESENT VALUE	100,000
EARNINGS RATE	8.00%

	AMOUNT	INCREASE
PAYMENT	20,000	0.00%
START AGE	30	
STOP AGE	65	

	AMOUNT	INCREASE
EMPLOYER MATCH	3,000	0.00%
MAX CONT. MATCHED	3,000	
INC. %	0.00%	

| TAXES & DEFERRALS |
| EFFECTIVE TAX RATE AT DEFERRAL AGE 30: | 36.77% |

GROSS ACCOUNT VALUE:
6,244,435

NET ACCOUNT VALUE: 6,244,435
NET CONTRIBUTIONS: 518,480

92%

8%

| CURRENT FEDERAL TAXES |
| FED. INC. TAX TABLE | 2023 |
| ALBERTA |
| ADDITIONAL INCOME | 150,000 |

FIGURE C.7

REGISTERED RETIRED SAVINGS PLAN REFLECTING THE IMPACT OF A 2% MANAGEMENT FEE

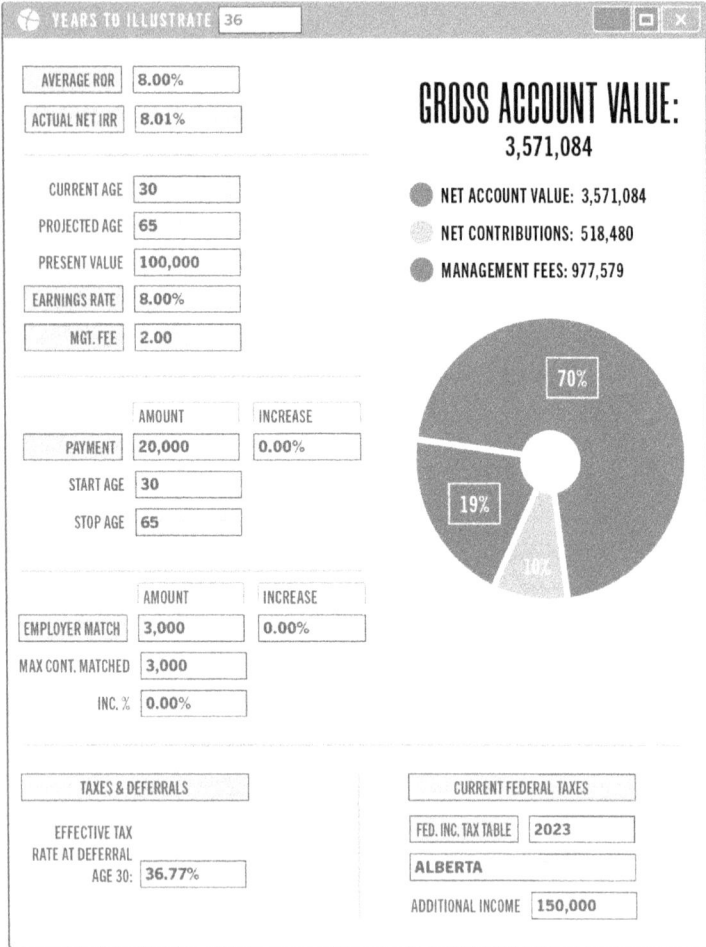

YEARS TO ILLUSTRATE	36	

AVERAGE ROR	8.00%
ACTUAL NET IRR	8.01%

CURRENT AGE	30
PROJECTED AGE	65
PRESENT VALUE	100,000
EARNINGS RATE	8.00%
MGT. FEE	2.00

GROSS ACCOUNT VALUE:
3,571,084

- NET ACCOUNT VALUE: 3,571,084
- NET CONTRIBUTIONS: 518,480
- MANAGEMENT FEES: 977,579

	AMOUNT	INCREASE
PAYMENT	20,000	0.00%
START AGE	30	
STOP AGE	65	

70%

19%

10%

	AMOUNT	INCREASE
EMPLOYER MATCH	3,000	0.00%
MAX CONT. MATCHED	3,000	
INC. %	0.00%	

TAXES & DEFERRALS
EFFECTIVE TAX RATE AT DEFERRAL AGE 30: 36.77%

CURRENT FEDERAL TAXES
FED. INC. TAX TABLE 2023
ALBERTA
ADDITIONAL INCOME 150,000

FIGURE C.8

REGISTERED RETIRED SAVINGS PLAN REFLECTING LOWER EARNINGS RATE TO 6%

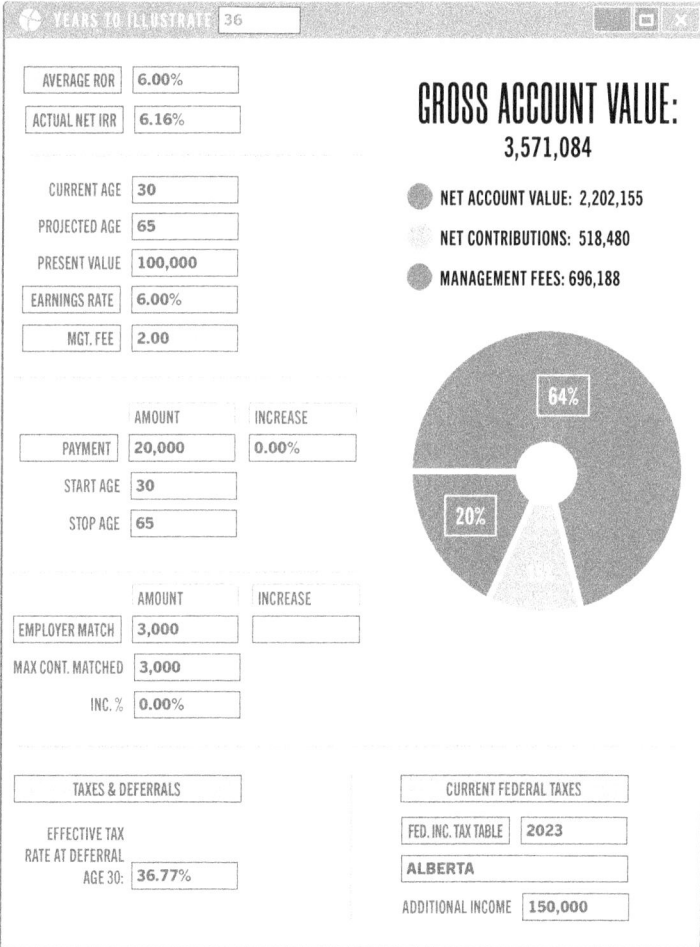

| YEARS TO ILLUSTRATE | 36 | | | ▭ ❐ ✕ |

AVERAGE ROR	6.00%
ACTUAL NET IRR	6.16%

CURRENT AGE	30
PROJECTED AGE	65
PRESENT VALUE	100,000
EARNINGS RATE	6.00%
MGT. FEE	2.00

GROSS ACCOUNT VALUE:
3,571,084

● NET ACCOUNT VALUE: 2,202,155

◐ NET CONTRIBUTIONS: 518,480

● MANAGEMENT FEES: 696,188

	AMOUNT	INCREASE
PAYMENT	20,000	0.00%
START AGE	30	
STOP AGE	65	

64%

20%

	AMOUNT	INCREASE
EMPLOYER MATCH	3,000	
MAX CONT. MATCHED	3,000	
INC. %	0.00%	

TAXES & DEFERRALS

EFFECTIVE TAX RATE AT DEFERRAL AGE 30:	36.77%

CURRENT FEDERAL TAXES

FED. INC. TAX TABLE	2023
ALBERTA	
ADDITIONAL INCOME	150,000

FIGURE C.10

QUALIFIED 7

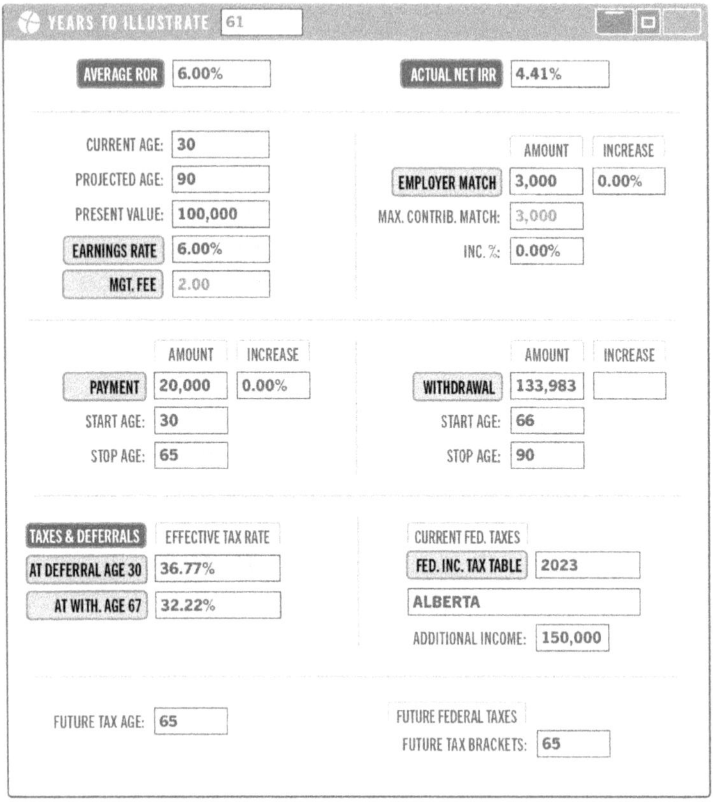

YEARS TO ILLUSTRATE	61		

| AVERAGE ROR | 6.00% | | ACTUAL NET IRR | 4.41% |

			AMOUNT	INCREASE
CURRENT AGE:	30	EMPLOYER MATCH	3,000	0.00%
PROJECTED AGE:	90	MAX. CONTRIB. MATCH:	3,000	
PRESENT VALUE:	100,000	INC. %:	0.00%	
EARNINGS RATE	6.00%			
MGT. FEE	2.00			

	AMOUNT	INCREASE		AMOUNT	INCREASE
PAYMENT	20,000	0.00%	WITHDRAWAL	133,983	
START AGE:	30		START AGE:	66	
STOP AGE:	65		STOP AGE:	90	

TAXES & DEFERRALS	EFFECTIVE TAX RATE		CURRENT FED. TAXES	
AT DEFERRAL AGE 30	36.77%		FED. INC. TAX TABLE	2023
AT WITH. AGE 67	32.22%		ALBERTA	
			ADDITIONAL INCOME:	150,000

FUTURE TAX AGE:	65		FUTURE FEDERAL TAXES	
			FUTURE TAX BRACKETS:	65

FIGURE C.10a

AGE	ANNUAL PAYMENT	TAX DEFERRAL	NET ANNUAL PAYMENT	EMPLOYER MATCH	ANNUAL WITHDRAW.	TAX PAYMENT	NET WITHDRAW.	EARNINGS RATES	ACCT. MGMT. FEES	END OF YEAR ACCT. VALUE
66	0		0	0	(133,983)	(43,164)	(90,820)	6.00%	(43,8445)	2,148,417
67	0		0	0	(133,983)	(43,164)	(90,820)	6.00%	(42,706)	2,092,594
68	0		0	0	(133,983)	(43,164)	(90,820)	6.00%	(41,523)	2,034,604
69	0		0	0	(133,983)	(43,164)	(90,820)	6.00%	(40,296)	1,974,365
70	0		0	0	(133,983)	(43,164)	(90,820)	6.00%	(39,016)	1,911,788
71	0		0	0	(133,983)	(43,164)	(90,820)	6.00%	(37,689)	1,846,783
72	0		0	0	(133,983)	(43,164)	(90,820)	6.00%	(36,311)	1,779,257
73	0		0	0	(133,983)	(43,164)	(90,820)	6.00%	(34,880)	1,709,110
74	0		0	0	(133,983)	(43,164)	(90,820)	6.00%	(33,393)	1,636,241
75	0		0	0	(133,983)	(43,164)	(90,820)	6.00%	(31,848)	1,560,545
76	0		0	0	(133,983)	(43,164)	(90,820)	6.00%	(30,423)	1,481,813
77	0		0	0	(133,983)	(43,164)	(90,820)	6.00%	(28,576)	1,400,229
78	0		0	0	(133,983)	(43,164)	(90,820)	6.00%	(26,844)	1,315,376
79	0		0	0	(133,983)	(43,164)	(90,820)	6.00%	(25,046)	1,227,230
80	0		0	0	(133,983)	(43,164)	(90,820)	6.00%	(23,177)	1,135,665
81	0		0	0	(133,983)	(43,164)	(90,820)	6.00%	(21,236)	1,040,547
82	0		0	0	(133,983)	(43,164)	(90,820)	6.00%	(19,219)	941,738
83	0		0	0	(133,983)	(43,164)	(90,820)	6.00%	(17,124)	839,095
84	0		0	0	(133,983)	(43,164)	(90,820)	6.00%	(14,948)	732,470
85	0		0	0	(133,983)	(43,164)	(90,820)	6.00%	(12,688)	621,708
86	0		0	0	(133,983)	(43,164)	(90,820)	6.00%	(10,340)	506,648
87	0		0	0	(133,983)	(43,164)	(90,820)	6.00%	(7,900)	387,124
88	0		0	0	(133,983)	(43,164)	(90,820)	6.00%	(5,367)	262,963
89	0		0	0	(133,983)	(43,164)	(90,820)	6.00%	(2,734)	133,983
90	0		0	0	(133,983)	(43,164)	(90,820)	6.00%	(0)	0
TOTAL	720,000	260,544	459,456	108,000	(3,349,586)	(1,079,089)	(2,270,497)	6.00%	(1,323,135)	0

Financial $potlight D: Buy Term and "Spend" The Difference

FIGURE D.1

DIVERSIFICATION ASSET A						

ILLUSTRATION PERIOD:	20		ACTUAL YIELD ON ASSETS	2.35%
PRESENT VALUE:	750,000		ACTUAL YIELD TO HEIRS	2.35%
ANNUAL SAVINGS	28,280			FEDERAL	STATE
FIXED RATE	5.00%		INCOME TAXES	53.00	
MGT. FEE			TERM INSURANCE DB		

BEG ■   END ☐   TAX CREDIT FOR LOSSES? ■   NET? ■

	SAVINGS AND EARNINGS				EXPENSES	RESULTS EOY	
YEAR	ASSET VALUE BEG. OF THE YEAR	ANNUAL SAVINGS BOY	ANNUAL EARNINGS RATE	ANNUAL INTEREST EARNED	ANNUAL INCOME TAXES	TOTAL VALUE OF ASSETS	TOTAL PROCEEDS TO HEIRS
1	750,000	28,280	5.00%	38,914	(20,624)	796,570	796,570
2	796,570	28,280	5.00%	41,242	(21,859)	844,234	844,234
3	844,234	28,280	5.00%	43,626	(23,122)	893,018	893,018
4	893,018	28,280	5.00%	46,065	(24,414)	942,948	942,948
5	942,948	28,280	5.00%	48,561	(25,738)	994,052	994,052
6	994,052	28,280	5.00%	51,117	(27,092)	1,046,357	1,046,357
7	1,046,357	28,280	5.00%	53,732	(28,478)	1,099,891	1,099,891
8	1,099,891	28,280	5.00%	56,409	(29,897)	1,154,689	1,154,689
9	1,154,683	28,280	5.00%	59,148	(31,349)	1,210,762	1,210,762
10	1,210,762	28,280	5.00%	61,952	(32,835)	1,268,160	1,268,160
11	1,268,160	28,280	5.00%	64,822	(34,356)	1,326,906	1,326,906
12	1,326,906	28,280	5.00%	67,759	(35,912)	1,387,033	1,387,033
13	1,387,033	28,280	5.00%	70,766	(37,506)	1,448,573	1,448,573
14	1,448,573	28,280	5.00%	73,843	(39,137)	1,511,559	1,511,559
15	1,511,559	28,280	5.00%	76,992	(40,806)	1,576,025	1,576,025
16	1,576,025	28,280	5.00%	80,215	(42,514)	1,642,006	1,642,006
17	1,642,006	28,280	5.00%	83,514	(44,263)	1,709,538	1,709,538
18	1,709,538	28,280	5.00%	86,891	(46,052)	1,778,657	1,778,657
19	1,778,657	28,280	5.00%	90,347	(47,884)	1,849,400	1,849,400
20	1,849,400	28,280	5.00%	93,884	(49,759)	1,921,805	1,921,805
TOTAL		565,600	5.00%	1,289,799	(683,593)	1,921,805	1,921,805

FIGURE D.2

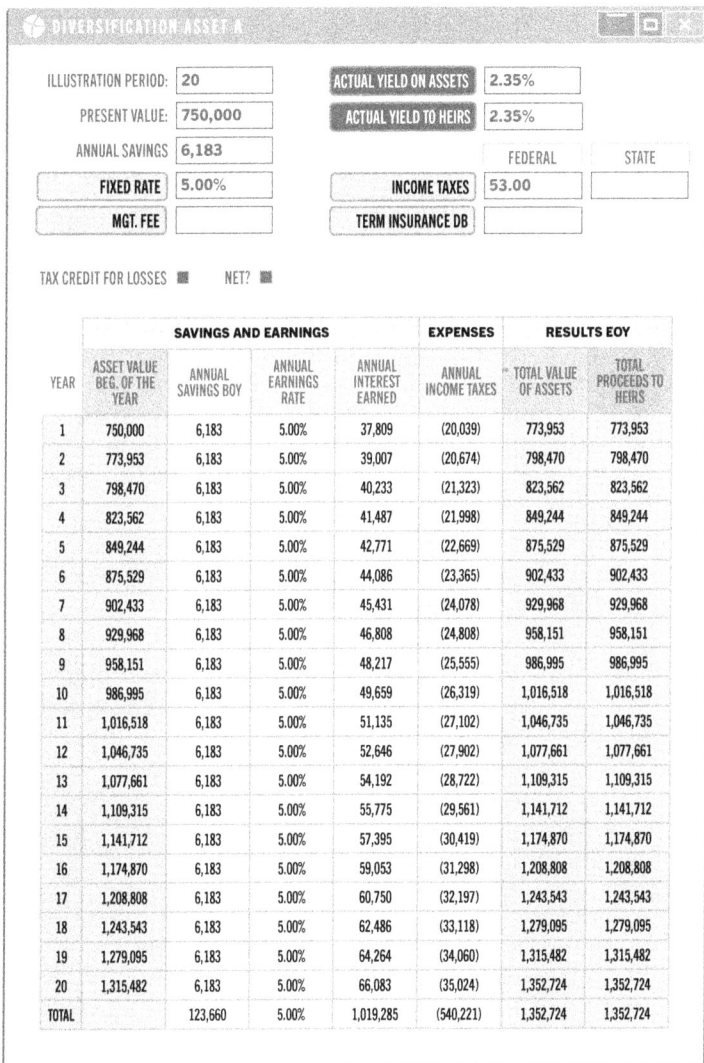

	DIVERSIFICATION ASSET A						

ILLUSTRATION PERIOD:	20		ACTUAL YIELD ON ASSETS	2.35%	
PRESENT VALUE:	750,000		ACTUAL YIELD TO HEIRS	2.35%	
ANNUAL SAVINGS	6,183			FEDERAL	STATE
FIXED RATE	5.00%		INCOME TAXES	53.00	
MGT. FEE			TERM INSURANCE DB		

TAX CREDIT FOR LOSSES ▨   NET? ▨

	SAVINGS AND EARNINGS			EXPENSES	RESULTS EOY	
YEAR	ASSET VALUE BEG. OF THE YEAR	ANNUAL SAVINGS BOY	ANNUAL EARNINGS RATE	ANNUAL INTEREST EARNED	ANNUAL INCOME TAXES	TOTAL VALUE OF ASSETS	TOTAL PROCEEDS TO HEIRS
1	750,000	6,183	5.00%	37,809	(20,039)	773,953	773,953
2	773,953	6,183	5.00%	39,007	(20,674)	798,470	798,470
3	798,470	6,183	5.00%	40,233	(21,323)	823,562	823,562
4	823,562	6,183	5.00%	41,487	(21,998)	849,244	849,244
5	849,244	6,183	5.00%	42,771	(22,669)	875,529	875,529
6	875,529	6,183	5.00%	44,086	(23,365)	902,433	902,433
7	902,433	6,183	5.00%	45,431	(24,078)	929,968	929,968
8	929,968	6,183	5.00%	46,808	(24,808)	958,151	958,151
9	958,151	6,183	5.00%	48,217	(25,555)	986,995	986,995
10	986,995	6,183	5.00%	49,659	(26,319)	1,016,518	1,016,518
11	1,016,518	6,183	5.00%	51,135	(27,102)	1,046,735	1,046,735
12	1,046,735	6,183	5.00%	52,646	(27,902)	1,077,661	1,077,661
13	1,077,661	6,183	5.00%	54,192	(28,722)	1,109,315	1,109,315
14	1,109,315	6,183	5.00%	55,775	(29,561)	1,141,712	1,141,712
15	1,141,712	6,183	5.00%	57,395	(30,419)	1,174,870	1,174,870
16	1,174,870	6,183	5.00%	59,053	(31,298)	1,208,808	1,208,808
17	1,208,808	6,183	5.00%	60,750	(32,197)	1,243,543	1,243,543
18	1,243,543	6,183	5.00%	62,486	(33,118)	1,279,095	1,279,095
19	1,279,095	6,183	5.00%	64,264	(34,060)	1,315,482	1,315,482
20	1,315,482	6,183	5.00%	66,083	(35,024)	1,352,724	1,352,724
TOTAL		123,660	5.00%	1,019,285	(540,221)	1,352,724	1,352,724

FIGURE D.3

BILL'S WHOLE LIFE POLICY ILLUSTRATION TO YEAR 20

DIVIDEND OPTION: PAID UP ADDITIONS

		GUARANTEED VALUES			CURRENT DIVIDEND SCALE NON-GUARANTEED VALUES		
AGE	YEAR	REQUIRED ANNUAL PREMIUM ($)	CASH VALUE ($)	DEATH BENEFIT ($)	ANNUAL DIVIDEND ($)	TOTAL CASH VALUE ($)	TOTAL DEATH BENEFIT ($)
46	1	23,816.95	0	1,000,000	1,043	1,022	1,003,328
47	2	23,816.95	0	1,000,000	1,377	2,404	1,007,584
48	3	23,816.95	0	1,000,000	1,943	4,384	1,013,407
49	4	23,816.95	0	1,000,000	2,678	7,142	1,021,193
50	5	23,816.95	0	1,000,000	3,531	10,836	1,031,138
51	6	23,816.95	4,500	1,000,000	4,470	20,059	1,043,341
52	7	23,816.95	12,000	1,000,000	5,481	33,407	1,057,857
53	8	23,816.95	20,250	1,000,000	6,549	48,769	1,074,658
54	9	23,816.95	31,500	1,000,000	7,671	68,433	1,093,739
55	10	23,816.95	44,250	1,000,000	8,833	90,964	1,115,060
56	11	23,816.95	59,250	1,000,000	9,989	117,250	1,138,424
57	12	23,816.95	77,250	1,000,000	11,177	148,003	1,163,780
58	13	23,816.95	96,750	1,000,000	12,349	181,734	1,190,975
59	14	23,816.95	118,500	1,000,000	14,030	219,716	1,220,996
60	15	23,816.95	143,250	1,000,000	16,130	263,368	1,254,487
61	16	23,816.95	186,000	1,000,000	17,989	327,310	1,290,761
62	17	23,816.95	233,250	1,000,000	19,826	398,060	1,329,620
63	18	23,816.95	286,500	1,000,000	21,697	477,187	1,370,987
64	19	23,816.95	345,000	1,000,000	23,593	564,374	1,414,695
65	20	23,816.95	409,500	1,000,000	25,596	659,763	1,460,890

FIGURE D.4

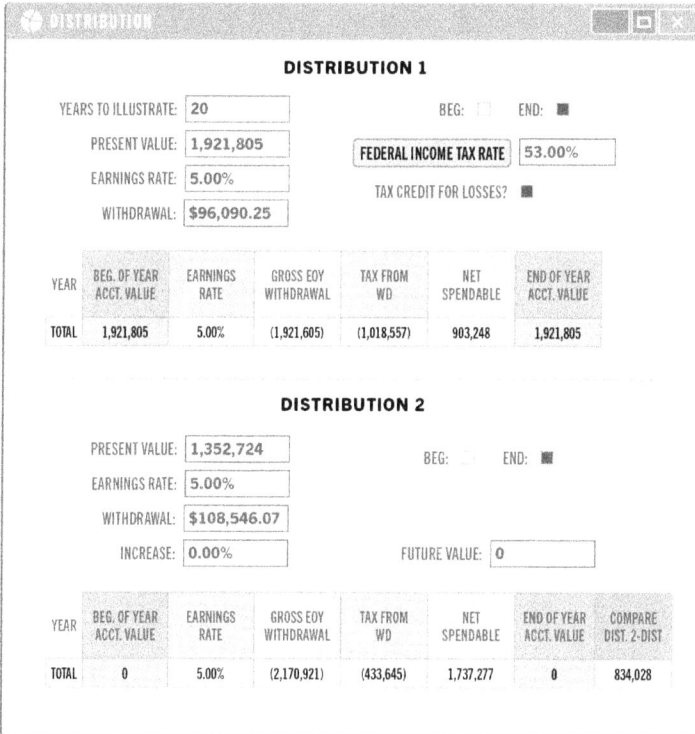

DISTRIBUTION

DISTRIBUTION 1

YEARS TO ILLUSTRATE: 20   BEG: ☐   END: ◼

PRESENT VALUE: 1,921,805   **FEDERAL INCOME TAX RATE** 53.00%

EARNINGS RATE: 5.00%   TAX CREDIT FOR LOSSES? ◼

WITHDRAWAL: $96,090.25

YEAR	BEG. OF YEAR ACCT. VALUE	EARNINGS RATE	GROSS EOY WITHDRAWAL	TAX FROM WD	NET SPENDABLE	END OF YEAR ACCT. VALUE
TOTAL	1,921,805	5.00%	(1,921,605)	(1,018,557)	903,248	1,921,805

DISTRIBUTION 2

PRESENT VALUE: 1,352,724   BEG: ☐   END: ◼

EARNINGS RATE: 5.00%

WITHDRAWAL: $108,546.07

INCREASE: 0.00%   FUTURE VALUE: 0

YEAR	BEG. OF YEAR ACCT. VALUE	EARNINGS RATE	GROSS EOY WITHDRAWAL	TAX FROM WD	NET SPENDABLE	END OF YEAR ACCT. VALUE	COMPARE DIST. 2-DIST
TOTAL	0	5.00%	(2,170,921)	(433,645)	1,737,277	0	834,028

FIGURE D.5

CASH VALUE AT 85

DIVIDEND OPTION: PAID UP ADDITIONS

AGE	YEAR	GUARANTEED VALUES			CURRENT DIVIDEND SCALE NON-GUARANTEED VALUES		
		REQUIRED ANNUAL PREMIUM ($)	CASH VALUE ($)	DEATH BENEFIT ($)	ANNUAL DIVIDEND ($)	TOTAL CASH VALUE ($)	TOTAL DEATH BENEFIT ($)
73	28	0.00	511,500	750,000	39,079	1,100,891	1,640,319
74	29	0.00	522,000	750,000	40,745	1,165,567	1,699,214
75	30	0.00	531,750	750,000	42,508	1,231,214	1,759,327
76	31	0.00	541,500	750,000	44,213	1,300,441	1,820,439
77	32	0.00	551,250	750,000	45,976	1,372,375	1,882,586
78	33	0.00	560,250	750,000	47,763	1,446,304	1,945,755
79	34	0.00	570,000	750,000	49,535	1,524,927	2,009,798
80	35	0.00	578,250	750,000	51,407	1,604,972	2,074,803
81	36	0.00	587,250	750,000	53,461	1,688,886	2,140,954
82	37	0.00	595,500	750,000	55,685	1,778,135	2,208,243
83	38	0.00	603,750	750,000	58,642	1,861,353	2,278,072
84	39	0.00	611,250	750,000	61,294	1,948,786	2,349,924
85	40	0.00	618,750	750,000	64,185	2,038,387	2,424,100

FIGURE D.6

BILL'S WHOLE LIFE POLICY ILLUSTRATION TO YEAR 100

			DIVIDEND OPTION: PAID UP ADDITIONS					
		GUARANTEED VALUES				**CURRENT DIVIDEND SCALE NON-GUARANTEED VALUES**		
AGE	YEAR	REQUIRED ANNUAL PREMIUM ($)	CASH VALUE ($)	DEATH BENEFIT ($)	WITH-DRAWAL	ANNUAL DIVIDEND ($)	TOTAL CASH VALUE ($)	TOTAL DEATH BENEFIT ($)
86	41	0.00	625,500	750,000	$96,090	67,259	2,034,721	2,390,537
87	42	0.00	633,00	750,000	$96,090	68,108	2,032,285	2,358,374
88	43	0.00	639,000	750,000	$96,090	69,080	2,027,359	2,327,681
89	44	0.00	645,750	750,000	$96,090	70,084	2,022,302	2,298,427
90	45	0.00	651,750	750,000	$96,090	71,153	2,015,752	2,270,626
91	46	0.00	657,750	750,000	$96,090	72,043	2,009,870	2,244,055
92	47	0.00	663,750	750,000	$96,090	71,765	2,000,509	2,217,354
93	48	0.00	669,750	750,000	$96,090	71,341	1,990,565	2,190,365
94	49	0.00	675,750	750,000	$96,090	71,079	1,978,755	2,163,238
95	50	0.00	681,750	750,000	$96,090	70,782	1,966,514	2,135,937
96	51	0.00	689,250	750,000	$96,090	70,652	1,954,120	2,108,614
97	52	0.00	697,500	750,000	$96,090	70,667	1,941,023	2,081,395
98	53	0.00	708,750	750,000	$96,090	69,242	1,942,734	2,053,045
99	54	0.00	724,500	750,000	$96,090	67,854	1,955,005	2,023,815
100	55	0.00	750,000	750,000	$96,090	65,064	1,992,789	1,992,789

FIGURE D.7

SEQUENCE 1

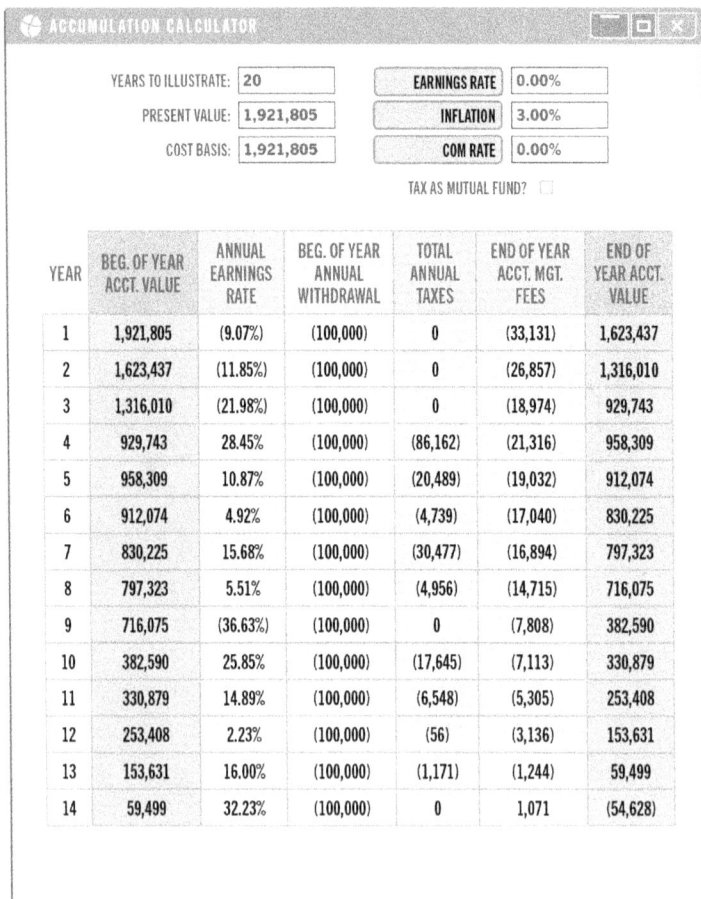

				ACCUMULATION CALCULATOR		
YEARS TO ILLUSTRATE: 20				EARNINGS RATE 0.00%		
PRESENT VALUE: 1,921,805				INFLATION 3.00%		
COST BASIS: 1,921,805				COM RATE 0.00%		
				TAX AS MUTUAL FUND? ☐		

YEAR	BEG. OF YEAR ACCT. VALUE	ANNUAL EARNINGS RATE	BEG. OF YEAR ANNUAL WITHDRAWAL	TOTAL ANNUAL TAXES	END OF YEAR ACCT. MGT. FEES	END OF YEAR ACCT. VALUE
1	1,921,805	(9.07%)	(100,000)	0	(33,131)	1,623,437
2	1,623,437	(11.85%)	(100,000)	0	(26,857)	1,316,010
3	1,316,010	(21.98%)	(100,000)	0	(18,974)	929,743
4	929,743	28.45%	(100,000)	(86,162)	(21,316)	958,309
5	958,309	10.87%	(100,000)	(20,489)	(19,032)	912,074
6	912,074	4.92%	(100,000)	(4,739)	(17,040)	830,225
7	830,225	15.68%	(100,000)	(30,477)	(16,894)	797,323
8	797,323	5.51%	(100,000)	(4,956)	(14,715)	716,075
9	716,075	(36.63%)	(100,000)	0	(7,808)	382,590
10	382,590	25.85%	(100,000)	(17,645)	(7,113)	330,879
11	330,879	14.89%	(100,000)	(6,548)	(5,305)	253,408
12	253,408	2.23%	(100,000)	(56)	(3,136)	153,631
13	153,631	16.00%	(100,000)	(1,171)	(1,244)	59,499
14	59,499	32.23%	(100,000)	0	1,071	(54,628)

FIGURE D.8

SEQUENCE 2

ACCUMULATION CALCULATOR

YEARS TO ILLUSTRATE:	20	
PRESENT VALUE:	1,921,805	
COST BASIS:	1,921,805	

EARNINGS RATE	0.00%
INFLATION	3.00%
COM RATE	0.00%

TAX AS MUTUAL FUND? ☐

YEAR	BEG. OF YEAR ACCT. VALUE	ANNUAL EARNINGS RATE	BEG. OF YEAR ANNUAL WITHDRAWAL	TOTAL ANNUAL TAXES	END OF YEAR ACCT. MGT. FEES	END OF YEAR ACCT. VALUE
1	1,921,805	31.29%	(100,000)	(250,714)	(47,835)	2,093,223
2	2,093,223	(4.28%)	(100,000)	0	(38,157)	1,869,704
3	1,869,704	21.64%	(100,000)	(153,183)	(43,054)	1,956,453
4	1,956,453	11.85%	(100,000)	(67,897)	(41,527)	1,966,949
5	1,966,949	1.46%	(100,000)	0	(37,883)	1,856,278
6	1,856,278	13.63%	(100,000)	(78,207)	(39,913)	1,877,509
7	1,877,509	32.23%	(100,000)	(252,767)	(47,010)	2,050,710
8	2,050,710	16.00%	(100,000)	(114,110)	(45,258)	2,103,539
9	2,103,539	2.23%	(100,000)	(731)	(40,963)	2,006,452
10	2,006,452	14.89%	(100,000)	(99,744)	(43,807)	2,046,809
11	2,046,809	25.85%	(100,000)	(214,365)	(49,001)	2,186,672
12	2,186,672	(36.63%)	(100,000)	0	(26,446)	1,295,850
13	1,295,850	5.51%	(100,000)	(9,982)	(25,235)	1,226,526
14	1,226,526	15.68%	(100,000)	(54,442)	(26,062)	1,222,614
15	1,222,614	4.92%	(100,000)	(7,309)	(23,556)	1,146,948
16	1,146,948	10.87%	(100,000)	(27,438)	(23,215)	1,110,084
17	1,110,084	28.45%	(100,000)	(111,144)	(25,949)	1,160,338
18	1,160,338	(21.98%)	(100,000)	0	(16,545)	810,719
19	810,719	(11.85%)	(100,000)	0	(12,530)	613,949
20	613,949	(9.07%)	(100,000)	0	(9,347)	457,987
TOT.	613,949	7.63%	(2,000,000)	(1,442,031)	(663,293)	457,987